MW01630565

The Karate-dō Manual

BARNES
& NOBLE
BOOKS
NEW YORK

The Karate-dō Manual

PMV Morris (4th dan)

BARNES
& NOBLE
BOOKS
NEW YORK

I dedicate this book to my teacher Shiro Asano. Chief Instructor of the SKI (GB) ant to my wife Evi.

This edition published by Barnes & Noble Inc.,
by arrangement with Tiger Books International
1993 Barnes & Noble.

First published in 1979 and reissued in 1982
by Stanley Paul & Co. Ltd.
An imprint of Random House UK,
20 Vauxhall Bridge Rd,
London SW1V 2SA

Created by The Wordsmiths Company Limited

Typeset by Gilbert Composing Services
Printed and bound in Italy by New Interlitho spa

ISBN 1 56619 493 8

The creators and publishers acknowledge:
PMV 'Vince' Morris (4th *dan*): authorship
Al Weiss (5th *dan*): consultant editorship
Alan Paul: Karate in America
David Mitchell, MAC: enthusiasm and advice
Sixpenny Studios: design and diagrams
Kay Williams: editing

My thanks to my wife Evi for coping with my terrible handwriting and turning it into typewritten copy, and to all who have helped in the creation of the book, including Richard Smith, David Hague, Philip Lhermette and David Babb who have helped secure the photographs.

PMV Morris
Newark 1978

contents

PROFILE—AL WEISS

Having been involved in karate for nearly twenty years, Al Weiss holds a prime vantage point over the martial arts scene in the United States. In addition to his practical martial arts experience, Mr Weiss has produced some fine publications dealing with the Oriental fighting arts. In 1962 he produced ***Karate,*** the first popularly priced book on the subject, followed by others including ***Tai-Chi*** and ***Kung-Fu,*** authored by Chinese master Alan Lee.

In 1968 he founded ***Official Karate*** magazine, the first American periodical devoted to exclusive coverage of karate. Mr Weiss continues to serve as Editor and creative head of ***Official Karate,*** which has grown in popularity throughout the years.

Mr Weiss began his karate training in the Shotokan style under John Kuhl, who had just moved to New York City from Canada. Initially sceptical, he started training and a few years later they switched to the more fluid ***goju*** style, in which Al Weiss presently holds a 5th ***dan***.

Though his schedule prohibits much time for training, Mr Weiss has remained active in other phases of the arts: he has promoted a number of tournaments under the auspices of ***Official Karate,*** and is a much sought-after referee and official for tournaments all over the country. Mr Weiss has received many awards and citations for his contributions to the martial arts over the years, and remains devoted and untiring in his efforts toward the promotion and development of karate in America.

Foreword

In the United States, Vincent Morris would be considered a 'purist', and that would place him in a highly controversial position. He would be respected and applauded by pioneers and serious students of karate who seek to retain the structure and philosophy of Japanese karate as it was originally taught by the Oriental masters. He would be jeered at by those who consider themselves innovators, modernists–those ***sensei*** who think the art should change to suit the needs and desires (as well as capabilities) of the student, rather than have the student work to meet the demands of the art.

The modernists are usually students of students. They are karate ka who never studied in the Orient and think most mental disciplines and all but the basic ***kata*** to be a waste of time. They are proponents of sport karate, full-contact bouts and quick self-defence courses. They often develop their own styles, their own uniforms and will acknowledge only the slightest relationship to the

Oriental arts.

Many of these ***sensei*** are sincere in their beliefs that karate must change to suit the times and Western attitudes, and in some cases their arguments do have merit, but they are supported by a large number of charlatans who find the modernist's way the opportunity to achieve quick success and recognition. One could declare himself a black belt without having to prove a connection with a recognized Oriental style.

The karate first seen by Westerners in Japan, Okinawa and Korea during and after the Second World War and the Korean conflict was an effective blend of physical and mental disciplines to form a unique and powerful human fighting machine. The Oriental masters seemed invincible, and a few inspired Westerners (the majority of them United States servicemen) begged to be taught the arts.

After years of strenuous, often torturous study, these dedicated few brought the fighting arts back to their countries, and they began teaching as they had been taught. They succeeded in retaining the purity of form and thought taught to them by their Oriental ***sensei,*** which meant that the martial arts community, though dedicated, was relatively small. Had we known then what we know now, we would have realized that these were the best of times. But Westerners, especially my own countrymen, are an impatient lot.

They crave instant success, instant knowledge. So the students of those who had studied in the Orient tried to capsulize and Westernize the information and training it took their ***sensei*** years to learn. They commercialized . . . often designing the art to suit their students.

Then came Bruce Lee, a talented martial artist and ***sensei*** whose films were more fantasy than fact. His success brought on a flood of cheap martial arts productions, mainly from Hong Kong, that showed men involved in improbable situations and using impossible techniques. Students rushed to ***dojos*** to learn these fantastic fighting arts - arts that only existed on film. This clamour for instruction brought out the parasites - the overnight ***sensei***, the instant black belts. And so the modernists, sincere as they may be, found themselves allied with the dregs of the karate community. Karate suffered what might be irreparable damage, disillusioned students, abandoned ***dojos***. A new drive to bring purity back to the arts began.

Great Britain has not yet suffered the 'range war' between purists and modernists that exists in the United States, thanks to the efforts of men like Vince Morris . . . men who work diligently to preserve the integrity of karate. In this book, Mr Morris stands solidly on the side of the purists, the Orientalists, although he states emphatically that Westerners 'no longer need bend a knee to Japan as far as practice and technique is concerned'. He leaves no doubt where his sympathies lie. He has painstakingly researched and thoroughly presented this detailed introduction to Japanese karate.

His message is clear. Karate is a way of life, a discipline that requires a spiritual devotion as well as technical skill. It is not a tournament win, a trophy, a championship title, and, though we all recognize the attraction of competition to test the effectiveness of techniques, it is not purely a sport.

Sensei Morris has produced a book that will prove to be extremely valuable, not only to Japanese stylists, but to all serious students of karate. It is informative without being long-winded, it is instructive without being pedantic. He has covered more ground than one would think possible in the space of one book and in doing so has performed a service to the ***sensei***, the student and the pure art of Japanese karate.

Al Weiss, 5th dan
Editor Official Karate

Foreword

Vincent Morris is the ideal choice as the author of a book on karate. On technical grounds he holds a high grade in Shotokan karate and is involved in both competition karate and the deeper aspects of the martial art.

On administrative grounds he is the Chairman of the Federation of English Karate Organisations and a karate representative to the Martial Arts Commission. From these positions he is well gifted to view all aspects of karate.

As a martial artist, though not myself a karate-ka, I found the book intensely absorbing and easy to follow. Vincent deals expertly with the basic movements and these, coupled with the excellent artwork, provide a step-by-step sequence.

The sections dealing with the philosophy of the martial art are well written and the would-be karate-ka is urged to study and consider this aspect.

All in all, the book is comprehensive and excellent value to the prospective or established karate-ka.

James Elkin
Chairman Martial Arts Commission

(James Elkin tragically died in 1982. He was succeeded as Chairman of the M.A.C. by the author. The current chairman is Baron John von Hoff.)

The Eastern concept of 'martial', in the term 'martial arts' or 'martial ways' (***budo***), has a much wider interpretation and significance than the Western definition of 'pertaining to war'. In essence, the Oriental concept includes such attributes as calmness, stoicism, courage, etc., as would be expected; but it also entails virtue, generosity of spirit, courtesy, respect for life, honesty and integrity. All true ***budo*** masters of today aim to promote the whole inclusive meaning of the martial ways, not simply the combative element.

Regrettably, this is not the case with all karate instructors, many of whom are young men with little or no deep understanding of, or concern for the history and practice of the real martial ways. In many instances, technically well qualified instructors - possessing ***dan*** (black-belt) grades awarded for fighting ability, duration of training, and technical expertise - may have been forced into accepting the responsibilities of passing on their knowledge by virtue of their rank. Such instructors, while genuinely doing their very best for their students, will acknowledge that they have just not had access to the teachings and example of a master exemplifying the more esoteric or philosophical sides of ***budo***. On the other hand, there are many instructors who deny their inadequacy. Maintaining that the moral, spiritual and philosophical aspects are of minor - at best, secondary - importance, they seek confirmation of their beliefs in the competition successes of their students.

With the proliferation of this latter view, and the increasingly widespread popularity of sport or competition-orientated karate, traditional karate-do - incorporating spiritual and philosophical values - stands in danger of being engulfed.

Quite understandably, young people, all over the world have flocked to join clubs practising this exciting martial art: and to the majority of them, to be successful in karate is equated with winning in competition, or beating their 'opponent' in free-style practice. The 'successful' club is the one which takes the most cups and medals in championships. This trend towards the competitive aspect of karate has been fostered by many, often well-intentioned, styles and organisations in Japan as well as in the West. It is my contention that this over-emphasis of sport karate is in danger of concealing from the karata-ka the tremendously important benefits which are to be gained from an understanding of the underlying philosophical basis of karate-do. While the Western karate world has undoubtedly shown that it no longer need 'bend the knee' to Japan as far as the practice of technique is concerned, it is as well to pause and reflect that Gichin Funakoshi, the 'father' of modern karate-do, continually stressed that karate-do is not a sport; indeed, he was severe in his comments about instructors 'of poor character' who 'thoughtlessly' placed the emphasis on technique rather than on the spiritual aspects. Karate was not devised as a sport; nor was it ever meant to become one. My fear is that the 'loss of face' the Japanese have incurred will press them even more urgently, in their desire to regain dominance, into the practice of sport karate to the exclusion of all else. It would be tragic if this came about, for although the West has demonstrated its capability in technique, the esoteric spiritual-psychological knowledge that karate also requires is mainly encapsulated in the traditions and philosophies which formed the basis for the way of life (and death) of the feudal-period Japanese warrior, and even now is more readily found maintained by the traditional ***ryu*** (schools) and ***budo-ka*** (martial arts practitioners) of Japan.

It should be food for thought that in the days when the ***samurai*** of Old Japan fought to the death in single combat, the man who mastered the mental and spiritual aspects of swordsmanship was considered to be a genius. Zen Buddhism has been called the warrior's religion: the ***samurai*** turned for support to Zen, which became the prop that enabled him to confront death fearlessly. Should it be any less effective today?

In terms of proficiency in combat, the mental disciplines promulgated by ***Bushido*** (the 'way' of the warrior) and Zen were to combine in the martial artist in such a way that his efficiency as a fighter would be increased. Can such disciplines by any less effective now?

Questions such as these surely cannot be dismissed or simply ignored. Recent masters of karate-do maintain that such concepts as courage, fortitude, integrity, courtesy and self-control are the prime objectives of karate-do; qualities which have little to do with strength of action and technique. Can the modern martial artist eagerly accept the technical teaching of these masters yet blithely dismiss their admonitions as to the supreme importance of the 'way'?

I have written this book because karate-do is my life. It has saved my life, it has changed my life, and it has changed me. I cannot believe that my little knowledge may honestly be said to do justice to the demands of the subject. Nevertheless, if even my mistakes provoke thought and discussion then the work has been worthwhile; or, in Zen terms:

'It is better to light a candle than to complain of the dark.'

A full account of the history of karate-do (literally, 'the way of karate'), and its underlying philosophy or ethic, Zen Buddhism, would require a lengthy book in its own right. What follows is a brief, selective account of the history of karate-do and of the nature and principles of Zen Buddhism, insofar as an understanding of the latter is indispensable to a follower of the former.

CHINA

The early history of Chinese martial arts is based upon tradition and later written references, but there is little doubt that systems of unarmed combat were in use as early as the Chou dynasty (1100-250 BC) and that they were used effectively in battle. The literature of the Han period (206 BC - AD 220) suggests that by this time unarmed combat was a highly developed art, one of whose features was the use of the head-butt as well as the more usual strikes, locks and throws.

Tradition has it that Bodhidharma (Japanese : Daruma-AD 470-543), an Indian Buddhist monk, 28th in line of descent from the Buddha, journeyed to China, where he was received in the year AD 527 by the Liang-dynasty emperor Wu-ti at his capital (modern Nanking). Bodhidharma's purpose was to establish the Zen (Chinese: Ch'an) school of Buddhism and after his meeting with Wu-ti he crossed the Yangtze river and travelled to the Shaolin temple (Japanese : Shorin-ji) in Honan province.

At the temple, Bodhidharma began to instruct the monks in Zen, but he found that many of them were too physically weak to endure the rigours of the ascetic and contemplative regime. Asserting that body and mind are indivisible, he is said to have devised a system of physical and mental training that would build up the strength and fortitude of the monks in order that they could continue with their Zen practice.

The techniques attributed to Bodhidharma to be found in a work purported to have been written by him, the ***I-chin Ching*** ('The Doctrine of Relaxing Tension'), concentrate mainly on various methods of breathing; they are essentially static in nature, involving no foot movements. Scholars,

Shin-no-shin-to-***ryu*** School of ***ju-jutsu***, 18th century. Sketches by Hokusai. (British Museum).

however, give no support to this tradition, holding that Bodhidharma had nothing to do with the fighting arts.

Whatever the truth of the matter, there can be no doubt about the existence of the Shaolin temple, and of the martial expertise of its monks; for from it sprang a famous fighting art, known as Shorinji ***kempo***, which spread throughout China.

Zen Buddhism

The connection between Zen Buddhist monks and the development of the fighting arts causes many a Westerner to raise his eyebrows. It should be realized, however, that Zen is not a religion as we would understand it, in that it has no deity as a central object of worship or devotion; nor is it concerned with such imponderables as Heaven and Hell. Zen imposes no moral preconceptions of 'good' or 'bad'; it stresses the true perception of reality, and the acceptance of life as it is, including, necessarily, its violent aspects.

Buddha

As it stems from the teaching of Buddha, the following section will perhaps help towards a better appreciation of the tenets of Zen Buddhism.

Buddha (Japanese:Butsu), born ***c.*** 565 BC, was the historical founder of Buddhism: Gautama Siddhartha, the Buddha Sakyamuni, son of Suddhodana, King of Kapilavasta (near Nepal).

As a young man, the Buddha had been acutely aware of the sufferings of humanity. When he set out to seek the cause of all distress in the hope of arriving at some remedy, he could gain no satisfactory answers to his questions. But one day, whilst sitting in meditation under a tree, he experienced a full and profound enlightenment: he discovered a 'way' of life based upon achieving a pure heart, full of love for all beings, and a mind entirely dedicated to seeing the truth, allowing no delusions or 'wishful thinking'. This way of life was based not upon God but on Man; though not upon the erroneous image of Man brought about by continual self-delusion. Rather was it dependent upon the true realization of Man, upon reality through meditation, and eventual understanding achieved by the transcending of physical or mental processes.

And it was this philosophy that formed the moral and spiritual foundations for the acceptance of the martial arts by the monks of the Shaolin temple. The techniques employed in Shorinji ***kempo*** were for the most part based on the premise that the monks would be unarmed; though use of 'natural' weapons, such as the staff (Japanese: ***bo***), was also practised.

During this period, China was ravaged by civil wars, which brought about the razing of the Temple on at least two occasions and the dispersal of the monks throughout the land. The scattering of the warrior-monks naturally led to a greater dissemination of ***kempo*** techniques, and the inevitable process of adaptation and a change began as ***kempo*** came to influence - and be influenced by - indigenous methods of fighting. In due course, this led to the subtle differences that can now be discerned between, for example, the styles of combat in Northern China, which emphasize kicking and evading techniques, and those of Southern China, which place a greater importance on upper body and hand techniques.

The ensuing centuries were to be characterized by civil wars, clan wars, piracy and lawlessness, not only in China but throughout Japan and Southeast Asia. Thus the martial arts became tried and tested in battle, and the survival of the fittest ensured that successful techniques survived and became systematized, whilst unsuccessful ones perished with their protagonists.

OKINAWA

The island of Okinawa (largest of the Ryukyu group, situated on the trade routes between Southeast Asia, China and Japan) was no exception to this general unrest. It, too, had developed rudimentary fighting arts. Although we cannot determine the precise nature or form of these, it seems that while the use of weaponry was quite common, unarmed combat was particularly emphasized.

Even in this early period, around the 7th century, it appears that there was already some Chinese influence, drawn from the knowledge and expertise of the multifarious visitors to the island, upon ***tode*** ('the hand arts') as they were termed.

In the 11th century, owing to the Taira-Minamoto wars in Japan, large numbers of Taira clan refugees fled from the mainland and settled in the Ryukyu islands. Many of these were warriors, well-skilled in their own martial arts— arts which were eagerly absorbed by the native systems. In 1372, Okinawa came under the feudal control of China; and thus began an era of cultural and social interchange, in which the Okinawans availed themselves of the more sophisticated and advanced philosophies and technologies of their feudal overlord. It was also a period of social intercourse, with Chinese families, merchants and diplomats visiting Okinawa and Okinawans travelling to the Chinese mainland.

It was inevitable that the Okinawans would pursue their search for information

H Kanazawa: knife-hand block (***shuto-uchi***).

regarding the martial arts, and that their indigenous systems would be influenced by what they learned. Many of the military attachés sent from China were themselves highly proficient in ***chu'an fa*** or ***kempo,*** and some of them taught their skills to local fighters.

In 1429, the three independent states of Okinawa were united under the sovereignty of Hashi, who decided to establish his seat of power at Shuri. One of his successors, Sho Shin, passed an edict confiscating weapons and banning their use throughout the country, as a safeguard against the island becoming embroiled in the sort of political and social upheaval that was taking place in Japan and many other Pacific nations. A natural consequence of this action was the promotion of interest in the weaponless fighting arts from China. The Okinawans' eclectic approach led them also to incorporate techniques from other Asian sources, revealed by travellers using Okinawan ports and possibly by the pirates (***wako***) who plied their trade in the surrounding seas.

In 1609, after bitter fighting, Japanese invaders defeated the Okinawans, who were greatly hampered by their lack of experience and skill in the use of weapons. The Japanese occupation led the islanders to concentrate even harder on developing and mastering effective weaponless techniques. Some even journeyed to the Chinese mainland itself to train themselves in Chinese forms of unarmed combat, which they could in turn pass on to their countrymen. The conglomeration of techniques, drawn from foreign and indigenous sources, became known as ***te*** ('hand' or 'hands'), later also termed ***bushi no te*** ('warrior's hand(s)').

Three main centres became known for the practice and teaching of distinct forms or variations of ***te***: the capital city, Shuri, gave rise to Shuri-***te***; another large city gave its name to Naha-***te***, and a third form, Tomari-***te***, was called after the port situated very close to Naha. Each developed a distinctive style, depending to a great extent upon the original characteristics of its prime source. Shuri-***te*** was apparently strongly influenced by the 'hard' Shaolin Chinese methods, whilst Naha-***te*** evinced characteristics of the 'soft' Chinese styles. Being a port town, Tomari was open to influences from a large variety of sources, and therefore was a mixture of many styles.

In 1669, after a further edict was issued banning once more the use of weapons and the practice of martial arts, Okinawa-***te*** went further 'underground' and was practised in great secrecy.

During the ensuing two centuries, many masters were to polish and refine the eclectic martial-art techniques into recognizable and efficient systems.

In 1871, Japan began to apply pressure to the Okinawans by means of imposing upon them the Japanese systems of law, government and education. This attempt to reinforce the Japanese claim to the island was fiercely resisted, and so began another period of unrest, riots and killings, in which local martial-arts groups figured prominently. Finally, the Japanese took the Okinawan king to Tokyo as a hostage, and completely annexed the island, naming it a province of Japan, Okinawa-***ken***.

During this period the term ***te*** fell into disuse and the name ***'kara-te'*** became popular. Although this can be translated as either 'empty hand(s)' or 'Chinese hand(s)', depending on the character employed (both are pronounced ***'kara'***), most experts and scholars agree that the reading 'Chinese hand(s)' is the more probable.

The distinctive terms designating the ***te*** of particular areas also fell into disuse. Tomari-***te***, probably because of its proximity to Naha, appears to have been subsumed by Naha-***te***, and the two generic names Shorin-***ryu*** and Shorei-***ryu*** came into use. Of these, the former utilized techniques more suitable for the small man, the latter being suited to big men. Shorei-***ryu*** taught an extremely effective form of self-defence but lacked the mobility of the speed-orientated Shorin-***ryu.***

In 1848, the Japanese authorities had begun the military conscription of fit male Okinawans. In later anticipation of the war between Japan and Russia (1904), great efforts were made to increase the health and strength of recruits, and to this end emphasis was given to sports and training in the martial arts. In 1902, following a demonstration arranged by Gichin Funakoshi (1868/70-1957; a student of Itosu and Azato of the Shorin-***ryu***), karate-***jutsu*** became part of the official schools' curriculum in Okinawa.

JAPAN

While the various forms of combat were proliferating and becoming systematized – ***chu'an fa*** or ***kempo*** in China, ***te*** in Okinawa – the situation in Japan was altogether different.

In the early periods of Japan's history, towards the end of the Han period in China (***c.*** AD 220), we find evidence of a fighting method that included kicking techniques. Known as ***chikara kurabe,*** this was a relatively unsophisticated art, relying to a large degree upon brute strength. There were originally no restrictions as to tactics or techniques, and fights were often to the death. ***Chikara kurabe*** was practised for employment on the field of battle, and naturally the development of armour served to render many of the techniques useless, the employment of grappling methods being more effective than ***atemi***-type attacks (punches, kicks, etc.).

The grappling methods evolved were termed ***yoroi kumi-uchi*** (wrestling in armour), and although they did employ the use of striking techniques these tended to be made with weapons rather than bare hands or feet. The utilization of ***yoroi kumi-uchi*** itself was only a tactic, a means to an end, the aim being to place the opponent in a disadvantegeous position so that a short-bladed weapon such as a ***yoroi-doshi*** (short dagger) could be thrust through a weak place in his armour.

Another factor that weighed heavily against the popularity of unarmed combat was the strict code of ethics which had evolved by the Middle Ages, and which normally determined the staging and procedure of combat between opposing factions. This implied that fighting without weapons was simply common brawling, and was therefore beneath the dignity and station of the warrior ***(bushi).***

The idea that karate has a long ancestry, and that it has direct connections with the ***samurai,*** or Japanese warrior, is therefore largely erroneous. Actual 'empty hand' methods of combat were only formally introduced into the martial ***ryu*** in the mid-16th century, as the wearing of armour became more infrequent. ***Yoroi kumi-uchi*** became ***kumi-uchi,*** a term denoting unarmoured forms of wrestling and from the ***kumi-uchi*** systems gradually developed the forms of combat known generally as ***ju-jutsu.*** These more accurately reflected the ethos and martial requirements of the Edo-period decline in the status of ***bu-jutsu,*** the classical forms of combat.

It was at this stage in the development of unarmed combat that certain Chinese ***chu'an fa*** or ***kempo*** techniques were incorporated into the repertoire, and in practice these tended to originate from the styles prevalent in Southern China.

The name ***ju-jutsu*** described a number of systems of fighting unarmed or lightly armed, which had begun in the relative peace of the Tokugawa (see Appendices) period. It was during this era, which saw the decline in the classical combative skills, that the martial ways ***(budo)*** came to assume a more important position, as the desire for self-perfection became stronger than the simple need for self-protection.

The martial ethic was further weakened, by a succession of Tokugawa ***shoguns*** (military dictators), to maintain the strength of their positions in the face of a less effective opposition. In some instances, the ***bushi*** were altogether forbidden to practise the classical martial arts; training in the arts of poetry and the tea ceremony ***(cha-no-yu)*** were substituted as more fitting.

There seems little doubt, however, that the death-knell of the classical warrior was sounded by the introduction of firearms. It became possible to equip and train commoners with muskets in a far shorter time than that required to prepare the martial skills of the ***bushi,*** who had spent years perfecting an expertise essentially designed for close-quarter confrontations. This technological advance meant that the classically trained warrior had not even a chance to employ his skills: he was simply slaughtered at long range.

These two main factors, then – the availability of firearms and the deliberate policy of promoting the decay of the classical martial arts – combined to hasten the metamorphosis of ***bu-jutsu*** into ***bu-do.*** And that change, together with the down-grading of the use of classical weapons, helped to ensure the growth and proliferation of unarmed combat systems. From this period onwards, therefore, ***ju-jutsu*** flourished. Techniques continued to evolve, and by the middle of the 19th century, defined methods of striking had been incorporated. These ***atemi-waza*** were blows aimed at specific points ***(kyusho)*** which, being now unprotected by armour, were particularly vulnerable to attack. The major emphasis was upon accuracy and speed, rather than (as in modern karate blows) upon speed and focused power ***(kime).*** The nature of the points attacked – such especially vital or weak areas as the testicles and eyes, etc. – ensured the blows' effectiveness.

Atemi-waza were considered useful, in the main, as part of a method of fighting which also included grappling, throwing and joint-twisting. Often, an ***atemi*** strike would be made as an introductory gambit, or as a distracting ploy to the main attack; or it would form part of the follow-through from a throw or joint hold. An ***atemi*** blow would, for example, constitute an effective first move in a sequence of techniques used to escape from a hold or an attempted throw. Seldom were ***atemi*** techniques considered to be sufficient in their own right, although in many instances they would indeed suffice.

This difference in the underlying principle serves to distinguish the earlier ***atemi-jutsu*** from karate techniques. Naturally, karate exponents recognize the importance of attacking the weak points of a human body; but up to the level of 2nd or 3rd ***dan,*** this is deemed secondary to the ability to deliver blows of great shocking power. Such blows, because of their great strength, have an immediate effect without requiring pin-point accuracy. The ***atemi*** points begin to regain their importance after the basic skills of delivering blows with maximum force have been acquired. They also figure significantly in the training of female karate-ka, older karate-ka, and those who suffer some physical impairment.

This then, was the situation in Japan at the beginning of the 20th century, when a school-teacher from Okinawa introduced the art of karate to the Japanese.

THE DEVELOPMENT OF KARATE-DO

Following the termination in 1906 of the Russo-Japanese war, Gichin Funakoshi continued his promotion of karate in Okinawa. He formed a demonstration group of experts and travelled the country, giving the first public displays of the art.

In 1917, he was selected as the representative of Okinawa province to give a demonstration in the Martial Virtues Hall (Butoku-***den***) in Kyoto. This was probably the first time that karate had been seen in Japan.

In 1921, Funakoshi was again selected to present a karate display, this time at Shuri Castle, and in 1922, karate was introduced into Japan in earnest when the Ministry of Education staged its first National Athletic Exhibition in Tokyo, and Funakoshi accepted the invitation to arrange and present a demonstration of karate. This event stimulated such interest that he was persuaded to stay in Tokyo and give further lectures and demonstrations, following which the popularity of karate spread rapidly. Funakoshi had soon established the art in many universities, military academies and even business organizations.

The growth of karate was accelerated by the arrival in 1928 of Kenwa Mabuni, a former student of Itosu (like Funakoshi) and of Higaonna (Naha-***te***). Mabuni began to teach his own style of karate, a combination of Shorin and Shorei. This he originally called Hanko-***ryu*** (half-heart style) but later changed it to an amalgam of the alternative readings of the characters representing the names of his former teachers, Shito-***ryu*** (Shi-Ito, from Itosu; to-Higa, from Higaonna). Mabuni, like his predecessor Funakoshi, found an eager audience, and Shito-***ryu*** flourished.

Later in the same year, yet another Okinawan master brought his particular style of karate to Japan. This was Chojun Miyagi, who taught mainly in the Kyoto area. He also had trained in the Naha-***te*** style under Higaonna; but he refined the system and added, to its basis of 'external' emphasis on conditioning and power, elements of the Chinese 'internal' systems, drawn from his experience of ***chu'an fa*** in China. This fusion he termed Go-ju (hard-soft), reflecting the basic concept of his style, the flexible interchange of hard and soft techniques.

At approximately the time that Mabuni and Miyagi came to Japan to establish their respective styles, another Okinawan – Kanbum Uechi – also began to teach karate. Uechi, who had been living near Osaka since 1924, had spent some 13 years in China practising the Pangai-noon system of fighting, and his particular style became known as Uechi-***ryu***, in his honour.

The period from 1922 to 1928, then, can rightly be considered as marking the introduction proper of karate to Japan. Correctly, the karate of this period was termed karate-***jutsu*** or 'Chinese hand art', reflecting the interpretation of the initial character, and using the suffix ***'-jutsu'*** to demonstrate that the art was directly orientated towards combat, not self-enlightenment.

In 1933, Funakoshi changed the first character reading 'Chinese' for another, which – although pronounced identically – meant 'empty'. He did this for a number of reasons. To begin with, he did not feel it appropriate to call an art which the Okinawans had so adapted and modified by a name that did not accurately reflect its history. At the same time, this was a period in which Japan was caught in the grip of a strong nationalistic spirit; and it seemed that retention of the Chinese character could be a serious obstacle to the free and unbiased acceptance of the art.

Perhaps even more importantly, the art of karate-***jutsu*** came into contact with, and under the influence of, that underlying philosophical ethic which played such a vital role in many of the Japanese traditional arts, martial and otherwise: Zen Buddhism, which as will be seen in Chapter 4, underpinned the whole concept of both the ***jutsu*** and the ***do*** forms of the martial art. Thus, Funakoshi, believing with the Buddhists that emptiness lies at the centre of all matter and all creation, found that the reading 'empty' was significant of more than just the fact that karate was a weaponless art in the traditional sense. Reflecting the change from the paramount need for an effective system of combat on the battlefield to the desire for personal enlightenment, he later also dropped the suffix ***'-jutsu'*** and

Sai kata. D Hague (2nd ***dan***), demonstrates the use of a traditional karate weapon, the ***sai.***

Ford
Ford
ENGINEERING
DESIGN
HALEWOOD TRANSMISSION
BASILDON RADIATOR PLANT

substituted *'-do'*. Thus, in 1935, karate-*do*, 'the way of the empty hand', properly became a new *(shin) budo*, described in Funakoshi's own words:

'Karate-do strives internally to train the mind to develop a clear conscience enabling one to face the world truthfully . . . mind and technique are to become one in true karate.'*

SCHOOLS AND STYLES

After its introduction to Japan, karate continued to evolve and develop into individual styles, according to the particular aspects emphasized by the respective senior instructors. Here follows a brief catalogue of some of the more important British and then American styles. The list is by no means exhaustive: it has been estimated that there are more than 70 different systems of Japanese karate.

GOJU-RYU (Hard-Soft)

A combination of the soft Chinese techniques with the hard Okinawan methods, this system was founded by Chojun Miyagi (1888-1953). It emphasizes the interchange of fast and slow movements, tension and relaxation, as appropriate to the situation – strong attack being deflected by a soft defence, for example. Goju training develops good body conditioning, and the *kata* stress tension/relaxation and deep abdominal breath control. Gogen Yamaguchi, present head of the Japanese Goju style, also places much importance on yoga exercises to supplement the karate training.

KYOKUSHINKAI (The Ultimate Truth)

This style was founded by a Korean, Masutatsu Oyama (*b.* 1923), who became familiar with Chinese *kempo* in Korea. After travelling to Japan, he studied Shotokan (q.v.) at Funakoshi's *dojo*. He also practised Goju-*Ryu*. In 1947, he won the All-Japan Karate Championship. Oyama spent two years living a solitary existence in the mountains to develop his self-discipline, and devised his own style from a combination of all the systems with which he was familiar. Kyokushinkai attempts to retain the features of a true *budo* form, stressing both the need for a realistic approach to combat and the necessity of mastering the self, in spiritual terms. To date, Kyokushinkai remains outside FAJKO and WUKO (Federation of All-Japan Karate Organisations and World Union of Karate-do Organisations, the international governing bodies), being unconvinced of the validity of 'no contact' competition. In training, much emphasis is placed on body conditioning, and on the importance of *hitozuki, hitogeri* – 'one punch, one kick' – to determine victory. The use of protective armour is allowed, in order to enable full-power techniques to be delivered, and 'knock-down' competitions are also held. *Tameshiwari* (the breaking of wood, tiles, bricks etc.) is stressed, as a test of technique and spirit.

SANKUKAI

Sankukai was founded in 1969 by Yoshinao Nambu (*b.* 1943), who had previously been active in the promotion of the Shukokai (q.v.) style. After winning the All Japan Students' Championship three times, however, he began to feel that too much importance was being placed upon competition. Having had much experience with most of the Japanese karate styles - Shotokan, Goju, Wado, Shito and of course Shukokai – Nambu synthesized his own style, which he called Sankukai, from these. One of the characteristics of Sankukai is the great use made of escaping techniques and of *aikido* defences.

SHUKOKAI (Way for All)

This style was developed in 1950 by Chojiro Tani (*b.* 1915), who first practised Shito-*ryu* under Kenwa Mabuni. Shukokai (way for all) is a very fast style: it has been claimed that it was in fact developed primarily for competition. It stresses no-contact in *shiai* (competition) and utilizes a relatively high stance, designed more for mobility than for power. Because of the body position assumed, the hips cannot be used in the traditional manner; a double-twisting action is used instead.

Following a split, two Shukokai organizations exist in Great Britain, the Shukokai Karate Union, under the direction of Shigeru Kimura, 7th *dan;* and the Shukokai World Karate Union, under the direction of Chojiro Tani and Y Suzuki.

SHITO-RYU

As explained in Chapter 2, the style originally called Hanko-*ryu* was changed by its originator, Kenwa Mabuni, to Shito. In some respects, this style was close to Funakoshi's Shotokan (q.v.,) for both had been students in the Shuri-*te* system. Mabuni, however, added elements of the Naha-*te*. Shito-*ryu* remains in essence more faithful to Okinawan than to Japanese karate, and its popularity has not spread far beyond Japan.

SHOTOKAN

The term means 'Shoto's house' or 'hall', Shoto having been the pen name used by Gichin Funakoshi. The style that Funakoshi originally brought with him, Shuri-*te*, had been characterized by close-range techniques intended mainly for self-defence, making frequent use of throwing methods and low-level kicks. He and primarily his son, Yoshitaka, modified this to include the practice of extended-leg kicking techniques to high targets *(mawashi-geri, yoko-geri, ushiro-geri)*, which demanded greater distance between combatants. The stances became more flexible and generally the throwing techniques were relegated to a

**Karate-do Kyohan*, by G Funakoshi, published by Kodansha

position of minor importance. Since its effectiveness purely in terms of combat then became questionable (many of the 'new' techniques being unsuitable for 'real' combat situations), the possibility was immediately opened up of karate becoming a sport.

In 1956, a group of Shotokan karate-ka, disagreeing with the strong sports emphasis being inculcated, broke away from the main body (see Shotokai). The remaining group formed the Japan Karate Association in 1957, with Masatoshi Nakayama, one of Funakoshi's best students, as chief instructor. The JKA is largely responsible for the world-wide promotion of karate and of its sporting elements. Another group of instructors, equally unwilling to continue with the promotion of a primarily sport-oriented form and disagreeing with the political ambitions of the JKA, resigned their affiliations with the parent body and formed the Shotokan Karate International (q.v.,).

Shotokan karate places great importance on ***kata*** training, and the use of low stances. It also fosters a strong, determined spirit. The techniques employed are well-suited to competition, being essentially strong and vigorous.

SHOTOKAI

Originally part of the Shotokan (q.v.,) group, Shotokai (Shoto's council) broke away in 1956 in an attempt to maintain the ***budo*** nature of karate, which they considered to be deteriorating owing to the emphasis currently given to the development of the sport aspect and the accompanying rise of commercialism and professionalism.

The technical differences between the two groups, while not great, are apparent. Shotokai make far greater use of flexible 'soft' application of techniques; and employ the one -knuckle fist, rather than the whole fore-fist, for punches. They do not commonly make use of the ***makiwara*** (striking post) or ***tameshiwari;*** nor do they take part in competition, believing it to be incompatible to the nature of true karate-do.

Shotokai also place a great deal of importance upon the practice of ***kata,*** and on the thorough understanding of each move.

SHOTOKAN KARATE INTERNATIONAL (SKI)

This group found itself – much like the Shotokai (q.v.,) – unable to continue to support the JKA. The cracks began to show in the mid-1970s, when many famous international instructors began to voice their dissatisfaction. Finally, in 1977, under the directorship of the legendary Hirokasu Kanazawa, former chief technical advisor and team coach to the JKA, the Shotokan Karate International formally parted from the parent group.

The aims of the SKI are to foster and develop the practice of karate as a ***budo*** form. SKI students take part in competitions, but the sport aspect is not allowed to take precedence over any other aspect of karate.

WADO-RYU (Way of Peace)

Founded in 1939 by Hironori Otsuka (***b***. 1892). Wado-***ryu*** ('way of peace') derived from Otsuka's long experience of the classical martial arts. He began to study ***ju-jutsu*** when very young, and also became one of Gichin Funakoshi's foremost students. An economical style, Wado karate stresses the concept of the 'soft' yielding to a 'hard' attack, and utilizes many tension-free 'snapping' techniques which depend upon speed for their power. Otsuka emphasizes the need for concentration upon ***kata*** training, rather than upon just the ***kumite.*** Like Shukokai, Wado-***ryu*** is well suited to the requirements of competition, and in height and position of stances it takes a middle course between Shukokai and Shotokan.

Though the authentic Japanese systems tend to dominate karate participation in Great Britain, the situation in the United States is quite different. Japanese styles had been the most widely practised in America until the mid-1960s, when the Okinawan and Korean fighting arts gradually began making their marks. Isshin-***ryu*** was probably the most popular of the Okinawan styles, with Shorin-***ryu*** next in line. Isshin-***ryu*** remains enormously popular today throughout the United States, but there has been a rapid growth of the Korean (***taekwondo***) systems, particularly ***moo duk kwan*** and ***tang soo do.***

Taekwondo styles had been relatively popular for some time on the West coast of the United States, and in the Northeast. This popularity spread outward quite rapidly to encompass the Southwest, and eventually the South and Mid-west.

Today ***taekwondo*** may well be the single most popular fighting art in America. The reasons for its rapid growth are varied, but American martial arts practitioners are basically attracted to it as a more 'dramatic' self-defence system. ***Taekwondo's*** emphasis on spectacular kicking techniques has undoubtedly been its prime selling point with American audiences.

One other major, non-Japanese style, ***kempo (kenpo),*** also enjoys a good deal of popularity in the United States.

TAEKWONDO

Taekwondo (literally 'the art of kicking and punching') is basically a combination of the abrupt, linear motions of Japanese karate and the more flowing, circular movements of the Chinese martial arts. Modern ***taekwondo*** owes its origins to a number of primitive styles which were being practised throughout the Orient as early as the first century AD. Two of these styles, ***kwon bop***

and ***soo bak,*** were brought to Korea by descendants of the original followers of Bodhidharma. They were incorporated into one style, and made mandatory training for warriors by the then military dictator, General Choi. In the latter part of the Yi dynasty – a peaceful period characterized by renewed interest in literature and painting – ***soo bak do***, as the system was then known, declined in popularity, not to rise again until the start of the Sino-Japanese war of 1894. At this time it came to be called ***tae kwon*** or ***tang soo do*** 'the art of the China hand'. Upon the liberation of Korea in 1945, ***tae kwon do*** was revitalized as both a means of self-defence and a national sport. ***Moo duk kwan*** is one of many schools which sprung from the basic principles of modern ***taekwondo.***

ISSHIN-RYU

Modern Isshin-***ryu*** karate is a conglomeration of the basic styles of Okinawan karate – Uechi-***ryu,*** Goju-***ryu,*** Shorin-***ryu,*** Matsubayshi-***ryu*** and Kobayashi-***ryu.*** Founded by Tatsuo Shimabuku after World War II, the system was considered a bastard by the Okinawan Karate-Do Association, which failed to recognize it. Shimabuku had learned Shuri-***te*** from his uncle, then took formal training in Kobayashi-***ryu*** under master Chotoku Kyan. Later he also studied Goju-***ryu*** with master Chokei Motobu, emerging as his leading pupil. Kyan and Motobu were among the first masters to begin teaching karate openly on Okinawa in the early 1900s. Shimabuku passed his art on to three Americans – Don Nagle, Steve Armstrong and Harold Long. Nagle is credited with opening the first commercial karate school on the East Coast of the United States, in Jacksonville, North Carolina, in 1957. Today, Isshin-***ryu*** is probably the most popular Okinawan style practised in the United States, one of the most popular of all the Oriental fighting arts.

KEMPO

Kempo (or ***kenpo***) karate derives from China. The kempo practised today in the United States and many other parts of the world was developed by Professor William K S Chow. Chow was one of five people who learned Kosho-***ryu*** kempo from Dr James Mitose. Mitose opened the Official Self-Defense Club at the Beretania Mission in Honolulu in 1942 and passed his art on to five selected students – Thomas Young, Chow, Paul Yamaguchi, Arthur Keawe and Edward Lowe – who in turn branched out to spread the teachings. American Ed Parker was a student of Professor Chow, and brought his own innovations to kempo when he too branched out on his own. Parker continued to refine the system, incorporating American boxing and street-fighting skills – something that had heretofore been unheard of in the history of the Oriental fighting arts as practised in America. Parker is credited with founding the first commercial karate school in the United States, in Provo, Utah, in 1954.

CHAPTER 3. KARATE IN AMERICA

Since its introduction to the United States in the 1950s, karate has had more peaks and valleys than the Rocky Mountains. Brought to the States by American servicemen stationed in the Orient, pockets of karate enthusiasm grew on both the East and West coasts, eventually spreading outward to enjoy popularity in all parts of the country. Americans had been familiar with judo, but karate was something entirely different. With its unusual punching techniques (which didn't really resemble American boxing) and flashy kicks, stateside Americans quickly became as enchanted by karate as did those who had first witnessed the art abroad.

Initially it was probably the 'mystique of the Orient' which first attracted Americans to karate. The Fifties were a time of relative peace and contentment in the United States, so people were generally not interested in the self-defence aspects of martial arts. They ***were*** interested in learning something new and exotic, and Americans have, of course, always been fighters. Oriental philosophy was as far from the minds of Americans as it could be; but the well-executed punch or kick . . . that was something they ***could*** relate to.

Robert Trias claims the very first ***dojo*** in the United States opened in 1946. Trias had been trained in Chinese, Japanese, Korean and Okinawan systems. He presently heads the USKA, one of the largest karate organizations in America. Ed Parker introduced karate (***kenpo*** karate) to the West coast in 1954, and, three years later, Isshinryu practitioner Don Nagle did the same on the East coast. Undoubtedly there had been some karate practised in America prior to the efforts of these three men, but the art was still practised underground – by Orientals, teaching Orientals. Parker and Nagle have been credited with opening the first 'commercial' schools in their respective parts of the country. Peter Urban brought goju karate to the United States, later developing his own style, called USA Goju.

Competition-minded American karate practitioners were most interested in the

fighting possibilities of karate, and this, more than anything else, was what they concentrated their energies upon. ***Kumite*** in the ***dojo*** rapidly expanded to inter-***dojo*** competition and eventually, toward the concept of invitational and open tournaments. The American karate community can probably be credited with the popularization of what today's practitioners know as the karate tournament. Isshinryu stylist Gary Alexander is believed to have held the very first tournament in America, the Karate Olympics, in the early Sixties.

Early competition was confined by style – that is, Okinawan stylists fought with Okinawan stylists, Japanese stylists fought among their own, Chinese-based styles did the same, and so forth. This was the beginning of the strict, and often rigid factionalization of karate in America which still exists today. It is the primary reason why there is no national karate organization which oversees a majority of styles and systems.

Finally, there grew some interaction – tournament-wise – among styles. This concept grew and flourished, though the intra-style concept continued to remain popular. Some Japanese factions, and the more recent Korean (taekwondo) styles (introduced by S Henry Cho), were the last to submit to competing in open tournaments. Today many of them still remain aloof, preferring to maintain a certain purity of style by limiting their interaction with others.

Karate grew slowly but steadily in the United States. It

Crab scissors throw – ***kani-basami.***

spread first southward from the East, then into the South-western states, and finally throughout the Mid-west. But still, relatively few Americans even knew what karate was, until the martial arts began to get some media exposure via television and the movies some ten or fifteen years after its introduction. Primary of course, to the rapid rise in popularity of the martial arts in America was the film and television work of the late Chinese martial arts superstar, Bruce Lee.

So, in actuality, it was kung fu, and not karate, that began to stir the enthusiasm of the lay American. But Americans tended not to differentiate between the Chinese and Japanese martial arts; to them, kung fu meant karate, and vice versa.

With the increased exposure of the martial arts, karate and kung fu schools began to grow and flourish. Enrollment doubled and tripled in schools all over the country, and the term 'martial art' became synonymous with 'big business' in America.

Tournament karate also continued to expand when, in 1968, Jim Harrison, a Mid-west black belt and karate pioneer, introduced the concept of 'professional karate'. His professional tournament featured prize money for winners, and prompted a similar tournament one year later on the East coast. This one, promoted by New York-based karate-ka Aaron Banks, is generally recognized as the first professional tournament. The event crowned champions in four weight divisions: heavy-weight (Joe Lewis), light-heavy-weight (Mike Stone), middle-weight (Chuck Norris) and light-weight (Skipper Mullins).

Tournament karate was later revolutionized by Washington, DC taekwondo instructor Jhoon Rhee. Rhee developed safety equipment - hand and foot pads made from foam rubber - for karate-type fighting. Initially the equipment was intended for use in non-contact fighting, merely as a form of protection against accidental injury. But a growing faction interested in full-contact sport fighting embraced the equipment as their own. This action more or less forced Rhee to further adapt gloves and foot pads which could be used in contact fighting. Since the inception of the Rhee equipment, a rash of other individuals and organizations have come out with their own full-contact gloves and boots.

Prior to the introduction of full-contact karate, however, a group of American karate-ka - weaned on American boxing and contact - began to hold what was termed 'American kick-boxing' matches. Patterned after Thai, and other forms of Oriental kick-boxing, the sport enjoyed a brief period of popularity, until it was finally pressured into obscurity by tradition-minded karate practitioners, who criticised it as being 'a desecration of the art'.

Kick-boxing all but disappeared from the American martial arts scene, but many American karateists still believed contact was the way karate should be played. In 1974, Oklahoma martial artist Mike Anderson founded the Professional Karate Association (PKA), and held his own version of the professional karate championships. The major difference between his event and Harrison's and Banks' was that now the competition was to be full-contact, to the knock-out or decision. The four champions established at that championship were : Joe Lewis (the only repeater from 1969), Jeff Smith, Bill Wallace, - all Americans - and Mexico's Isias Duenas. Of the four, only two - Wallace and Smith - still hold their crowns.

Today the PKA is under the direction of non-karate practitioners Don and Judy Quine. After a shaky beginning, they have managed to stay with the concept, and have made much progress. Presently the PKA is by far the major organization producing full-contact bouts, but by no means the only one. Still, they have made the greatest strides toward international acceptance of professional karate, and their champions are widely recognized as legitimate.

Mike Anderson's 1974 professional championships were very well received by most in the karate community and a large portion of the lay public. The programme was carried over national television, and shown a total of three times on WABC-TV's ***Wide World of Entertainment*** programme. It was reportedly the most popular production ***Wide World*** had ever aired.

The reception gained by those championships had karate-ka all over the country excitedly speculating over the future of this new American sport . . . but their excitement was short-lived. Subsequent professional programmes which reached national prominence were vastly less 'professional' than the original. In a rush to latch onto the full-contact band-wagon, promoters all over the country (themselves ill-prepared for the task) hastily put together full-contact cards with poorly trained and conditioned fighters. What resulted were embarrassing bouts whose participants most closely resembled bad amateur boxers.

In addition, events sprung up featuring boxing vs. karate bouts. The representatives from the Oriental fighting arts most often ended up on the losing end of these bouts. In one of the mixed-matches, a female boxer (Jackie Tonawanda) actually knocked-out a male karate-ka (Larry Rodania). The young sport of pro karate had reached an all time low.

Having seen the mystical Oriental fighting arts in action, the lay public in America was at once repelled by them. This reaction not only hurt the fledgling sport of full-contact karate, but also the ***dojo***-owner. The laughable publicity garnered by early pro karate bouts convinced Americans that karate and its cousin arts were probably not all they were cracked up to be. Potential students stayed away from neighborhood ***dojos*** in droves, and the martial arts all but died out as an activity in the United States.

As a result of the full-contact karate experience in America, the martial arts community began to fall into two general categories - those that believed properly handled full-contact was the future of karate in America, and those that totally shunned the full-contact off-shoot and sought to bring karate back to its Oriental roots.

While full-contact karate is only now beginning to enjoy the acceptance which was hoped for it some years ago, karate as a practised art also seems back on the road to popularity in the United States. For years, prominent American ***sensei*** have believed that unification was the only way toward a healthy growth; they are now coming to understand that unification is virtually impossible. Owing to the incredible proliferation of styles - not just of karate, but seemingly countless other martial arts as well - in America, it has been difficult at best for any sort of move to unification (that is, bringing all styles together under one overall governing body). In addition to the vast numbers involved, those interested in unification were also met by often insurmountable 'ego problems' in any attempts - even on a small scale - to unify.

The trend today seems to be heading toward a total separation of martial arts factions. (The situation in the US has always featured factionalization, but now there is a more or less organized effort toward that end.) Heads, of each style are drawing their members inward, intent on concentrating all their efforts in the area of developing their own style to its maximum potential. Rather than attempting any merger now, individual styles are coming to recognize their separateness,

H Kanazawa and S Asano: combination downward block and lunge punch (***gedan-barai, oi-zuki***).

even relish it.

Unlike the situation in England, the American system of a federal government has also contributed to the fact that there is no single national governing body for martial arts in the country. Each state is essentially responsible to govern itself, regulating its offices and agencies as it sees fit. For this reason, the practice of martial arts generally comes under the authority of the state boards of athletics, and the situation is often grossly dissimilar from state to state.

It is only recently, in fact, that states have at all been attempting to regulate martial arts participation within - and this, too, is a direct result of the growth of the professional sport. The state of California, for example, was the first to institute a regulatory programme for martial arts. Primarily they were concerned about control of full-contact, professional fighting. California initiated their programme in 1976, and New York is presently involved in exploring the probability of similar legislation. Since the state athletic commissions form a loose national network, it can be assumed that most will adopt control measures in the not-too-distant future.

On the amateur side of karate competition (non-contact fighting and ***kata*** competition) the only major national organization which has attempted regulation, standardization and control is the Amatuer Athletic Union (AAU). The AAU is one of two organizations (the other being the NCAA, National Collegiate Athletic Association) which more or less control non-professional sports in the United States.

Though the efforts of the AAU and its supporters within the karate community have been substantial, there is much controversy - and very little actual support - surrounding it. It's backers are aiming toward eventual acceptance of karate as a world-wide sport by the Oympic Committee, to be included in the Olympic Games.

One other group, called Martial Arts Rating Systems (MARS) has made strides in the area of tournament standardization and organization nationally, on an amatuer level. The group, headed by Cecil Kitchens, employs the use of computers to keep a record of tournament participation and relative standings of its member athletes. The group is relatively small at present, but appears to be gaining support quite rapidly.

During the past few years in the United States, there has arisen a large degree of

H Kanazawa, 8th ***dan***, executes a reverse roundhouse kick (***gyaku-mawashi-geri***).

nationalism with respect to karate. That is to say, a good percentage of American ***sensei*** - particularly those who have accepted and been involved in full-contact - have been making a concerted effort to 'Americanize' the martial arts - to adapt them more to the characteristically American temperament, physical attributes and way of life. These people feel that karate as it was devised by Easterners so many hundreds of years ago, is, today, relatively ineffective. They cite the results of early full-contact (and karate vs. boxing) bouts as examples of this allegation, adding that today's more highly polished pro and amateur karate fighters have incorporating boxing and street-fighting techniques into their repertoires.

The 'purists' on the other hand, are quick to say that traditional karate ***is*** effective, but that it has been diluted and diminished in translation from the Oriental ideal. They say that traditional karate can be effective, both as a fighting art and a means of practical self-defence, if it is learned and practised properly - something that short-cut-minded Americans find difficult to do. One group of traditionalists has even gone so far as to say that karate was never intended as a sport - not even a non-contact sport - and have almost totally de-emphasised tournament competition.

In summary, karate has undergone many dramatic changes since it first began to prosper in the United States nearly twenty-five years ago. Certainly, given the nature of the American philosophy and way of life, change was inevitable. Americans have always been experimenters, rebels, if you will; the very nature of American society was founded upon rebellion. Karate in America is practised like nowhere else in the world, and American ingenuity has brought much - both good and bad - to the art.

Hopefully, the years ahead will prove fruitful and prosperous for all aspects of the martial arts in the US (early signs seem to indicate this). Hopefully, also, both purist and modernist will learn to co-exist and collectively (if not harmoniously) contribute to the growth of the martial arts.

But predictably, American martial artists will continue to yield at least as much controversy and confusion as positive contribution. For better or worse, the phenomenon coming to be known as "American Karate" is here to stay.

Kanazawa and Asano demonstrate basic one-step sparring, ***kihon ippon kumite:*** Side thrust kick, ***yoko-geri-kekomi.***

So far, we have looked briefly at the history and development of Zen Buddhism (Chapter 2). For a realistic view of Zen as it applies to karate-do, however, it is necessary to understand some of the underlying principles. Being intuitive in essence, the nature of Zen is particularly difficult to describe in intellectual terms.

In this chapter we consider also Shinto, Confucianism and Bushido, 'way of the warrior'.

Zen Buddism in Japan

According to one tradition, Buddhism was first introduced to Japan from Korea in the mid-6th century. Essentially influential among the nobility, it appeared as an advanced form of culture in China, and its acceptance by the highest ranks of Japanese society began the close association between Buddhism and the State.

The word ***zen*** itself is the Japanese form of the Chinese ***ch'an,*** which in turn represents the Sanskrit ***'dhyana',*** meaning simply'meditation'.Zen Buddhism differing from other forms of Buddism basically in its extension of the practice of meditation into a sect in its own right – was introduced into Japan in more than one form by two main personalities. The two schools came to be known as the Rinzai sect and the Soto sect.

Rinzai Zen was brought to Japan from China by a Japanese priest called Eisai, who in 1187 had travelled to China to further his studies. He returned in 1191 and was instrumental in establishing a temple at Kamakura and another at Kyoto. Here he began the teaching of his concept of Zen, which emphasized the importance of gaining enlightenment through continual meditation upon ***koan*** (questions or problems that baffle the intellect and force the student to make the intuitive 'leap').

Rinzai Zen, with the patronage of the Kamakura shogunate (see Appendices), soon gained general acceptance with the newly ascendant military classes.

Soto Zen was introduced to Japan shortly afterwards by Dogen (1200-1253), also a Japanese priest who had journeyed to China to attain enlightenment. Unlike Eisai, however, Dogen kept away from the major centres of population and established a temple in the remote province of Echizen (now part of Fukui province). The Soto school puts its emphasis simply in the action of ***za-zen***, meditation in a cross-legged position. The act of ***za-zen*** itself brings enlightenment: shallow practice in ***za-zen*** brings shallow enlightenment (Japanese ***satori***); deep practice, deep enlightenment.

The discipline of Zen is self-reliant and ascetic, treating life and death with equal indifference; yet flexible, having no specific doctrine or philosophy. It emphasizes single-mindedness, will-power and the determination never to look backward. The Kamakura ***samurai*** had a natural predilection for this austere and simple religion:

'For the samurai to learn
There's one thing only,
One last thing —
To face death unflinchingly.'

Tsukahara Bokuden (1490-1572)

This verse, by one of the greatest Japanese swordsmen, exemplifies the major concern of the ***samurai:*** 'to face death unflinchingly'.

For these early warriors, the threat of death was ever-present; it could come anywhere, at any time. But fear of dying could weaken the resolve, and perhaps delay reactions in a moment of crisis. This was to be cowardly, and to be a coward was to be without honour, which was to be no man. Consequently, although the thought of death might be constantly in the forefront of the ***samurai's*** mind, Zen pointed out the transience and impermanence of all things, and so enabled him to come to terms with his mortality and to transcend it.

Karate-do and Zen

The connection between Japanese karate-do and Zen Buddhism is in a sense almost unavoidable. It is true that, in the ***-jutsu*** form, karate in Okinawa was relatively uninfluenced by Buddhism; but upon its acceptance into the Japanese martial ethos, it became more and more subject to the traditions and philosophies of the classical martial arts and ways. Funakoshi recognized this and (as described in Chapter 2) changed the character reading 'Chinese' for a homophone reading 'empty', giving his reason for so doing as an attempt to reflect the new philosophical aspect which had permeated his concept of the art. When, two years later, he re-emphasized the nature of the change by dropping the suffix ***'jutsu'*** and substituting ***'do'***, karate-do became just as the classical martial ways had become, an acknowledged path to self-enlightenment; and the same Zen principles that pervade the classical forms quite naturally gained meaning and importance within it, reinforcing certain shared aspects such as the concept of the 'mind like water' ***(mizu no kokoro),*** and the need for the protagonists to transcend the fear of death in order to act instinctively and not intellectually.

The purpose of Zen is to attain the intuitive awareness that comes when the intellect is transcended and perceiver and perceived merge. The Zen practitioner aims to realize a 'one-ness' with creation. In denying that the intellect can provide the answers to all problems, in asserting that intellect is finite, Zen emphasizes direct awareness. The importance of the intellect is in no way denied; but emphasis is on the existence of vital areas where the faculty of direct awareness is of far greater importance.

'The forceps of our minds are clumsy things, they crush the truth in their attempt to grasp it.' Simply – we 'know' what we feel, but in attempting to communicate that knowledge we are forced, by the limitations of speech and intellect, to describe only a partial, incomplete version of the total experience. We know, for example, what constitutes a cup of tea. We understand the processes that led to the making of the tea leaf, the mechanics of brewing the tea; we can describe the type of leaf, the temperature of the water, and whether the milk – sterilized, pasteurized or whatever – is from a goat or cow. All this we can communicate to another, who might, through the use of his intellect, understand all that we say. What we cannot do, however, is describe the taste/texture/temperature, etc., in the way that will equal the awareness/knowledge to be gained by the direct experience of actually tasting the tea.

The aim of Zen is ***satori*** – enlightenment: a state which – by its nature of being beyond pure intellect – no words can adequately describe. This is not at all to say that the mind is in the clouds, divorced from reality. On the contrary, to attain ***satori*** is to experience a 'oneness' with reality – an awareness of the 'wholeness' of the here-and-now.

To some people, **satori** happens all at once, to others a little at a time; but once experienced, it is never forgotten. The Rinzai sect hold that a person's intellect must be forced to the limit by ***mondo,*** a form of question and answer between master and pupil, and ***koan,*** a word or phrase presenting a puzzle insoluble by simple intellect: processes that push the pupil 'over the edge' of the intellect and leave no alternative for him but to 'let go' and make the leap to enlightenment.

The Soto school, on the other hand, maintains that by the simple practice of meditation ***(za-zen)*** in a regular and

Asano ***sensei*** executing jumping side thrust kick (***yoko tobi geri kekomi***).

disciplined fashion, ***satori*** is achieved. The term 'meditation', however, ought not to be construed in the manner in which Westerners understand it, implying the active contemplation of specific thoughts. In fact, the opposite is nearer the truth. Thoughts may, in the first instance, come and go, but eventually they are stilled and the meditator simply sits. Zen master Ummon said to his monks: 'If you walk, just walk; if you sit, just sit - but don't wobble!'

For the martial artist, the ability to transcend the intellect and make use of total awareness is vital. In simple terms, if his mind is continually appraising his opponent's movements, at least two major obstacles arise to hinder his success in combat. First, his mind will incessantly 'see' openings in the opponent's guard and opportunities for a decisive blow, but inevitably his body will be too slow to react and the moment will be lost. Secondly by seeing his opponent in dualistic terms, rather than as an extension of himself, he stands the chance of allowing rage or fear or other emotions to further influence his abilities and actions. In other words, he will have a 'stopping mind'.

Hui-neng (The Sutra of Wei Lang) describes the calmness and serenity of the Zen practitioner thus:

'Imperturbable and serene, the ideal man practises no virtue;
Self-possessed and dispassionate, he commits no sin:
Calm and silent, he gives up seeing and hearing;
Even and upright, his mind abides nowhere.'

This Zen concept of the mind's abiding nowhere - 'no-mind' ***(mushin)*** - has been compared with the calm surface of a pond, which accurately reflects every movement and ripple ***(mizu no kokoro):*** the state of utter awareness seen as a prerequisite for the mastery of swordsmanship.

One of the most renowned swordsmen in Japanese history was Yagyu Tajima no Kami Munenori (1571-1646), whose skills were such that he became the teacher of the Shogun himself. This famous swordsman studied Zen under master Takuan, and was emphatic in his insistence that the martial artist attain 'no-mind' ***(mushin)*** or 'immovable mind' ***(fudoshin)***, in which state thoughts of life or death obtruding between perceiver and perceived vanish like the darkness when the moon slides from behind the clouds and is reflected in the waters of a still pond:

'However well a man may be trained in the art, the swordsman can never be the master of his technical knowledge unless all his psychic hindrances are removed and he can keep the mind in the state of emptiness, even purged of whatever technique he has obtained. The entire body together with the four limbs will then be capable of displaying for the first time and to its full extent all the art acquired by the training of several years. They will move as if automatically, with no conscious efforts on the part of the swordsman himself . . . with the self vanishing nowhere anybody knows, the art of swordmanship attains its perfection, and one who has it is called a genius.'

Another famous swordsman, almost a contemporary of Yagyu Tajima no Kami Munenori, Odagiri Ichiun, also stresses the Zen approach:

When with a sword you confront the enemy, advance towards him, if the distance is too far, and strike . . . if the distance is just right, strike him from where you are. No thinking is needed.'*

Simple and direct advice; but Ichiun goes on to point out that in most cases this is not how matters proceed. As the combatants take up their stances and begin to work their minds 'in the busiest possible way', they reflect on the various techniques and strategies - and perhaps they also allow their thoughts to dwell upon their chances of success:

'The great mistake in swordsmanship is to anticipate the outcome of the engagement; you ought not to be thinking of whether it ends in victory or defeat. Just let nature take its course, and your sword will strike at the right moment.'

In fact, Ichiun gives further advice, to the effect that the martial artist should enter every contest with the idea that it will end in a 'mutual striking down', ***(ai-uchi),*** because in this attitude of mind the question of coming out of the affair alive does not arise. Unencumbered, the mind is at its most resolute and fearless.

To practise Zen with the aim of becoming a perfect martial artist, however, is completely to misunderstand the situation. Practice with such an aim implies the achievement of an 'end product'. Zen is not at all concerned with an 'end product', it has no goal. The desire for success is the effect of the ego which will only make the path to enlightenment that much more difficult; for Zen is, if anything, 'acceptance' not 'ambition'.

This point is of great significance to the student of the martial ways, for, when judged in terms of Zen, practice for the master and for the student become equally valid. In most cases, the complete beginner, even if unknowingly, can with proper guidance enter Zen and start along the way. Indeed, the beginner unaware of ***satori*** will not be able to fall into the trap of actively seeking it - an activity that only ensures its remaining out of reach.

How does this early concern for the ***-do*** (the 'way') of karate have a bearing on present-day karate-do? It is to be hoped that

*(from ***Zen and Japanese Culture,*** D T Suzuki, Routledge and Kegan Paul and Princeton University Press).

the thoughtful reader will already have begun to see the implications. Karate-do has had such a tremendous growth-rate that it might be described as an infant prodigy – if a deformed one! The proliferation of styles and clubs, with a few direct ties or contacts with the sources of knowledge and the concomitant explosion in the number of 'instructors' has meant that, while the techniques of karate have spread at an enormous rate, the 'way' of karate is largely unknown.

Hirokasu Kanazawa ***sensei*** (instructor), 8th ***dan***, Chief Technical Adviser and team coach to the JKA, and Chief Instructor in Europe for SKI, is probably one of the world's best-known Shotokan instructors. A former student of master Funakoshi and winner of the All-Japan Karate Association Championship in both ***kumite*** (fighting) and ***kata*** (forms), he clearly recognizes the problems inherent in this rapid development:

'Although karate has reached a high standard in Britain, many people are being trained only for *kumite* — to win contests. Our aims at the Shotokan Karate International organization are to return to Mr Funakoshi's teachings and train for spirit, character and for health. Of course we also train for championships but we feel we must encourage the *budo* spirit.'*

Another acknowledged master, president and chief instructor of the Shotokan of the Japan Karate-do Shoto-kai, Shigeru Egami, who also was a pupil of Funakoshi and of his son, Yoshitaka, states categorically:

'The karate practised today is quite different from that of forty years ago . . (and) . . while it can be said that there are certain groups in the United States and Europe that . . place emphasis on the spiritual side of karate, the sad truth is that many styles teach only the fighting art and neglect the spiritual aspects. And the practitioners themselves, who offer lip-service to the spirit of the art, have as their real objective the winning of matches.'**

Kanazawa and Egami are saying, basically, that karate-do is becoming a sport. ***Shiai*** (competition), or rather success in ***shiai***, has become the major concern of the majority of karate-ka. This does not apply solely to the formal competitions held by associations or the like, but is equally true of individual contests held every day in the ***dojo***, when two karate-ka engage in ***ju-kumite*** (free style practice). Undeniably, ***shiai*** and ***kumite*** provide the student with the opportunity to test his techniques against another while under pressure, enabling him to learn from the results and improve his standard. But the essential point, so often forgotten, is that winning itself is secondary; what matters is that the experience is used as an adjunct to basic training, that the student becomes aware of his strong and his weak techniques and acts accordingly.

Much of this situation stems, as has been mentioned, from a basic lack of instruction in the 'way' of karate; but often this is compounded by a lack of understanding of the very real differences, in both purpose and practice, between ***kumite*** and ***shiai*** to which we shall return later.

Once the student realizes the truth of the present situation, however, in which the sporting element in karate has gained the ascendancy, it is to be hoped that he will re-evaluate the direction in which his own practice is taking him. Some of the differences between sport karate and karate-do are dramatic. For example, most karate-ka tend to avoid risking injury in practice immediately prior to a competition. This is understandable, of course; but to practise karate-do properly is to recognise the totality and enormity of each moment's being the supreme moment; each block is the most important block, each strike or thrust should be full and total commitment. Karate-do is a continual series of life-or-death encounters; thoughts of what may happen next, or later in the training session, are completely irrelevant: life itself depends upon the reaction to the immediate blow, strike, thrust or kick. Likewise, thoughts of next week's competition must be of no concern. My own experience of this situation will perhaps prove enlightening.

In the week before the 1976 SKI Open Championship, I was practising free-style ***(ju-kumite)*** with my teacher, Asano ***sensei***, when I received an injury to my leg. As it happened I was a member of the team that had won the championship the year before, and was favourite to win in the forthcoming event. At this stage, I wondered whether I should call ***sensei's*** attention to the fact that I was injured, and that it might be better if I rested in order to recover in time for the championship. Suddenly, however, I could see in ***sensei's*** eyes that he knew my thoughts and he immediately attacked me harder and harder, forcing me to revert to being concerned only with the immediate problem of sheer survival. Naturally, on the day of the championship I had not properly recovered, and the team as a whole suffered quite severely from injuries.

Was Asano ***sensei*** right or wrong? If I had not been injured, perhaps I could have won my fight in the finals, instead of drawing. Of course, the answer depends entirely upon whether you are concerned with sport karate or karate-do. Zen and karate-do are concerned with the immediate present, the here-and-now, not with the future

****Combat***, Volume 2 Number 11

*****The Way of Karate***, Shigeru Egami, Ward Lock and Kodansha

Gingaku-ji, The Silver Pavilion. Constructed in 1482 for Ashikaga Yoshimasa, combining Chinese and Japanese elements to become a forerunner of the Zen-inspired traditional Japanese house. (Japan Information Centre)

and its possible benefits. The future will continue to be the future all our lives until, suddenly and finally, there is no future! Better savour the continual stream of here-and-now, and remember master Ummon's advice: 'If you walk, just walk; if you sit, just sit – but don't wobble!'

A final thought: to emphasize the sporting and competitive aspect of a martial way is necessarily to restrict it to the young and fit. And that is not the intention of the way, which is open to all.

Shinto

As we have seen, Zen is not a religion in its truest sense, since it does not concern itself with God or gods. The religious aspect of the ***samurai's*** life was catered for by Shinto, whose deities are called ***kami***. Originally, anything that inspired awe was termed ***kami***; rivers, trees, mountains, rocks, even extraordinary human beings (the emperor, for instance). The Shinto view of a man differs from that upheld by traditional Christian theology, in that it sees him as essentially pure and good; evil is a secondary accretion, eradicable by ritual purification.

Shinto shares common ground with Zen in its view of the nature of man, and its concern with transcending worldly entanglements. The Shinto temples themselves further pressed the similarities between their philosophies, for inside them the object of worship was often simply a mirror. Traditionally regarded as a symbol of authority, handed down to her descendants by Amaterasu (mythical ancestress of the imperial lineage), the mirror was considered to represent the presence of the ***kami*** herself. In addition, it signified that the inner spirit of man was of supreme importance, and that every man was to look into his own depths to perceive his inner 'condition'.

Like Zen, Shinto was readily acceptable to the hierarchy of the feudal system, preaching as it did the basic tenets of patriotism and loyalty, reverence for ancestral memory and respect for authority.

Confucius

The congruent philosophies of Zen and Shinto were further enhanced by the teachings of

Rock Garden at Ryoan-ji, Kyoto (Zen Buddhist Temple c. 1490). The rocks in the sea of gravel invite the mind to enter a state of tranquil contemplation. (Japan Information Centre)

the great Chinese philosopher and scholar Confucius (550 - 478 BC).

In a sense, because Buddhism could be construed as having little or no concern with the outward show of the world, Confucianism, with its acceptance of worldly conventions and institutions, was assimilated even more readily into the traditional Shinto ethic. Confucius also held that all men were inherently good, and that good order in society was dependent upon the practice of proper respect and behaviour between lord and retainer, parent and child, older children and younger, husband and wife, and friend and friend.

Thus, while Zen and Shinto were essentially concerned with the inner man and his spirit, Confucianism was concerned with external man and his relationships in society; and these three philosophies formed the basis of what came to be known as 'the way of the warrior' - Bushido, in which the embryonic concept of 'the way' was defined and given contemporary relevance.

Bushido

The code of Bushido was originally an unwritten one. Nevertheless, it was common currency among the élite of the social hierarchy from the 12th century to the mid-19th century. The ***samurai*** were taught that just as rank has its privileges so it also has its duties, and therefore they were expected to conduct themselves as models of dignity and virtue. They were required to lead austere lives, devoting themselves unswervingly to the service of their feudal lord ***(daimyo).*** They were expected to be courageous (courage was defined as simply seeing what had to be done and doing it, even if it resulted in death), and in this connection they were expected to be capable of determining the right moment to die, and to have a right reason. Anyone could rush blindly into battle and be killed, but unless the cause was right this was deemed a 'dog's death'. In this light, we see that the practice of ***seppuku*** or ***hara-kiri*** (suicide by cutting open the belly, followed by beheading by a 'second') was not the last resort of a warrior pushed beyond his limits by the vicissitudes of fate; but an honourable act of ultimate free-will. Often demanded by the *daimyo* or state in the form of lawful sentence of death, it allowed the nobleman to atone for his transgressions and enable his lineage to continue without dishonour.

Although Bushido was not passed on initially by the written word, a book called *Hagakure* ('Hidden among the Leaves') has come down to us from the early 18th century. This work, although often contradictory, contains the thoughts and precepts of an ex-*samurai* priest, Jocho Yamamoto (1659-1719). His words - noted down and preserved by his student Tsuramoto Tashiro (in spite of instructions to the contrary) - give us invaluable insight into the *samurai's* concept of Bushido. This book was never made freely available, but was kept and treasured as a system of practical and moral teachings for the lord and *samurai* of the Nabeshima clan. One or two examples from its pages will clearly reveal the profound effect of the centuries of Bushido influence:

'In a 50-50 life or death crisis, simply settle it by deciding on immediate death. There is nothing complicated about it. Just brace yourself and proceed.' (Book One)

'The best conduct with regard to speaking is to remain silent.' (Book Three)

'If you must fail, then fail splendidly.' (Book Two)

'Lord Naoshige said, 'The Way of the Samurai is a mania for death. Sometimes 10 men cannot topple a man with such conviction.' (Book One)

Regarding the aims and abilities of the individual *samurai* in the martial arts, Jocho quotes the words of a master swordsman, to the effect that a *samurai's* training lasts a lifetime. Initially, all the training seems to no avail as the student never seems to improve. At the next stage, he begins to realise his deficiencies, and the shortcomings of others. The next highest level is attained when the *samurai* is competent and confident enough to rely on himself. In this stage, he is pleased to receive praise and laments the failings of others. Above this is the level that demonstrates true mastery, in which the *samurai* never reveals his feelings or emotions by facial gestures and the like, nor does he continually exhibit his skill: on the contrary he pretends ignorance and incompetence whilst truly respecting the skill of others.

This, the master supposes, is the highest level that most can aspire to, but there is yet one more stage; the stage in which the one who reaches it realizes that his training will have no end, and that he will never achieve perfection. Here he quotes Yagyu Tajima no Kami Munenori: 'I do not know how to excel others, I only know how to excel myself. Today I am better than I was yesterday, tomorrow I will be better than I am today.'

Perhaps understandably, the Hagakure became a huge best-seller during World War II and one of its slogans 'I found that the Way of the Samurai is death' was taken to heart by the kamikaze suicide pilots. It was also a formative influence on the life and works of Yukio Mishima, Japan's best-known post-war novelist, who lived and died according to the Hagakure morality.

Naturally enough, with the Allied victory, the book was quickly abandoned as 'dangerous and subversive'. It is not, however, a manual of death. It exemplifies correct behaviour in all circumstances, and surely it has something to say to the modern Western *budo-ka;* for even if, at first sight, it portrays a staggering approach to our taboo subject of death, it also demonstrates categorically that there are ways of coming to terms with this fear of death. Again one must urge the Western karate-ka to look beyond the practice of technique and seek that calm acceptance of the inevitable which was an integral feature of the *samurai's* psychological make-up. Karate-do, like Bushido, is not to be confined to the *dojo* or the battlefield; it is for life.

CHAPTER 5. THE DOJO, ETIQUETTE AND CONVENTION

Dojo means, literally 'the way place': a place where students learn 'the way'. The name originally designated a room or hall of worship in a Buddhist temple, but now has come to denote any place set aside for the practice of the martial arts.

Usually, a *dojo* is a hall with a flat (generally wooden) unobstructed floor, of reasonably large proportions. It should be scrupulously clean and well ventilated, and smoking should not be allowed. Its atmosphere should reflect the serious intent of the *budo-ka* (martial arts practitioners): quiet, calm, with an air of respect and decorum. A sloppy, ill-lit, untidy *dojo* is indicative of the attitudes of its instructors and students, and the prospective student would be well advised to seek instruction elsewhere.

Many *dojo* (Japanese words can be interpreted as either singular or plural) have an area set aside for auxiliary training, with kick and punch bags, the *makiwara* (striking post) and weights. One wall may have large mirrors attached, to aid in checking for faults in stance and technique. Some *dojo* have club rooms for the students to relax in after training; but all *dojo* should have a proper shower,

Mokuso – meditation after training (author 2nd right).

toilet and changing facilities.

The ***dojo*** instructors (***sensei***) line up at the start of a training session in the traditional kneeling position (***seiza***), on the left-hand side of the ***shomen*** (front wall: in Japan, the place of honour), facing the line-up of students on the opposite side, who also kneel, in descending order of rank or grade (highest on the left, lowest on the right).

When everyone is still, the highest-graded student or junior instructor in the line facing the instructor(s) says in a loud voice: 'Sensei, ni rei' – 'Bow to the teacher(s)'. The whole class then bows formally to the instructor(s), who gravely return(s) the bow.

The strict discipline of a well-run ***dojo*** is maintained as much by the higher-ranked students, who set an example for the rest to follow, as by the instructors. Though this may at first appear unwelcome to the Western student, it is a fact that the majority of students learn to understand and even to demand the discipline, for it is based upon respect; indeed, in the main it is self-discipline. It soon becomes obvious to the student that sincerity and honesty of effort are two of the main criteria by which he or she is judged; and that mutual respect engenders courtesy and self-discipline.

Although training sessions vary, according to the emphasis placed on the various elements of karate by the different styles and individual ***sensei,*** a typical session begins with general calisthenics under the direction of the senior student. The teacher then takes the class

SKI *dojo* training.

through *kihon* (basic) training, in which the stances, blocks and attacking techniques that form the bedrock of the art are practised. This may well last for a whole session in the case of a beginners' class, or for only a proportion of the session in the more advanced classes. Then the students generally pair off and practise one-step or five-step sparring or the like, where basic defence techniques are practised against a pre-arranged attack.

After this, the teacher may move on to a more advanced technique, which the partners will practise over and over again until they have grasped it correctly. In advanced classes, the higher grades might practise semi-free sparring, in which the attack is pre-determined but the response left to the individual; after which there may be a period set aside for free-sparring itself, where both partners practise defence and attack in a spontaneous manner.

The final period is often devoted to the practice of *kata,* the formal sequences of karate techniques, in which the class will usually perform the sequence to the teacher's count and then at speed without count. This can be extremely tiring, as each mistake means that the whole *kata* will be repeated. In a high-grade class, the teacher will often ask the black-belt students to perform individually their *tokui* (favourite) *kata* which he will scrutinize and correct.

At the end of the whole session (generally 90 minutes), the class re-forms its original line(s) and in response to the senior student's command, 'Mokuso', they kneel in quiet meditation for a few minutes. This is brought to an end by the further command, 'Mokuso yame'. The senior student will then repeat the command he made at the start of the session, 'Sensei ni rei', and all the students bow formally to the *sensei,* who will reply: 'Go-kuro-san' (a contraction of the more formal 'Go-kuro-sama-deshita'; 'Thank you for your efforts.').

In some *dojo* the session closes with the class reciting the *dojo kun,* or oath, of which there are many. A typical one (a JKA *kun*) is:

To strive for perfection of character.

To defend the ways of Truth.

To foster the spirit of effort.

To honour the principles of etiquette.

To guard against impetuous courage.

The students then turn and bow to the *shomen* (a sign of respect made upon entering and leaving the *dojo*) as they depart. In some *dojo,* the lowest-graded students clean the floor quickly in readiness for the next session. To try to evade this duty is considered to be a sign of pride and misapprehension of its purpose, which is not one of punishment but of inculcating the attitude of helpfulness and social conscience students of the way of karate should exemplify.

CHAPTER 6. GRADING SYSTEMS

The degree of expertise of a karate practitioner is indicated by the colour of his or her belt *(obi).* The different styles have slightly different systems of grades and colours; but in the main, a brown belt indicates a student approaching the level of black belt. The ranks below black belt are called *kyu* grades (literally, 'boy' or 'pupil' grades), and there are normally between six and ten, depending on the style. Given below are two UK systems of *kyu* grades for comparison, one used by the British Karate Kyokushinkai, and the other by the SKI (GB).

BKK

10th *kyu* **white**
9th *kyu* **white**
8th *kyu* **light blue**
7th *kyu* **light blue**
6th *kyu* **yellow**
5th *kyu* **yellow**
4th *kyu* **green**
3rd *kyu* **green**
2nd *kyu* **brown**
1st *kyu* **brown**

SKI

ungraded **red**
9th *kyu* **white**
8th *kyu* **white**
7th *kyu* **yellow**
6th *kyu* **green**
5th *kyu* **purple**
4th *kyu* **purple with white stripe**
3rd *kyu* **brown**
2nd *kyu* **brown**
1st *kyu* **brown with white stripe**

Three major American grade systems are as follows.

Isshin-*ryu* (6 *Kyu* system)

6th *kyu* **white**
5th *kyu* **green**
4th *kyu* **green**
3rd *kyu* **brown**
2nd *kyu* **brown**
1st *kyu* **brown**

Goju-*ryu*

10th *kyu* **white**
9th *kyu* **white**
8th *kyu* **white**
7th *kyu* **white**
6th *kyu* **green**
5th *kyu* **green**
4th *kyu* **purple**
3rd *kyu* **brown**
2nd *kyu* **brown**
1st *kyu* **brown**

Correct distance - ***ma-ai.*** It is vital to maintain balance, posture, flexibility and defence whilst manoeuvring into attacking distance.

Taekwondo

9th ***kup***	**white**
8th ***kup***	**yellow**
7th ***kup***	**yellow**
6th ***kup***	**green**
5th ***kup***	**green**
4th ***kup***	**green**
3rd ***kup***	**red**
2nd ***kup***	**red**
1st ***kup***	**red**

In the ***kyu*** grades, the higher numbers indicate the lower grades and vice versa. In the black-belt or ***dan*** (literally 'man') grades, the higher numbers represent the higher grades.

Just as there are differences in the ***kyu*** systems of the different styles, so there are in the black-belt ranks. Some styles give appreciably higher ***dan*** grades than others: for example, top instructors and competition fighters in the SKI, with the exception of the chief instructors, are all of 2nd and 3rd ***dan*** rank, with the chief instructor being 8th ***dan***. Other styles go up to 10th ***dan*** or more, and grade upwards accordingly.

The American colour system for ranks of black belt vary from karate style to style, but basically they are as follows:

1st - 4th ***dan***	**black belt**
5th - 8th ***dan***	**white and red belt**
9th & 10th ***dan***	**red belt**

The black-belt grades also have courtesy titles. The senior instructor of a world-wide style organization is known as ***kancho,*** the 'master of the house'; 6th ***dan*** instructors and upward are called ***shihan*** or 'master'; 2nd to 5th ***dans*** are called ***sensei*** or 'teacher'; and 1st ***dans*** (and senior ***kyu*** grades if no dan grades are present) are called ***sempai,*** meaning 'senior'. In general, the grades beyond 5th and 6th ***dan*** are awarded for services to the art; top competition men tend to be 3rd to 5th ***dans*** who are still relatively young.

Contrary to popular opinion the black belt itself does not signify that the wearer is a master, or is expert in all the karate techniques. What it does indicate is that the ***yudansha*** – the holder of a black belt – is considered to have progressed from the ranks of the novices and is now a serious student.

To move from one rank to another, each student takes part in regular 'gradings', which test his level of competence in basic technique and ***kata.*** Generally, the time period between ***kyu*** gradings is three months, with perhaps six months between 1st ***kyu*** and 1st ***dan.*** The intervals between ***dan*** gradings are longer; normally, a period of one year has to elapse before a 1st ***dan*** can try for 2nd ***dan,*** and a minimum of two years before a 2nd ***dan*** can attempt 3rd ***dan,*** and so on.

Most styles have a similar format for their gradings: students line up and perform basic techniques relevant to their grade, to the command of the examiner. The higher ***kyu*** grades then pair off and demonstrate basic one-step sparring. Following this, each performs the ***kata*** mandatory for the grade attempted. If they have been successful, the examiner will promote them to the next grade. Sometimes, a temporary grade can be awarded if the student has satisfied most of the requirements but needs to overcome a weakness in one area before progressing.

The gradings for black belt are significantly more demanding than those for ***kyu*** grades. The formula of basics, sparring and ***kata*** is maintained, but a higher degree of expertise is demanded. The student will also have to demonstrate greater accuracy and power of technique, and instead of one-step sparring he will generally have to fight some of the other contenders. The aspiring black-belt will normally be graded as much for his spirit as for his technique, and is expected to show courage, controlled aggression and mental alertness.

A drawback of the belt system of grading is that occasionally students become 'belt-hunters'. This not only gives rise to egotism but can also mean that the student is wrongly seeing the colour of his belt as an end in itself. Remember: the belts themselves mean absolutely nothing; it is the person wearing the belt that is important.

CHAPTER 7. MECHANICAL PRINCIPLES

The techniques of karate are based upon sound scientific principles. Throughout its long history, the art of karate has undergone refinement. More recently, it has also benefited from advances in the understanding of physical and mechanical laws.

There is nothing in the physical universe that is not subject to the physical laws of nature; the human body is, of course, no exception.

The physical laws upon which the techniques of karate are based are, in brief:

Every mass (body) continues in its state of rest or uniform motion in a straight line unless an external force is applied. (Newton's First Law).

Force is proportional to the rate of change of momentum (mass x velocity). (Newton's Second Law).

To every action there is an equal and opposite reaction. (Newton's Third Law).

When we stand, we experience the force of gravity as weight, and when we move about we gain a momentum, which is the product of mass (m) times velocity (v).

Mass is a constant factor, basically taken to be the amount of matter in an object. In practice, we normally recognize this as weight, which is mass under the attraction of gravity. Thus, while weight can vary according to the force of gravity, mass remains unchanged. As we have seen, mass x velocity = momentum. By Newton's First Law we know that objects with momentum will continue forever at the same speed unless another force acts to alter the situation. This is known as inertia, the property of an object to maintain its current state.

Let us consider the human fist: as an object propelled by a force, it has momentum. Naturally, the fist can travel only as far as the limits imposed by a full extension of the arm; the intention of the puncher, however, is to make contact with a target before this limit is reached. If the fist collides with a stationary object, or with one moving more slowly than the fist (the head, for example), there is a transference of momentum from the faster to the slower object.

It follows, then, that if the fist has a low momentum (is moving slowly) it will transfer only a small degree of force at the moment of impact. If, however, the fist is moving very quickly (possessing a high momentum) it will impart a greater degree of force to the target.

If the target is indeed the head, and if the fist has developed considerable momentum, a high degree of force will be transferred to the head, which will attempt to move in the former direction of

Kanazawa (8th ***dan***) and Asano (7th ***dan***) demonstrate a roundhouse kick to the head and double block (***jodan-mawashi-geri*** and ***morote-uke***).

the fist. Of course, it cannot do this very effectively, because of its considerably more restricted range of movements. But for a short space of time this is what happens - and it leads directly to brain concussion, as the brain encased within the skull is subjected to 'whiplash' injury against the hard, bony substances surrounding it.

As momentum is the product of mass x velocity, it is obvious that although we can do little to alter the former it is perfectly possible to increase the latter, with the result of generating a much higher transference of force upon impact. And this, to a large extent, accounts for the dramatic results of karate blows. They are light, but very fast - and the power of a blow depends upon the speed of its delivery.

An analogy may help to demonstrate Newton's Second Law: if someone picked up a bullet and threw it at you it might cause a slight bruise, but would be unlikely to do much major damage. If, on the other hand, the same bullet were loaded into a gun and fired at you, the result would be all too certain. But what has changed? Certainly not the bullet. The only difference is that it has developed a much greater momentum: it hits the target at a much higher speed. To increase force, therefore, one must increase velocity to its maximum.

Newton's Third Law, which holds that for every force produced there is automatically an equal and opposite reaction, is supremely important in a consideration of the techniques of karate, for a number of separate but inter-related reasons.

First, it should be well understood that in the execution of all techniques of punching, kicking and striking, and in the use of hard (as opposed to soft/parrying) blocks, the muscular force of the body is primarily effective only in as much as it affects the speed of execution of the technique. Of course, muscles not directly concerned with the technique are brought into play in a secondary role, to maintain balance and to act as a base upon which force-producing muscles react to institute the force. But the prime concern of the muscles is to bring the

Downward elbow strike - ***otoshi-empi-uchi***.

attacking body weapon into contact with the target as fast as is humanly possible, because the effectiveness of the blow depends upon its speed.

In complex motions, such as those involved in the delivery of a karate technique, maximum momentum is created if forces are produced sequentially rather than simultaneously. Muscular force, then, must be cumulative to produce maximum effect. This means that the relatively slow but powerful muscles of the waist and abdomen must be brought into play before the weaker but faster ones of the extremities. This is significant in the light of the Third Law, since for the muscles of the extremities to have the desired effect they must derive a reaction from the application of force against the stronger, less resistant, muscles of the torso, which must, therefore, be contracted (tensed) beforehand. (NB: It is important to note that after the initial muscular contractions the muscles should be relaxed so as not to interfere with the ballistic momentum.)

In achieving maximum momentum, the principle of reaction force is also utilized in the following ways: (a) in creating a force with linear motion, (b) in creating a force with circular motion and (c) in creating a force with pendular motion. In many instances (a), (b) and (c) are combined to a greater or lesser extent, and the consideration of a specific technique - the basic reverse punch ***(gyaku-zuki),*** for example - will make the principles clear.

First, the linear force T(a) generated by the leg muscles thrusts against the floor to create forward linear impetus. This imparts a momentum M, which is present equally in all parts of the body, including the attacking limb, in this case the right arm.

Second, the forward motion V of the arm is supplemented by the centrifugal force C generated by snapping the hips in a circular motion (b) in the direction of the blow*. This movement is itself strengthened by the reaction force R, created by the rapid withdrawal of the non-punching arm.

Basically, then, thrust T and linear motion (a), reaction force R, centrifugal force C and circular motion (b) combine to produce momentum in the body and attacking limb, to which is added V, the velocity created by muscular contraction.

In some kicking techniques - front kick ***(mae-geri),*** for example - the hips are sometimes used in a forward-and-backward, pendulum-like motion (c), which also adds impetus to the blow.

The fact that every action produces an equal and opposite reaction does also mean that when the fist strikes the target, it will be subject to a force equal to that which it imparts. For this reason, it is important that blows be aimed below surface level, or 'through' the target, as the continuing momentum nullifies the reaction force. Again, it is necessary to ensure that at the moment of impact the body is in a strong and stable position, and that the wrist and arm joints - which are relatively weak - are strengthened, or the force of the blow will be dissipated.

In order to ensure that the body is in optimum condition to effect a successful transfer of the fist's momentum force to the target, karate-ka practice ***kime,*** or focus, in which the muscles that have been relaxed after the initial contraction to launch the technique are sharply tensed at the moment of impact.

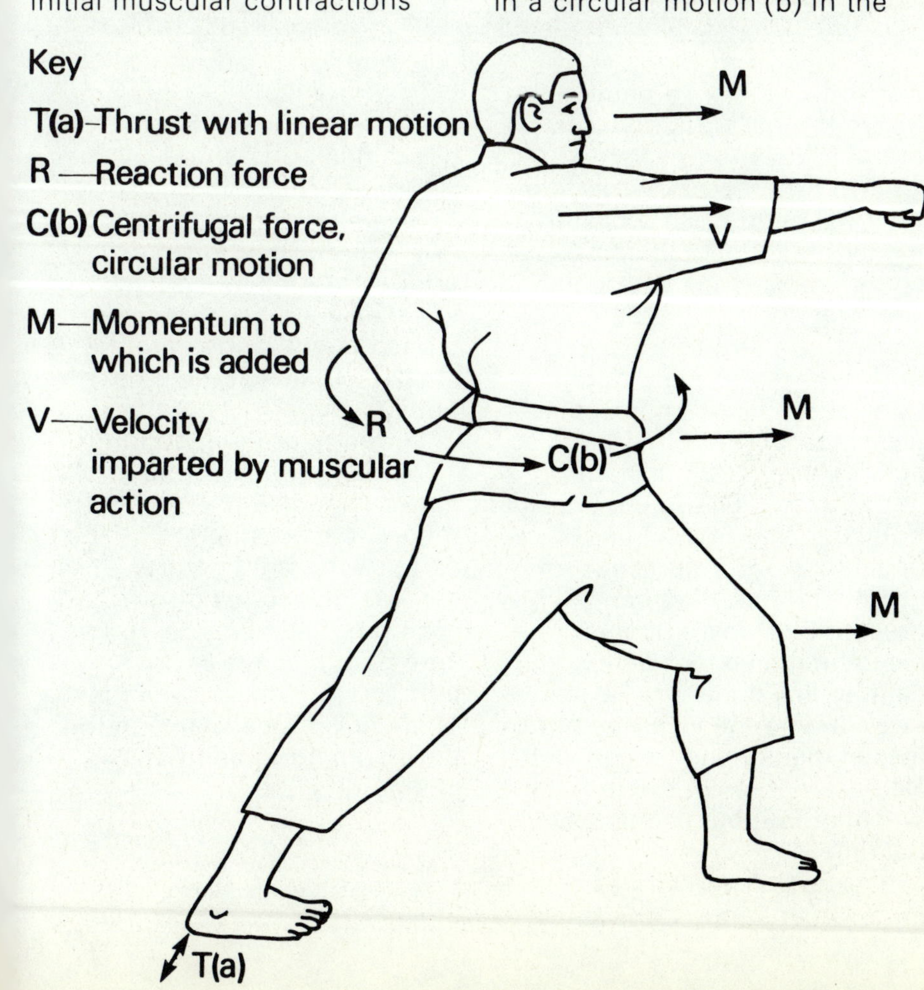

*Most karate styles facilitate this by assuming a half-front-facing stance. Others - Shukokai, for example - use a double twisting action from a squarer front-facing stance, the hips first twisting in an opposite direction to the intended thrust; the reaction force thus created is then utilized to snap the hips back again.

Kime (focus)

Researches into the function and operations of the muscles of the human body, have discovered that muscles can produce a force of approximately 42lb per square inch of cross section. On this basis, it has been estimated that if all the muscle fibres comprising the muscles could be made to contract simultaneously, a force could be generated in excess of six tons! It seems that the body has built-in inhibitors which prevent the generation of such a degree of force, which would of course entail a total and massive contraction that would have extremely harmful effects. It has happened that perfectly ordinary men and women, in times of overwhelming stress, have performed some almost superhuman feat of strength; but this may be credited to the temporary over-riding of the inhibitory mechanisms.

As well as sending signals to the muscles causing them to act (i.e. contract), the nervous system apparently sends signals that ensure they do not act at full power. Since it has been proved that hypnotism, for example, can improve strength and muscular endurance, and that in times of stress the inhibitory mechanisms can be over-ridden, it would seem that much athletic training produces its effect as much by weakening or removing these blocks as by improving bodily strength and endurance.

The great speed with which karate techniques are delivered is the result of strenuous long-term training. The speed is largely generated by the rapidity of muscle contraction, from relaxed to tensed; the faster the delivery, the more successful has been the removal of inhibitory responses.

The trained karate-ka, by continually practising ***kime*** – the abrupt and powerful tensing of all appropriate muscles at the split second of impact or full extension – in all suitable techniques over a period of years, should be able to generate considerably greater force without harming his or her own body than an untrained person.

At the moment of impact with the target, the drive and speed (momentum) of the attacking limb is converted into destructive power by the instantaneous application of ***kime,*** which lasts for only a split second and aids the transference of momentum to the target. This ability to snap out extremely fast techniques that culminate in a forceful muscular contraction accounts to a great extent for the tremendous power of karate blows and blocks, and is based firmly upon the scientific application of Newton's three laws.

S Asano with a variation of minor outer reap (***ko-soto-gari***) against back kick (***ushiro-geri***): stepping inside the kick and sweeping away the leg from the rear.

CHAPTER 8. THE ESOTERIC PRINCIPLES

In the previous chapter, karate techniques were considered in terms of mechanical principles. There are, however, other factors which have a bearing on the effectiveness of any technique: the esoteric, or spiritual and psychological aspects.

Hara

In the traditional martial arts, ***hara,*** which can be looked upon as the spiritual (as opposed to the physical) centre of gravity of a body, is the spiritual essence responsible for maintenance of the alert, calm self-control considered essential in achieving any degree of mastery.

As it happens, oriental philosophy places the centre spot of this spiritual force in exactly the place occupied by the physical centre of gravity, in a person standing erect; that is, in a hypothetical point some two to three inches behind and below the navel (hence the literal translation of ***hara*** as 'belly'). Whereas, however, the physical centre has no fixed location – indeed, in some circumstances (as with pole-vaulters, sprinters, etc) it even shifts to a point outside the body altogether – the ***hara*** is considered to be immovable, and it is from here that all actions and motions stem. Through the ***hara,*** mind and body become unified and capable of resolute action:

'He who has Hara can be prepared for anything and everything, even for death, and calm in any situation. He can even bow to the victor with no loss of dignity and he can wait. He does not resist the turning wheel of fate but calmly bides his time.'*

Basically, ***hara*** is an essential factor in ensuring consistent success. Skill in technique is necessary, of course, but does not in itself guarantee success. However well-controlled or executed a technique, as long as the performer is subject to doubts, moods and other stresses, he may be master of his technique but cannot be master of himself: his skill is open to the effects of his uncertainty or intimidation.

In a sense, development of ***hara*** is not only a requisite for the martial artist; it should be an aim. The fighting arts – like the arts of ***ikebana*** (flower arranging) and ***cha-no-yu*** (tea ceremony) – have as their ultimate aim the transcendence of sheer physical skill and the development of spirit and character.

**Hara. The Vital Centre of Man,* Karlfried Graf von Dürckheim, Unwin Paperbacks (George Allen and Unwin) and Samuel Weiser.

Ford
DAGENHAM FOUNDRY
ENGINEERING
Ford
DESIGN

Ki

Accompanying the concept of ***hara*** is the idea of a 'life force' that activates and permeates all living creatures. The ***hara*** is considered to be the central point of this spirit, which in Japanese is called *ki* (from the Chinese *ch'i*). Completely natural and in no way magical, ***ki*** may be thought of as the spirit that distinguishes the living from the dead. To many martial arts masters, ***ki*** and its conscious control lies at the heart of all traditional and modern ***budo.***

The development of ***hara*** and *ki* are inextricably linked to the practice of deep abdominal breathing, such as that utilized in ***za-zen*** (sitting meditation). To be effective, the breathing should be slow and regular, the air inhaled through the nostrils and 'pushed' firmly down into the lower abdomen, the chest remaining uninflated. The ***hara*** should be slightly tensed, with everything else above the waist relaxed and free of tension. Exhalation should be done slowly, through the mouth. The body should be erect, generally seated cross-legged; though if necessary the practice can be carried out in a standing position.

A competition demonstration of lunge punch (*oi-zuki*) to the head.

Kiai

The technique of harnessing the inner power, and using it effectively to augment physical power ***(chikara),*** is called ***kiai-jutsu. Ki*** means spirit, internal force; ***ai*** comes from a contraction of the verb ***awasu,*** meaning 'to unite'. Many astonishing claims have been made about the ability of advanced exponents of the art to kill with the power of their ***kiai.*** But very few non-Japanese instructors are capable of teaching the art and principles of ***ki*** and ***kiai;*** and one suspects that there are not all that many Japanese who really understand them fully.

In karate-do, the ***ki*** is summoned up and united with the physical power, normally at the instant of ***kime*** (focus), by uttering a piercing shout. This acts as a trigger, co-ordinating neural and muscular responses so that everything, spirit and power, is concentrated in the same split second. Physically, it has also the effect of tightening the muscles of the torso and lower abdomen, thus enabling them to be used to provide reaction force (explained in chapter 7).

The ***kiai*** is also used to psychological effect: to deter or intimidate an opponent; or to startle him into a reaction that may be used to advantage.

One of the major problems to be overcome in the practice of ***kiai*** is simply one of shyness. The student may be unwilling to attract attention to himself by uttering loud, fierce shouts. Such hesitancy must be surmounted, for with practice he will experience the tremendous difference in power gained by uniting ***ki,*** strength and technique.

CHAPTER 9. STUDENT AND TEACHER

It may be fairly stated that the majority of those who join a karate club do so initially for the wrong reasons. The greatest wish of many young men, attracted by the myth of the invincible karate expert who takes on and defeats all-comers and smashes bricks and wood with ease, is to wear the magical black belt and themselves become 'invincible'. A large number of young women join because they are persuaded by the media that karate is a weapon guaranteed to protect against the would-be rapist.

Of course, to some extent, both dreams are based on reality. But what is not appreciated is the degree of discomfort, the amount of sweat and the years of dedication the young man or woman will have to survive before he or she has the skill necessary to make either objective feasible. Yes, karate techniques can be used to smash objects and defeat opponents; but if this is the chief objective – or rather, if this ***remains*** the chief objective – of the male student, then he would be well advised to follow Asano ***sensei's*** advice and go and buy a shotgun, which certainly would ensure his success in combat. And the female student would better prepare to protect her honour by enrolling in a self-defence class.

Karate-do is not a sport, nor is it primarily a system of self-defence; these are merely facets of a multi-sided diamond, the heart of which is 'the rough, rugged and painstaking quest for the answer to the meaning of existence, undertaken by a master and his pupils in their ***dojo***'. To understand this point is to make a great step forward, and to ensure clarification of many of the problems that may arise during the course of training.

If his ***sensei*** is Japanese, or has been thoroughly trained in the Japanese spirit, the student may sometimes feel he is being selected for harsh treatment, that the instructor is not being 'fair' to him; all he ever seems to do is criticize. In fact, the student should welcome this; the ***sensei*** is now showing that he has accepted him as a serious student and therefore worthy of criticism.

Sometimes the ***sensei*** will test the student's spirit by pressing him to his limits and beyond in stamina, courage and willpower. The exhausted

Whirlwind defence and counter: M Mura (6th ***dan***), S Kato (5th ***dan***). The jump and spin add power and impetus to the techniques of small karate-ka.

Y Shinohara with a jumping roundhouse kick (*mawashi-tobi-geri*).

pupil should notice, however, that, severe though the ***sensei*** has been, he has also been totally impersonal; and is just as demanding with every other student. Clearly, the master can have no friends in the ***dojo:*** by not offering the 'prop' of friendship, he forces the student to rely solely upon himself.

My own recollections of such experiences are vividly etched. Every time my teacher called me out for free-style with him, my heart would sink! I knew just what was to come. ***Sensei*** would keep me out, blocking my attacks and showing up my weak defences by the occasional (non-too-gentle) blow, until I began to develop asthma (from which I suffered quite badly). At this stage, instead of taking pity on my wheezing and gasping, he would begin to press his attacks until I was almost unable to stand. Still ***sensei*** kept up the pressure, until I could only stagger around, offering a token defence. After a while, I passed beyond all care of life or death, my only remaining thought rapidly assuming supreme importance: I would not give in! And only then, as I launched desperate 'do or die' attacks with total commitment, did ***sensei*** call a halt and allow me to drag myself away.

Why? The answer only really came after I myself became a teacher. Asano ***sensei*** was always aware of the possibility of my 'hiding behind' my asthma; making it an excuse for not training as hard as other members of the class, or using it as a psychological balm, to soothe my pride by excusing a poor performance. By continually denying me these indulgences, ***sensei*** made me realize that the powers of mind and spirit are always adequate to cope with and overcome limitations imposed by the body. (Incidentally, we never spoke of this after a training session. Only after nearly nine years did ***sensei*** laconically remark: 'Better now, neh?')

The majority of students are perfectly healthy; but the lesson to be learned remains the same. The student must cultivate the ability to see things in their true perspective, and to be completely honest with himself. This means never making excuses for a bad performance, nor being content with 'coasting along' in training. Eventually, he will be led to understand that it is just as egotistical to be concerned overmuch with defeat as it is to rejoice in victory.

The traditional ***budo*** master will, in fact, make very sure that he continually 'knocks down the nail that sticks up'. He will seldom, if ever, compliment his best pupils on their performance; indeed, those who achieve success in competition will more than likely find that the ***sensei*** is at pains to demonstrate in free-sparring that they still have much to learn! In his eyes, success carries with it the chance that the student will react incorrectly and place a false value upon it; for, in truth, each win gives further opportunity for ultimate failure, just as each meal gives opportunity for future hunger.

From time to time, every student will experience the 'plateau effect' – a period of dissatisfaction with his performance. It may seem that, in spite of all his efforts, he has achieved no consequent improvement in skill; indeed, it may even seem he is regressing.

It helps to understand that, during such a period, the body is actually assimilating the new knowledge gained from the training. It will reveal itself eventually, and the student will suddenly find that things begin to go right. The plateau effect ***will*** pass. It will also return; though of course each time the effect is maintained at a higher skill level.

During periods of physical difficulty, the spirit receives its hardest training. Remember: to meet continually with success is never to learn how to cope with failure. If setbacks and difficulties were never to arise, they never could be overcome.

Students may find it helpful to remember that indomitable spirit, particularly in the context of the martial arts, is as much a heritage of Western society as Japanese, as these lines from an early poem, describing a battle between the English and their Danish invaders in the year AD991, clearly indicate:

'Spirit shall be the harder,
Heart the keener,
Courage the greater,
as our strength grows less.'

'The Battle of Maldon' (my translation)

This conveys, over many centuries, precisely those attributes of courage and determination which distinguish the true ***budo-ka*** of today.

In principle, any hard part of the body can be utilized as a weapon of defence or attack. In practice, however, it is sensible to concentrate on mastering the use of those parts most manoeuvrable and effective. The head, for example, though an extremely powerful close-range weapon, is naturally less useful than the fists or feet, which are capable of a much wider range of movements. In karate, the techniques can be broadly classified as hand techniques ***(te-waza)*** and leg techniques ***(ashi-waza).***

STANCES

It is difficult to over-emphasize the importance of assuming correct stances when executing karate techniques. No matter how strong the karate-ka, and regardless of his speed and accuracy, all will be to no avail if he is not firmly settled in a strong and stable position at the moment of execution. Lacking a firm base, the technique will lack power and the deliverer will be in danger of being caught in or forced into, an off-balance position by his opponent. And when off-balance the karate-ka is vulnerable, for he can perform neither offensive nor defensive techniques effectively.

Some styles of karate (Shotokan, for example) insist on low stances at all times during basic technique training. Other styles (Shukokai) tend to train in higher stances. Yet others (e.g., Wado-***ryu***) utilize stances which are neither so low as those of Shotokan, nor as high as those used in Shukokai. These differences reflect to some extent the varying emphasis placed on such things as straight as opposed to circular techniques, hip movements, and sport karate, where speed assumes more importance than power.

Briefly, proponents of the low-stance styles maintain that the muscular effort required to keep in a low stance while training strengthens hips, legs and allied musculature, so that when a higher stance is adopted (in free-style, for example) the karate-ka's kicking techniques should be stronger than those of one whose leg muscles have not been so strengthened. Many low-stance stylists also consider that it is easier (particularly for a 'puncher') to get in under the attacks of someone in a higher stance; that after long low-stance practice, attack and defence in general are easier since they present a smaller target; and that, in blocking from low stance, the hands have to travel through a smaller range of movements.

Those who practice from the higher stances hold that what they lose in power they gain in mobility. Styles that emphasize competition and sport karate generally adopt the latter view, since, because of the rules of competition, the ability to deliver powerful, conclusive blows (especially to the head) becomes secondary to the need to deliver fast, snappy techniques that score points.

While the most practical approach to training will involve a variety of stances, with perhaps a bias toward low stance, the student beginning karate-do would do well to consider the differences between the styles and evaluate them in the light of their underlying philosophies, and with due consideration to his own aims and physical characteristics. Then, whatever his final choice, he will be aware of the fact stressed by all karate styles: that assuming the right stance at the right time is of great importance.

The descriptions of stances which follow have been selected as being – with minor modifications – common to all the major karate styles:

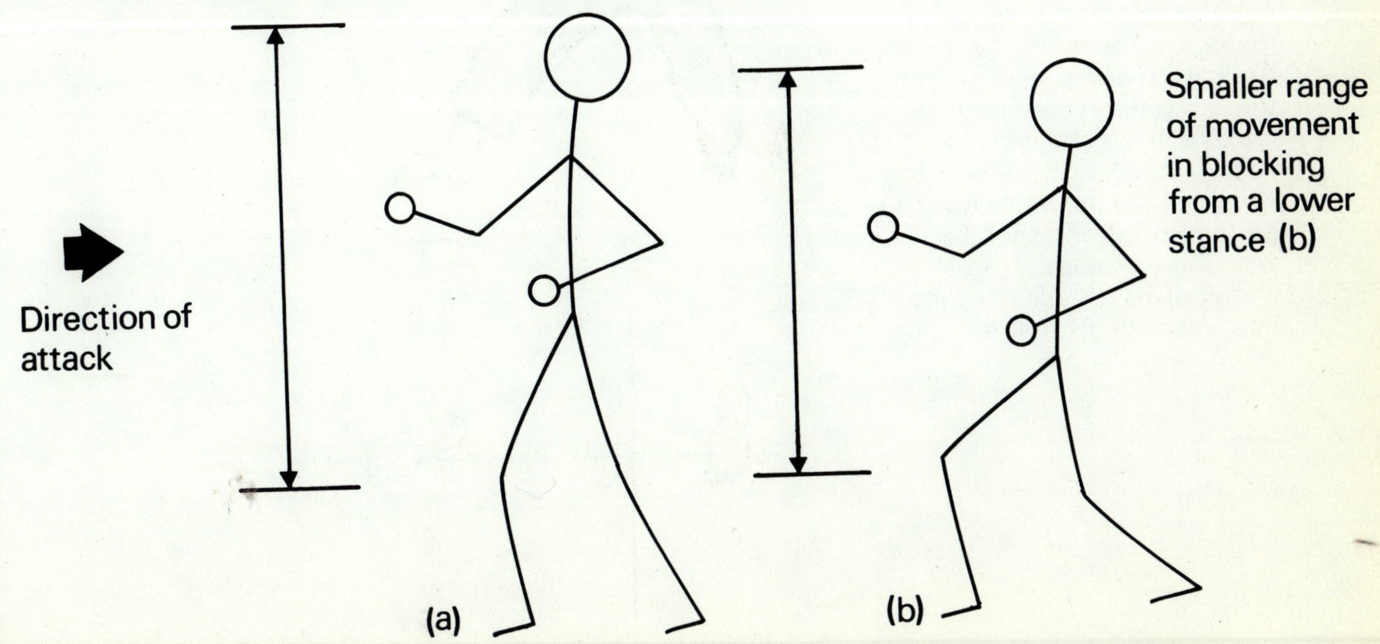

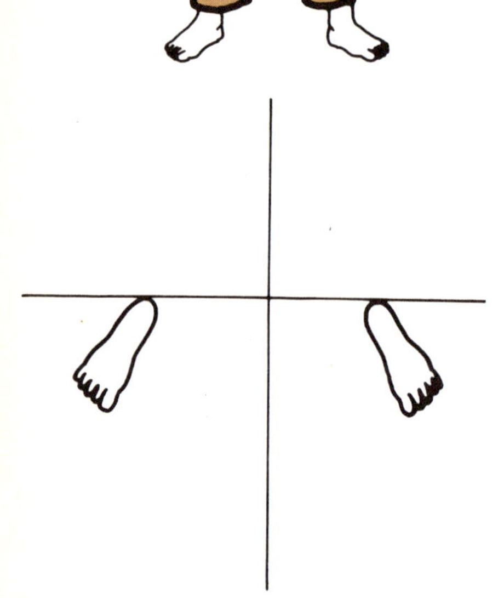

Hachiji-dachi the 'natural' stance. Feet are roughly shoulder-width apart, with toes pointing slightly outward. This stance was once assumed with muscles tensed; nowadays, all tension is eliminated and breathing is slow, gentle and relaxed. In this stance, the karate-ka should maintain an air of quiet alertness.

Heisoku-dachi In this stance the body is as in ***hachiji-dachi,*** but the feet are together. This is the position usually taken before bowing.

Kokutsu-dachi back stance. Formerly a sideways-facing stance, now usually half-facing with the hips 45° to the front, this strong defensive stance enables counter-attacks to be made even stronger by using the bent rear leg as a spring, thrusting the hips forcefully into the front stance. Approximately 65–70% of the weight is on the back leg. The general position assumed is with the feet about twice shoulder-width apart front to back, with heels in line.

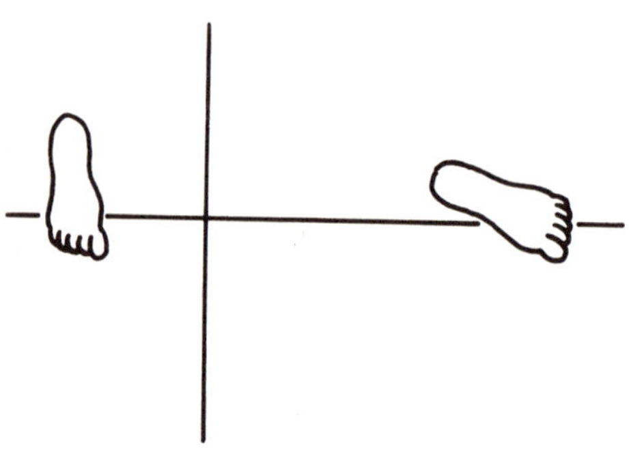

Zenkutsu-dachi front stance. One of the most utilized stances. It allows strong blocks, attacks and counters to be made in a forward direction. The weight is approximately 60% on the front leg. The body is kept upright, facing either directly to the front, or half-front. The head faces the front in either case. The front foot points forward, rear foot is turned as near as possible in the same direction. Front leg is bent, knee directly over the toes, while rear leg is kept straight and tensed. Feet should be approximately shoulder-width apart left to right, and roughly twice shoulder-width apart front to back.

Nekoashi-dachi cat stance. A shorter version of back stance, with 90% of weight on the rear leg. Front foot rests on the toes, front knee is turned slightly inward to protect the groin. This is an ideal position for the execution of fast front-foot kicking techniques, and for rapid evasive and counter-attacking movements.

Fudo-dachi (sometimes called *sochin-dachi*) the immovable stance. This is not a traditional stance, but one devised after much discussion in the mid-1930s, when the original comparatively high stances derived from Okinawan karate were modified by some styles. Essentially, *fudo-dachi* is a modification of the front stance with the rear knee bent and tensed in an outward direction. The body is half front-facing. This is a very strong and stable stance, facilitating powerful blocks and counters.

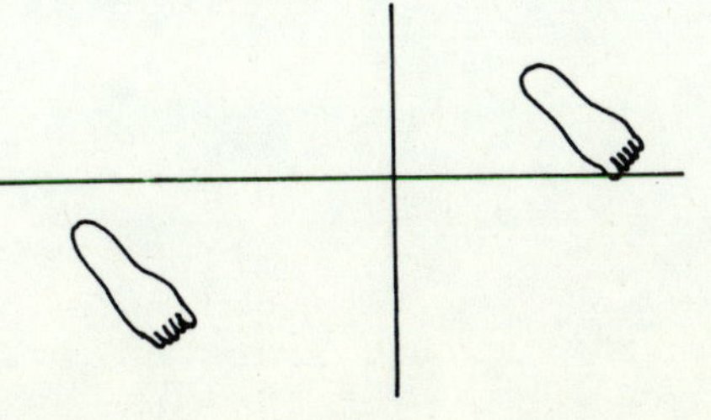

Ju-dachi free stance. This, too, is a relatively new stance; basically, a slightly shorter, more flexible version of the front stance. Approximately 60–65% of the weight is on the front leg, as in front stance, but the distance between front and rear leg is shorter, and the rear leg is bent slightly at the knee. The body is upright, generally half front-facing, thus presenting a smaller target. Some styles (e.g. Shotokan) assume a low free stance, while others (e.g. Shukokai) adopt a higher position. This stance enables extremely fast movements in most directions, and particularly favours the totally committed lunging attack.

Three versions of *ju-dachi* (free stance): Shotokan (left), Wado-*ryu* (centre) and Shukokai (right).

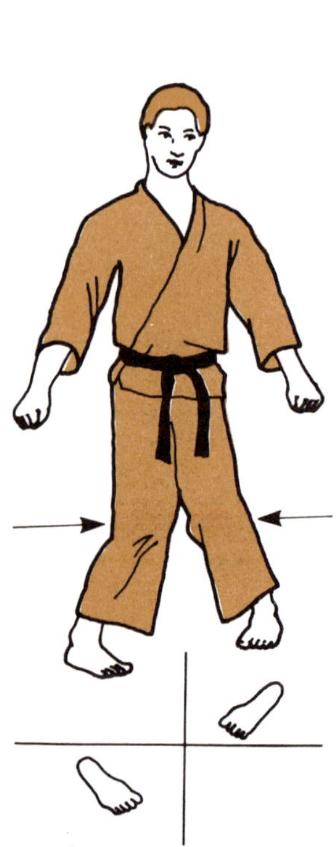

Sanchin-dachi hourglass stance. In this very strong defensive stance (little practised by most styles outside the *kata*), the toes of the rear foot are in line with the heel of the front foot, the knees are flexed inward, and the body is kept upright. The toes of both feet are pointed slightly inward.

Hangetsu-dachi half-moon stance. This is similar to the *sanchin-dachi,* but the position of the feet is closer to that of the front stance. Again, the knees are strongly flexed inward. A useful stance for both attack and defence, it is mostly used for the latter, since it favours powerful punching and striking techniques.

Kiba-dachi straddle or horse stance. A strong sideways stance, comparatively weak and unstable to front and back, this position facilitates side techniques such as ***uraken*** (back fist), ***yoko-empi*** (side elbow), and ***yoko-geri*** (side kick). Generally, the feet are approximately twice shoulder-width apart, with the hips lowered and the knees strongly flexed outward. Weight is equally distributed on both legs.

This stance is occasionally used as a fighting stance, despite the fact that it restricts the range of effective techniques. One drawback is its vulnerability to fast leg-sweep and lunge-punch attacks; though the advanced karate-ka can turn this to his advantage by creating apparent openings in his defence and countering the forthcoming attack.

It is a useful exercise to practise alternately tensing and relaxing all the muscles in the various stances, to develop strength and gain familiarity with the optimum body position and muscular tension for effective ***kime*** (focus), vital for the correct execution of karate techniques.

CALISTHENICS

Stretching exercises to loosen the joints and make the muscles supple should be performed at the begining and end of every training session. For maximum benefit, each exercise should be performed smoothly and rhythmically. 'Bouncing' the body is not recommended; best results are obtained by holding the stretch position for a brief period before relaxing.

Students should not be in too much of a hurry to achieve suppleness: 'little and often' should be the maxim.

There are many variations used in different ***dojo***; but whatever the style of karate practised, make sure to thoroughly and briskly loosen the major muscle groups before commencing the basic training.

PARTS OF THE BODY USED

Te-waza (zuki-te = hand attacks, *uke-te* = hand blocks)

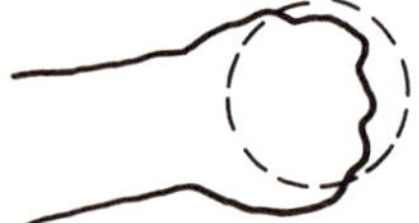

Back fist *(uraken)*
Formed in the same way as ***seiken,*** used in snapping attacks against opponent's head and body.

Fore-fist *(seiken)*
This fist used to be formed in the usual clenched-finger manner, but with the thumb pressed over the index finger, the top joints of which were kept extended. Now the regular method used is simply to clench the fist in the normal manner. A general principle of karate technique is always to use the smallest striking surface possible to deliver a blow; this concentrates the force over a small area. (The effectiveness of this principle can be easily demonstrated. Place your hand flat, palm downward, on a flat surface. Now put the palm of your other hand on top and push down hard. Next form the upper hand into a one-knuckle fist and press down equally hard. The difference, even with the same degree of force being utilized, will be immediately noticeable).

In order to make use of this effect, only the two large knuckles of the index and middle fingers are used in ***seiken*** to attack the opponent's vital points (generally head, chest and stomach).

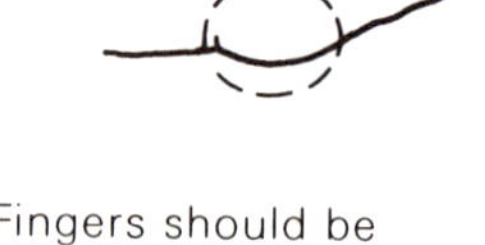

Knife-hand *(shuto)*
Fleshy area at base of little finger is used to attack opponent's face, temple, neck, body or the vital points of the limbs. Fingers should be firmly tensed together and thumb slightly bent but pressed against base of index finger.

One-finger spear hand *(ippon-nukite)*
Index finger is extended, others are bent at centre finger joints, to give support to extended finger. Used to attack opponent's eyes.

Middle knuckle fist *(nakadaka-ken)*
Fist is firmly clenched, with centre knuckle joint of middle finger protruding. Used mainly to attack opponent's temples, solar plexus and other vital points.

Two-finger spear hand *(nihon-nukite)*
Similar to ***ippon-nukite,*** but using both index and middle finger to attack opponent's eyes.

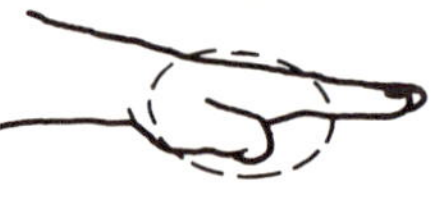

Ridge-hand *(haito)*
Hand position is similar to that in shuto, except that thumb is bent and folded into palm. Used to attack opponent's face, neck and ribs.

Hammer fist
(tetsui)
Using fleshy area at base of little finger, ***tetsui*** is used to attack opponent's head, neck, body and joints.

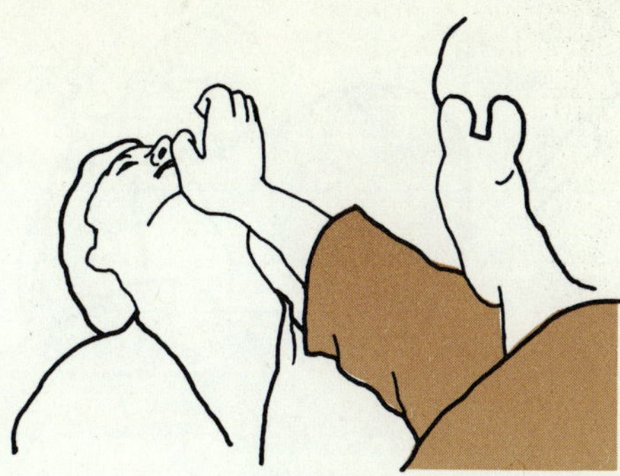

Palm-heel
(teisho)
Fingers and thumb are folded, and wrist bent sharply upward. Used to attack opponent's nose, jaw and stomach. Also used for blocking.

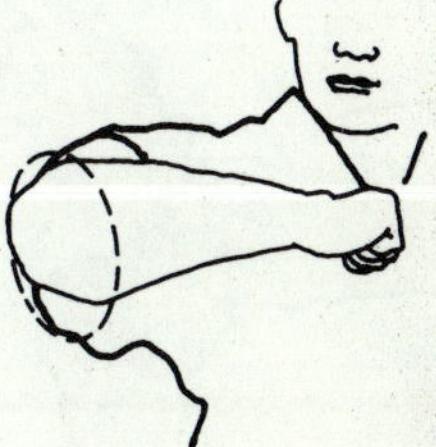

Elbow
(empi)
Point of the elbow is used to attack opponent's face, chin, chest, ribs and stomach.

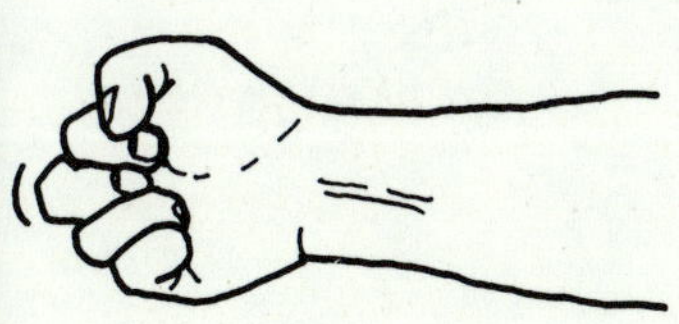

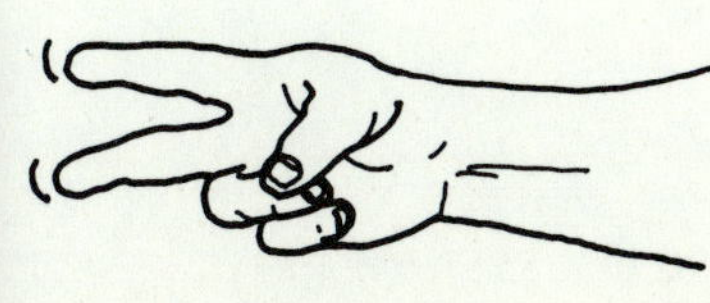

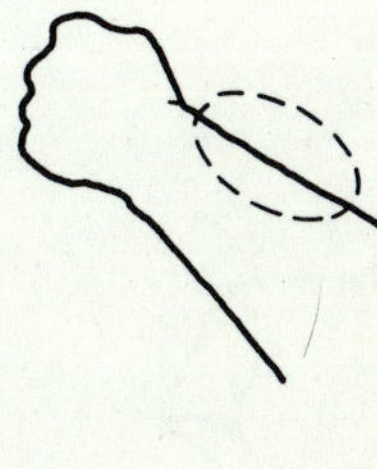

Forearm
(ude)
All parts of the forearm are used; occasionally to attack opponent's face or neck, but primarily for blocking.

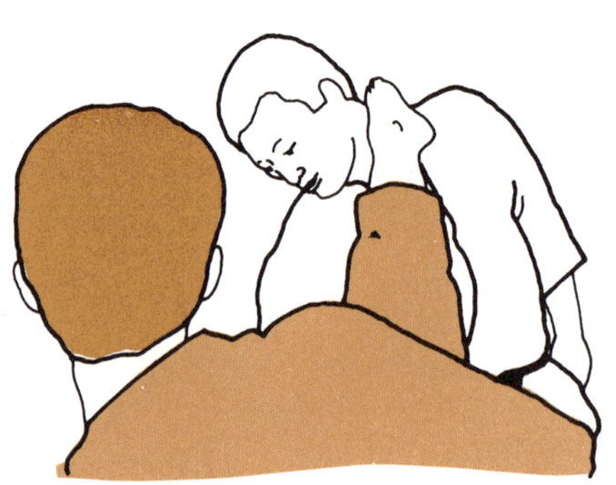

Instep
(haisoku)
Toes are fully extended, or flexed slightly downward, and top of foot is used to attack opponent's head, neck, ribs, stomach, and groin.

Ashi-waza
Ball of foot
(koshi)
With toes curled upward, ball of foot is used to attack opponent's head, neck, ribs, stomach and groin.

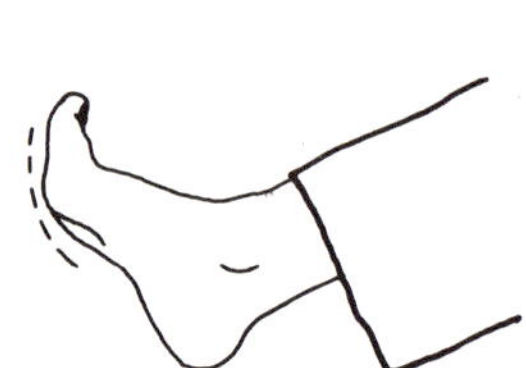

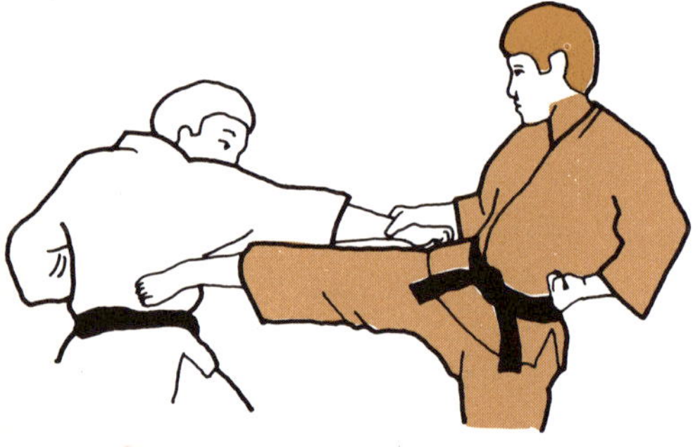

Edge of foot
(sokuto)
Foot should be bent to form right angle with leg, and outer edge used to attack opponent's face, neck, jaw, ribs, stomach, groin and joints.

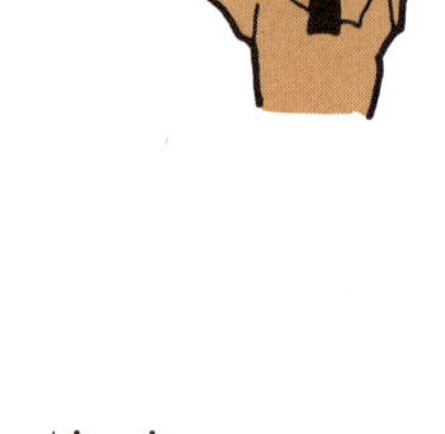

Heel
(kakato)
Heel is used to attack opponent's head, jaw, chest, ribs, kidneys, stomach, groin, joints and instep.

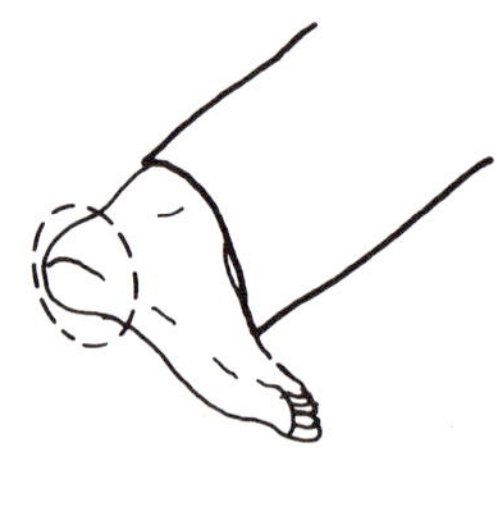

Knee
(hiza)
Knee is used to attack opponent's face, stomach or groin.

CALISTHENICS

Solo Exercises

Neck

Loosen neck muscles by turning head from side to side, then rotating it clockwise and anti-clockwise.

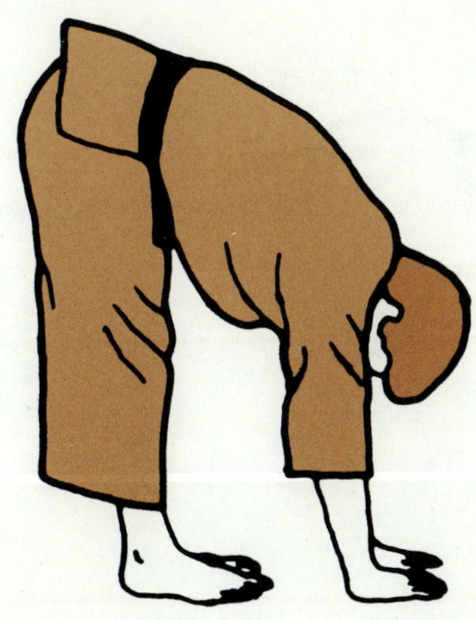

Hip, Waist and Back

Feet apart, legs straight, alternately touch toes of both feet.

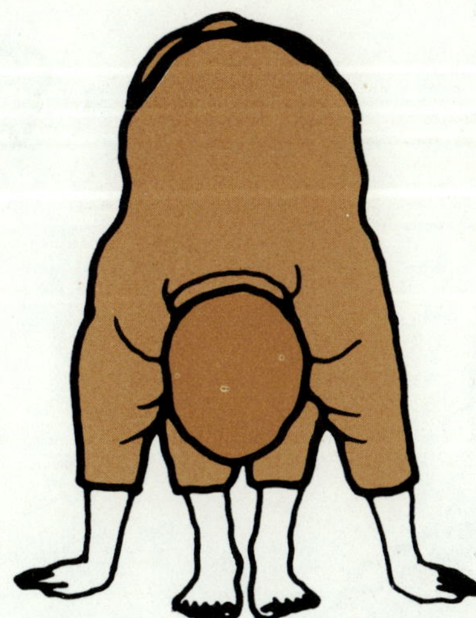

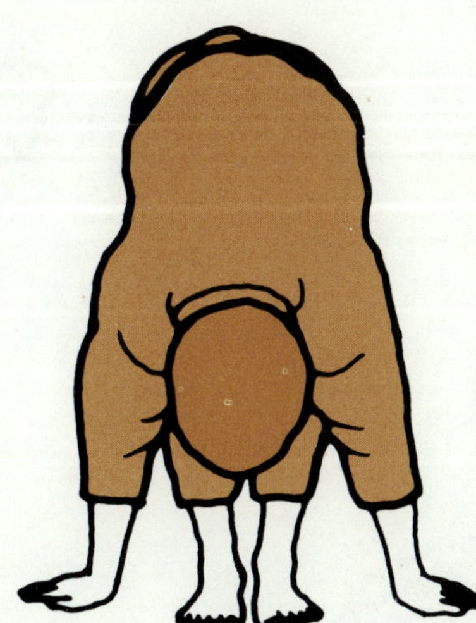

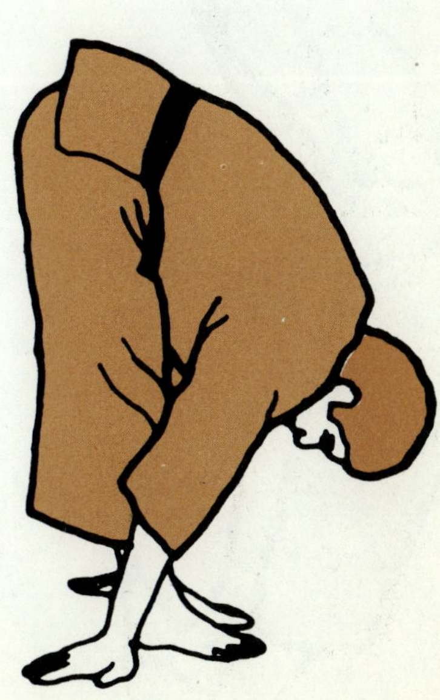

Hip and Hamstring

Place palms of hands on the floor in front of feet. Straighten legs. Bobbing up and down, place hands by heels.

Hip, Legs and Trunk

1. Feet wide apart, legs straight, clasp hands behind head and bend backwards and forwards.

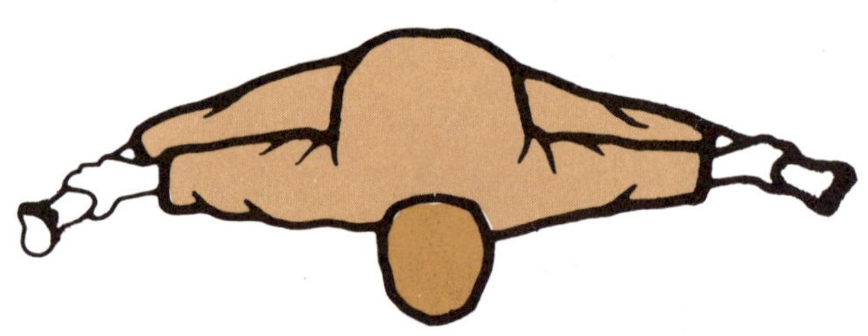

3. From the same position, grasp ankles and press head down to floor.

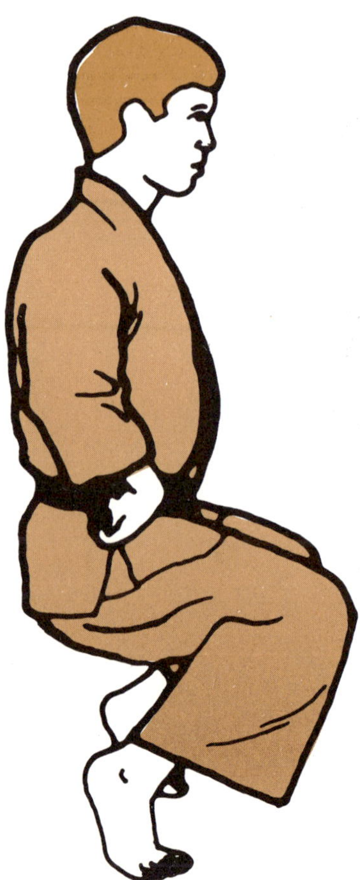

Back, Waist and Hips

Clasping feet, press knees firmly outwards. Maintain and pull head down to feet.

Achilles Tendon

From the squat position, snap the legs straight and rock back onto the heels.

2. Feet wide apart, legs straight, sit down and touch head alternately to both knees.

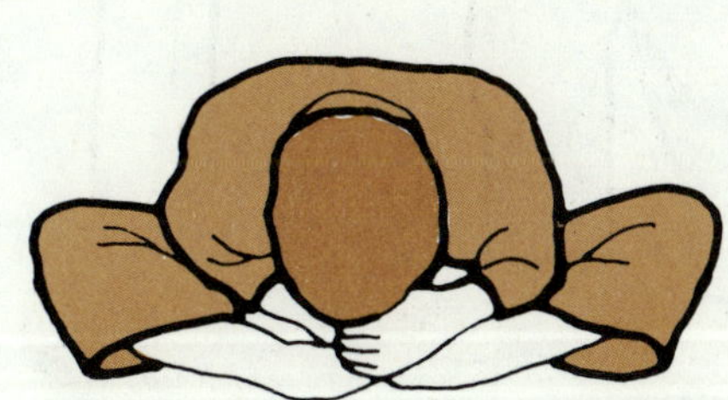

Knees
Bending the knees, circle to left and right.

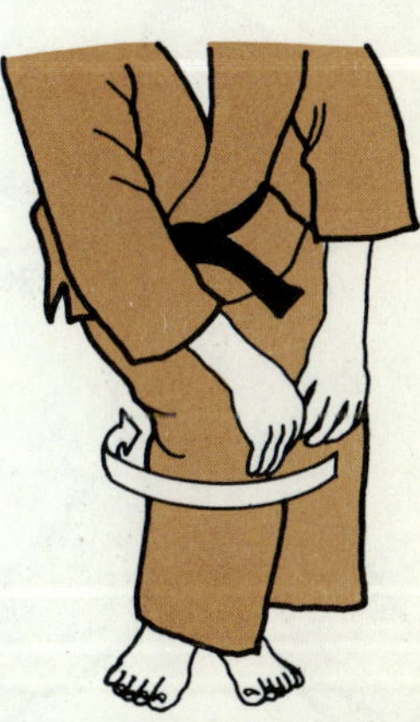

Legs
Squatting on one leg, push knee of other leg straight. Alternate legs, and also change foot positions of extended leg: (a) toes up, (b) side of foot.

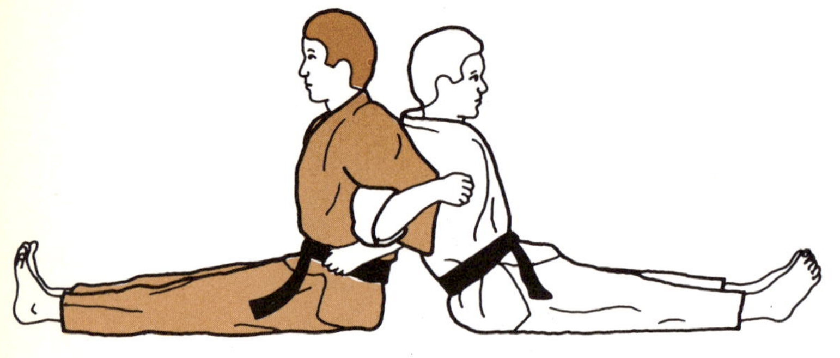

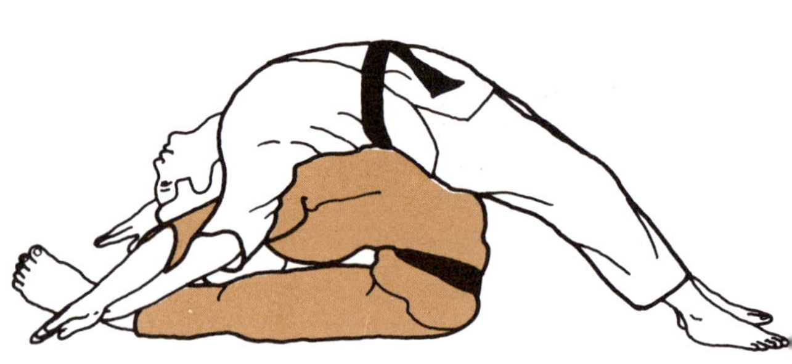

Exercises with a partner

Seated back-to-back, arms linked, ***b*** arches himself backwards over ***a,*** holding final position for count of 8-10.

b places leg in side-kick position on ***a***'s shoulder. ***a*** slowly rises, keeping his hands on ***b***'s leg to ensure it remains straight.

In side-splits position, ***b*** places his feet on inside of ***a***'s ankles and, grasping him by the belt, rocks him backward and forward. If ***a*** is not flexible enough, ***b*** can grasp him by the wrists.

b places leg in front-kick position on ***a***'s shoulder. ***a*** slowly rises, supporting ***b*** by elbows.

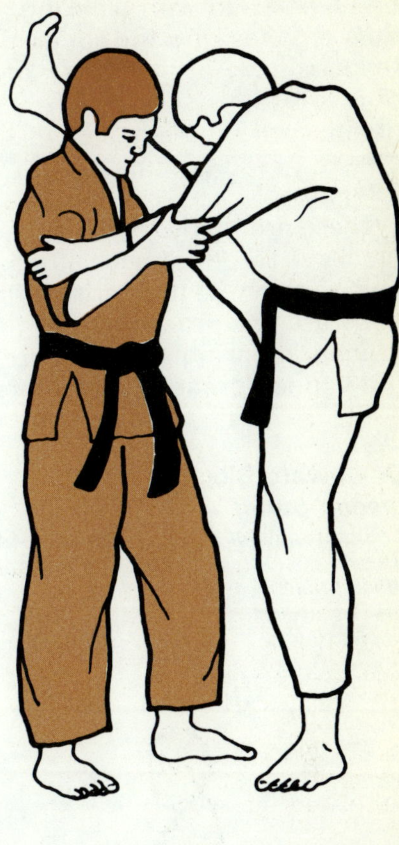

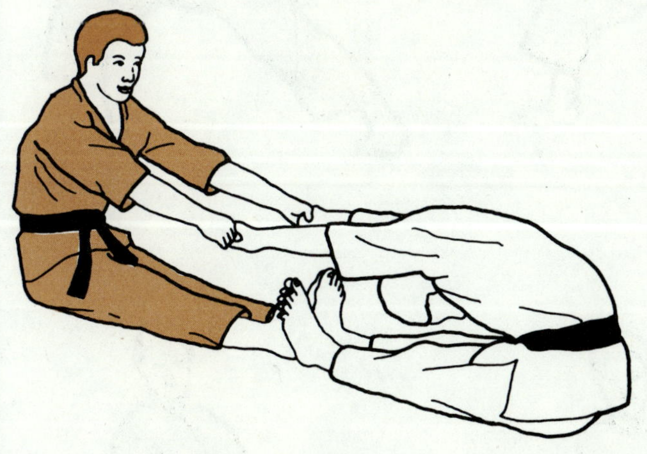

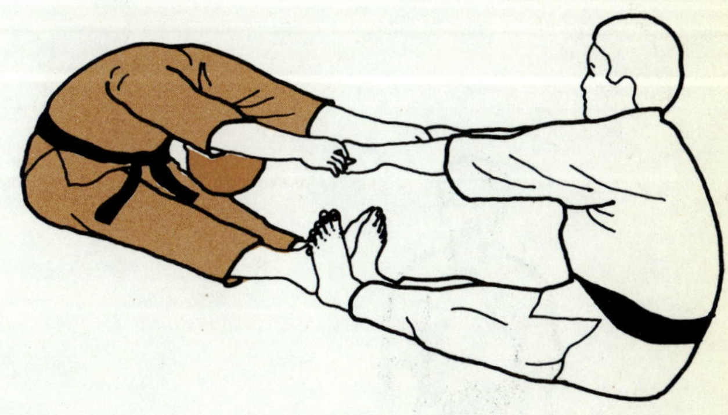

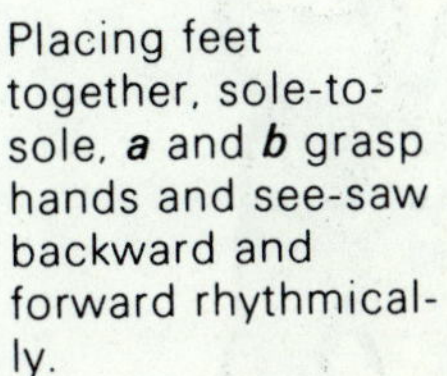

Placing feet together, sole-to-sole, ***a*** and ***b*** grasp hands and see-saw backward and forward rhythmically.

The art of karate-do is said to begin and end with blocking, thus emphasizing the social responsibility of the karate-ka only to use his skill in self-defence, or in defence of others, never as a means of offence.

There are many methods of blocking an opponent's attack, and a variety of the parts of the body are used to do so; but the primary blocking weapons are the hands, forearms and, more occasionally, the feet. Different styles of karate emphasize slightly different variations of blocking technique, some preferring circular movements, others more linear movements. Most, however, share certain common methods of defence, in which the attacking limb is struck, hooked, swept or pressed to deflect it from its intended course.

In general, blocks can be classified as either 'soft' or 'hard'. Soft blocks deflect an attack rather than meet it with force, while the aim of a hard block is to strike the attacking limb with force enough to render further use unlikely. In practice, most styles include both methods; indeed, a style that did not would be singularly lacking in all-round effectiveness.

A selection of the more commonly utilized blocking techniques is given. Remember

Downward Block
(gedan-barai)

Beginning in ***yoi*** (ready) position ***(hachiji-dachi)***, the blocking hand is raised to a position near the opposite ear, with the back of the fist facing outward. From here it is swung across the body, rotating at the last moment so that the back of the hand is uppermost. The outside edge of the forearm is used to strike and deflect the opponent's punch or kick. As the blocking hand sweeps downward the other hand is withdrawn strongly to the hip, with the back of the fist downward. At the moment of impact, the arm is straight and all the muscles

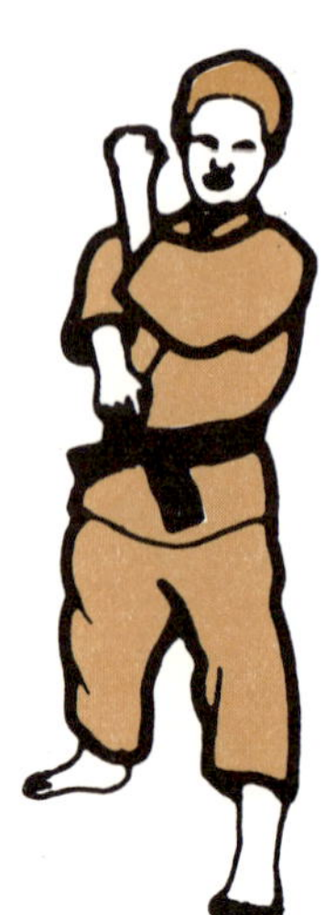

that to be effective a block must be executed from a stable, well-balanced stance, and that blocking techniques should be practised not as an end in themselves but as the first element of a counter-attack. This means that each block should end with the karate-ka in a good position to thrust home an effective counter blow.

Points to remember

a. If possible, use your opponent's strength and impetus against him.

b. Do not follow the block through so that the blocking arm is away from the body.

c. Try not to lean away from the upright position; rely upon the blocking technique itself. Too much leaning will delay your counter-attack.

d. Keep the upper body in the half-front-facing position.

e. When applying a focused block, remember to ***kime*** from the stomach, and also to tighten the muscles of both armpits.

f. Do not always step straight backward when blocking and retreating, side-step and move away from the direction of your opponent's momentum.

g. Keep your eyes on your opponent's face, not on the attacking limb.

h. Higher grades should cultivate an aggressive blocking technique of simultaneous block and counter-attack.

are strongly focused. Practise in front stance.

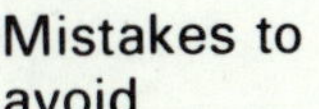

Mistakes to avoid

(i) failing to clench blocking fist, which endangers wrist.
(ii) failing to ***kime*** (focus) at moment of impact.
(iii) failing to focus with all the muscles, not just those of the blocking arm.
(iv) leaning forward, thus weakening stance and leaving the head open to attack.

Upper Rising Block *(age-uke)*

From ***yoi*** position, front hand is extended and blocking hand clenched at the hip.
Moving into front stance, blocking hand is swung close to body, in front of face, to a position three to four inches from forehead. As arm approaches final position, it is rotated so that back of fist is toward the forehead.
Front hand is withdrawn simultaneously across front of face to the hip.

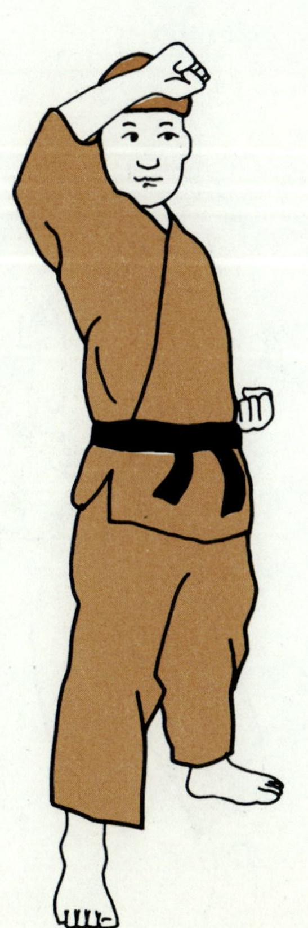

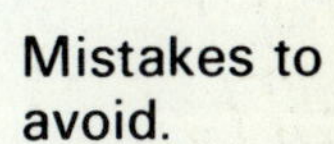

Mistakes to avoid.

(i) blocking too far in front of forehead, allowing opponent opportunity to attack over the block.
(ii) lifting shoulder of blocking arm, making it impossible to focus muscles of chest and armpit properly.
(iii) raising the elbow of the blocking arm too high, again making it difficult to focus correctly.

Forearm block *(ude-uke)*

(a) From outside inward *(soto ude-uke).*
(b) From inside outward (uchi ude-uke).

(a) soto ude-uke

From ***yoi*** position, moving into front stance, front hand is extended and blocking hand (clenched) is moved to a position behind ear on same side of the body, with back of fist facing inward. Front hand is strongly withdrawn to the hip while blocking arm simultaneously swings in an arc to a position approximately 18 inches in front of centre-line of body. Hips turn body strongly into half-front-facing position. In ***soto ude-uke***, striking area is outside edge of forearm.

Mistakes to avoid

(i) following block through too much, thus weakening focus and placing body in a disadvantageous position for countering.

(ii) not fully rotating fist, so that weaker inner surface of forearm is used instead of outer edge.

(iii) over-extending blocking arm (to an angle greater than 80° to 90°), thus leaving an opening for a follow-up attack.

(b) *uchi ude-uke*

From ***yoi*** position, moving into front stance, front hand (fist clenched) is extended in front of body, while blocking fist goes under opposite armpit. Blocking arm is swung strongly across body, with elbow at fulcrum, rotating so that in final position back of fist faces forward in a mirror-image of ***soto ude-uke.*** Striking area is inside edge of forearm.

Mistakes to avoid

As for ***soto ude-uke.***

Knife-hand Block *(shuto-uke)*

From ***yoi*** position, stepping into back stance, non-blocking hand is thrust directly forward, fingers extended, palm down. Blocking hand, fingers firmly pressed together, is placed beside opposite ear, palm inward. Using elbow as a fulcrum, arm is snapped into a position about 18 inches in front of centre-line of body, fingertips at shoulder height. Angle of blocking arm should be approximately 90° As arm swings into final position it rotates, so that little finger edge is downward and slightly outward. As usual, other hand is retracted strongly.

Mistakes to avoid

(i) not maintaining half-front-facing position.
(ii) allowing blocking arm to straighten, or allowing elbow to stick out, which will weaken effectiveness of block.
(iii) bending wrist, which also tends to weaken block.

X-Block
(juji-uke)
From *yoi* position, moving into front stance, thrust both hands (fingers extended) in a straight line forward and upward, until they reach and cross at a point level with, and approximately 18 inches in front of, top of head. Normally, right-handed karate-ka

place right hand on top of left. This block can also be used in a downward direction, to block kicking attacks; in this case, the hands are generally clenched into fists, to prevent possible injury.

Mistakes to avoid

(i) allowing elbows to bend too much, weakening block so that it gives way under a strong attack.
(ii) swinging arms into position through an arc, rather than in a straight line.
(iii) leaning upper body forward, weakening balance. Not focusing strongly at moment of impact.

Scooping Block
(suki-uke)

From *yoi* position, retreating into front stance, blocking hand swings in an arc across the front of the body to catch the kicking leg with open hand. The opponent's leg is then jerked upward and to the side. This block can be applied in two directions:

(a) from outside

Mistakes to avoid

(i) forgetting to jerk the captured leg to unbalance opponent.

(b) from inside

Hooking Block
(kage-uke)

From ***yoi*** position, moving into front stance, blocking hand is placed in front of body, palm downward. With elbow as fulcrum, arm pivots across

front of body and rotates until it reaches final position with palm upward. Striking area is back of hand, close to wrist. Hand hooks attacking limb and deflects it downward and slightly outward.

Mistakes to avoid

(i) not tensing muscles around armpit sufficiently.
(ii) allowing elbow to stick out, thus weakening block.

In karate, a distinction is made between punching techniques and striking techniques, although in many cases the differences between them are subtle. Basically, punching techniques are delivered in a straight line to the target, whilst striking techniques are generally executed with a snapping motion, with the arm pivoting around the elbow.

It is most important that at the moment of impact all the muscles of the body are sharply contracted and then relaxed; especial care must be taken to tense the muscles of the abdomen and armpits.

Although presented here as attacks, many of the techniques can be used effectively as blocks.

The straight punch ***(seiken-choku-zuki),*** probably the most widely used of all karate hand techniques, is normally practised from the natural stance ***(hachiji-dachi)*** at the beginning of most training sessions. In practice, however, it is most commonly and effectively practised as either lunge-punch ***(oi-zuki)*** or reverse punch ***(gyaku-zuki).***

In principle, the straight punch is delivered in a straight line to the target, moving from a position - generally near the hip in basic practice - with the back of the fist downward, to a final position with the arm fully extended at a point in line with the centre-line of the body with the back of the fist rotated into an upward position. As the punch is executed, the opposite hand is withdrawn to the hip and at the moment of completion all the muscles of the body are momentarily tensed.

Lunge Punch
(oi-zuki)

From ***yoi*** position, moving into front stance, non-punching hand is extended to front. As front foot advances, front hand is retracted and attacking fist (on same side as front foot) brushes side and is thrust strongly forward. As body moves forward, rear leg is driven forcefully into ground, imparting greater momentum to technique. As arm nears full extension, fist is rotated strongly into final position with back of fist upward.

Mistakes to avoid

(i) over-emphasizing role of arms and shoulders instead of concentrating on thrusting forward powerfully with hips, thus leaning forward and diminishing strength of punch.
(ii) moving forward in an up-and-down motion instead of keeping hips on an even plane.
(iii) not concentrating power into wrist on contact.
(iv) allowing shoulder to move forward with punch hindering strong focus.

Vertical Punch
(tate-zuki)

A variation of the straight punch, except that fist is only rotated through 90°. Especially useful for close-range attacks.

Mistakes to avoid

(i) allowing elbow of punching arm to move away from body, which results in punch moving in as arc rather than straight line, imparting a tendency to skate off target.

Reverse Punch *(gyaku-zuki)*

From ***yoi*** position, moving into front stance, non-punching hand is extended to front. As front foot advances, front hand is retracted and the attacking fist (on opposite side to front foot) brushes side, and with strong twist of hips is thrust powerfully forward. As body moves forward, rear leg drives forcefully into ground. As arm nears full extension, fist is rotated strongly into final position with back of fist upward.

Rising Punch *(age-zuki)*

As for reverse punch ***(gyaku-zuki)*** except that fist moves in an upward arc to contact target (usually the chin) with top part of knuckles.

(ii) leaning forward, thus inhibiting twisting motion of hips.
(iii) allowing shoulder to move forward with punch, thus hindering strong focus

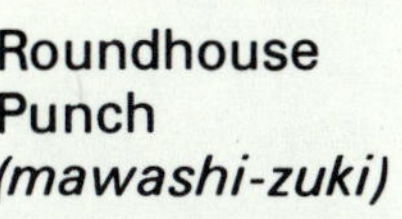

Roundhouse Punch *(mawashi-zuki)*

In this technique, fist moves in arc to target, aided by strong rotation of hips. It is important to focus sharply at moment of impact.

Especially useful for close-range attacks, often used after grasping opponent with other hand.

Close Punch
(ura-zuki)

Especially effective for close-range attacks, punch is delivered as the reverse punch, except that the fist is not rotated at all, but drives forward in a straight line to target.

Hook Punch
(kage-zuki)

Commonly used from side-facing stance (e.g. ***kiba-dachi***) to attack solar plexus, ribs, face, etc., from close range. Can be considered short-range version of ***mawashi-zuki.***

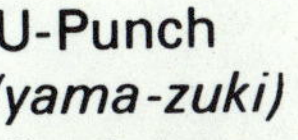

U-Punch
(yama-zuki)

Simultaneous attack to opponent's head with ***choku-zuki*** and stomach with ***ura-zuki***. Especially useful for close-range simultaneous defence and attack.

Back-fist strike *(uraken-uchi)*

Used from many stances, but most effective in a side-facing stance *(kiba-dachi,* etc.), to attack head, face and chest.

Striking techniques are usually executed as counter-attacks, immediately following the blocking or deflecting of the opponent's attack, making full use of the force generated by strong rotation of the hips to their former position, following their utilization in the blocking action itself. In most instances, the transmission of the force follows a circular rather than linear path, much of the power coming from the speed of the technique, which is augmented by rapid withdrawal of the non-striking arm.

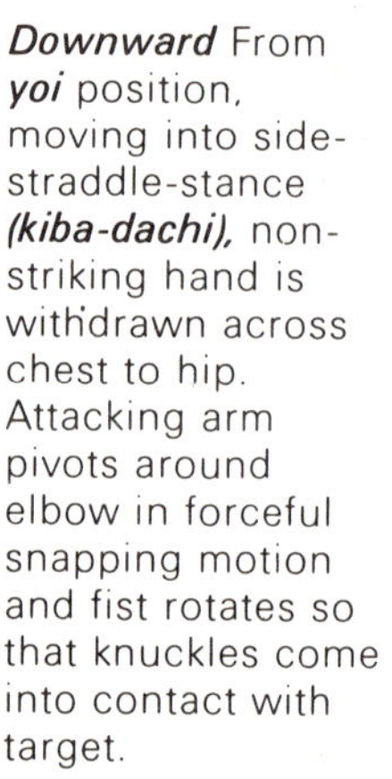

Downward From ***yoi*** position, moving into side-straddle-stance ***(kiba-dachi),*** non-striking hand is withdrawn across chest to hip. Attacking arm pivots around elbow in forceful snapping motion and fist rotates so that knuckles come into contact with target.

Lateral As downward strike, except that attacking arm follows an arc parallel with the floor.

Knife-hand strike *(shuto-uchi)*

This strike, using little-finger edge of hand, is directed against opponent's temple's, face, neck and abdomen, and also against limbs.

From ***yoi*** position, moving into front stance, non-striking hand is thrust forward and then rapidly retracted to hip.

Striking hand, fingers pressed firmly together, is raised – palm upward and outward – to a position beside ear on same side. As front hand is withdrawn, striking hand simultaneously swings in an arc around elbow joint so that at point of impact it is in line with centre of body. As strike is executed, hips are rotated strongly in direction of blow, to generate greater speed and power.

Bottom-fist strike *(tettsui-uchi)*

Also called 'hammer-fist strike', like ***uraken-uchi*** this can be used downward or laterally, and is especially useful when attacking hard targets, since there is little risk of damaging the fist. Can be considered a variation of ***uraken-uchi,*** contact area being fleshy pad at base of little finger.

Mistakes to avoid

(i) raising shoulder of attacking arm, which interferes with ability to focus correctly.
(ii) not ensuring that fingers of attacking hand are tightly together, thus allowing possibility of injury.

Mistakes to avoid

(i) failure to withdraw non-attacking arm strongly enough, thus weakening the focus.
(ii) not snapping attacking fist back again immediately target is struck.
(iii) putting too much tension in striking arm, thus inhibiting development of full speed and power.

Elbow strike
(empi-uchi)

An extremely powerful close-range weapon, used in a variety of ways to attack chin, chest, ribs and solar plexus.

Forward elbow strike
(mae-empi-uchi)

Generally executed from reverse front stance.

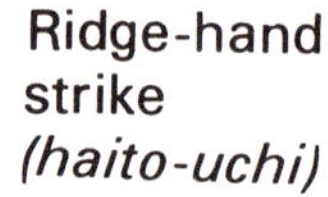

From left front stance, front (left) hand is withdrawn to hip while right elbow is thrust directly forward at target. A major variation is to allow striking elbow to swing out and describe an arc to the target instead of following a straight line. This, called ***mawashi***

Ridge-hand strike
(haito-uchi)

A circular strike to temples, neck, ribs, etc., using area at base of index finger.
From ***yoi*** position, moving into front stance, non-striking hand is extended to front and then rapidly retracted to hip. Attacking hand projects to rear, palm downward, and as the other hand is withdrawn it is swung forward in a wide arc, gathering force from momentum and rotation of the hips, until it strikes the target directly in front of the body.
(In basic practice this is a large movement, but is perhaps more effectively used with the attacking hand starting from its normal position in front of the body - in ***ju-dachi*** - and describing a shorter arc to the target but also utilizing an inward snapping motion from the elbow.)

Mistakes to avoid

As for ***shuto-uchi.***

empi (roundhouse elbow), is extremely effective if combined with strong rotation of hips.

Backward elbow strike
(ushiro-empi-uchi)

In effect, this is the movement executed each time a correct punching attack is made with the opposite hand. Generally useful in close-quarter fighting, from most stances but often from hourglass *(sanchin)* or side-straddle *(kiba)* stances, it is shown here in an augmented version moving from front stance to back stance, with added power gained through the other hand's pressing backward on the fist of the attacking arm.

From *yoi* position, stepping backward into front stance, fist of attacking arm, on same side of body, is covered by the other hand. As stance changes into back stance, elbow is thrust strongly alongside body and arm is rotated so that back of fist is downward.

Side elbow strike *(yoko-empi-uchi)*

Generally executed from side-straddle stance.
From ***yoi*** position, sliding into ***kiba-dachi,*** attacking elbow is driven directly sideways, arm rotating so that at moment of impact back of fist is upward. Movement of arm should be parallel to floor and close to chest. Basic technique is performed with non-attacking arm being retracted strongly to hip. A major variation utilizes the non-attacking hand in much the same manner as ***ushiro-empi.***

Downward elbow strike *(otoshi-empi-uchi)*

Used against a low target, often as follow-up to a throw or joint-lock. From ***yoi*** position, moving into immovable stance ***(fudo-dachi),*** attacking arm is raised; as knees are sharply bent, elbow is brought vertically down onto target. Other hand is simultaneously withdrawn strongly to hip. Care must be taken to keep hips low and back as straight as possible.

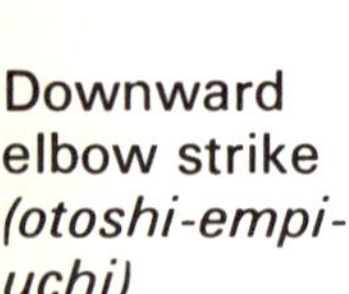

Mistakes to avoid

(i) raising shoulder of attacking arm, making it difficult to focus correctly.
(ii) raising hips and therefore weakening stance.

Upward elbow strike *(age empi-uchi)*

As ***mae-empi,*** except that the stance favoured here is normally front, not reverse, and elbow is swung powerfully upward so that at point of impact with target fist is close to the ear.

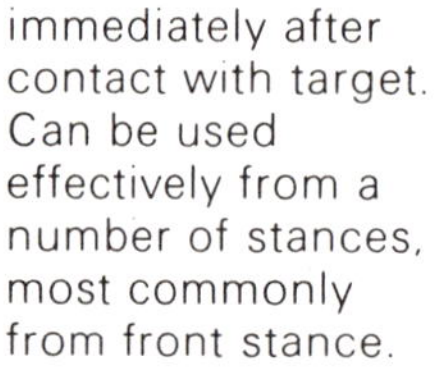

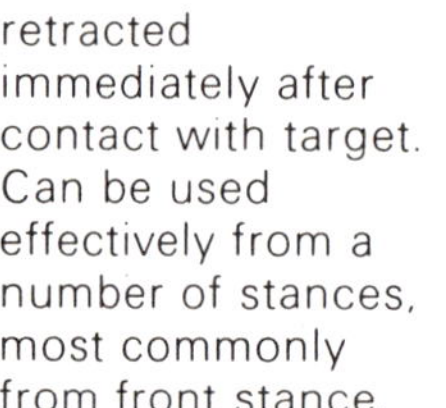

Front Kick
(mae-geri)

Normally, the ball of the foot is used to strike the target, and the technique can be executed as either a thrust or a snap, depending on the circumstances.

Shown here from ***yoi*** position, kicking leg is brought rapidly up and kicked strongly forward, utilizing pendular motion of hips, and is retracted immediately after contact with target. Can be used effectively from a number of stances, most commonly from front stance.

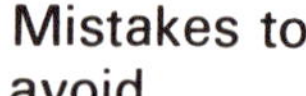

Mistakes to avoid

(i) lifting foot of supporting leg.
(ii) not thrusting hips forward.
(iii) not lifting knee high enough.
(iv) not tensing foot and ankle on impact.

The effective use of kicking techniques requires constant practice of the basic forms. It is particularly important to pay due attention to the supporting leg, which, to withstand the shock of impact, should be slightly bent. After kicking, the attacking leg should be withdrawn as rapidly and smoothly as possible to avoid possible counters by grabbing or sweeping.

There are basically two distinct types of kick: the thrust kick and the snap kick. The most basic rule to be observed in executing the majority of ***keri-waza*** is to lift the knee of the attacking foot as high as possible in preparation for the technique.

Originally, all karate kicking techniques were directed at relatively low targets. The high kicks, though aesthetically pleasing and undoubtedly effective in many instances, are not to be considered the most important, since they tend to leave the attacker in a vulnerable position. This applies also to the jumping techniques.

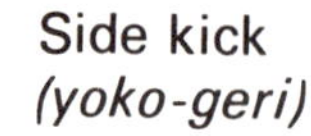

Side kick
(yoko-geri)

Outside edge of foot is used, in either snapping or thrusting motion, to attack low.

Roundhouse kick (*mawashi-geri*)

Ball of foot or instep can be used to attack high and middle-level targets in circular snapping motion. From ***heisoku-dachi***, knee of kicking leg is raised high to side of body. As hips are strongly rotated, knee is driven forward in an arc parallel with floor, then straightens so that foot snaps round to strike target. As hips turn towards target, upper body moves in reverse direction to maintain good balance.

Mistakes to avoid

(i) bending body too much, inhibiting hip movement.
(ii) failing to snap leg back immediately after impact.
(iii) lifting supporting foot.

A variation of this technique is the back-roundhouse kick, ***ushiro-mawashi-geri***, where heel of attacking foot is used to strike target. Leg is driven forward, almost in manner of side kick, and heel is then snapped in at target. This technique requires good balance and much practice.

middle-level or high targets. Most commonly used from a side-facing stance.

Side thrust kick *(yoko-geri-kekomi)*

From ***heisoku-dachi,*** knee of kicking leg is raised high to chest, ankle and foot tensed. Utilizing strong thrusting motion of hips, foot is driven directly sideways to target.

Mistakes to avoid

(i) leaning body away from direction of kick.
(ii) not lifting knee high enough.
(iii) failing to thrust through target.
(iv) not withdrawing foot rapidly enough.

Side snap kick *(yoko-geri-keage)*

As for thrust kick, except that knee of kicking leg is pointed diagonally towards target, and foot is snapped upward so that edge strikes target. Not normally as useful a technique as thrust kick.

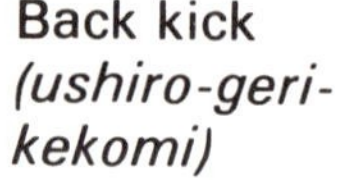

Back kick *(ushiro-geri-kekomi)*

Using heel as striking area, this is a very powerful technique.
From ***heisoku-dachi,*** knee of kicking leg is

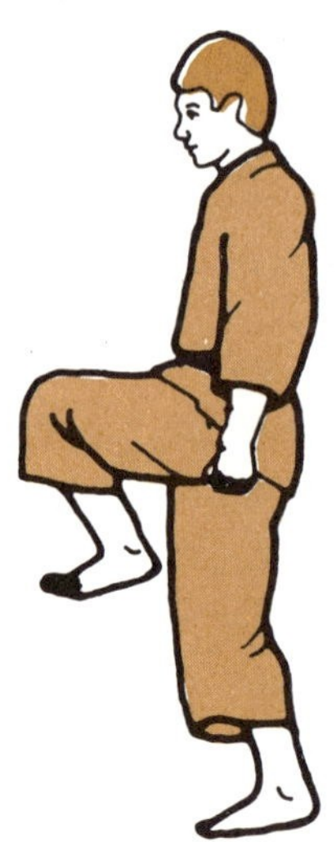

Jumping kicks
(tobi-geri)

Many of the kicking techniques can be executed following a jump, while karate-ka is still in mid-air. When effective, these are excellent for surprise attacks; but they do leave the attacker in an extremely vulnerable position, and it is far more important to master the basic techniques.

raised to front. Bending slightly forward, foot is driven directly backward to target in strong thrusting motion. A variation ***ushiro-geri-keage,*** utilizing upward snapping action of heel, is used at close-range.

Mistakes to avoid

(i) leaning too far forward.
(ii) not retracting foot quickly enough.
(iii) not kicking directly to rear.

Sequential and combination techniques

Basic techniques are normally practised at the beginning of every training session. Each student works first on his own, then with a partner, to increase speed, power, rhythm and co-ordination. Each technique is executed while moving forward and backward. When a certain degree of skill has been acquired, a number of techniques are combined (e.g. ***age-uke*** and ***gyaku-zuki***); combinations too are practised first individually and then with a partner. Here are a very few examples of the more regular sequential and combination techniques the student could expect to practise in most ***dojo.***

Sequential Practice

(Each of the following techniques should be repeated five times, forward and backward.)

Rising block ***(age-uke)***

From ***gedan barai,*** step forward into right ***zenkutsu-dachi,*** blocking with right arm.

Step forward into left ***zenkutsu-dachi,*** and block with left arm.

Rising block reverse punch ***(age-uki gyaku-zuki)***

From ***gedan barai,*** step forward into right ***zenkutsu-dachi,*** blocking with right arm.

Outer/inner forearm block, side elbow ***(soto/uchi-ude-uke yoko empi)***

From ***gedan barai,*** step forward into right ***zenkutsu-dachi,*** blocking with right hand. Without stepping forward, change to ***kiba-dachi*** stance and attack with right ***yoko empi.*** Step forward and repeat on left side.

Immediately punch forward with left ***gyaku-zuki.*** Step forward and repeat on left side.

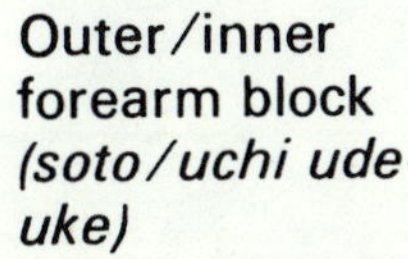

Outer/inner forearm block *(soto/uchi ude-uke)*

From ***gedan barai,*** step forward into right ***zenkutsu-dachi,*** blocking with right arm.

Step forward into left ***zenkutsu-dachi*** and block with left arm.

Knife-hand block
(shuto-uke)

From ***kokutsu-dachi,*** step forward into right ***kokutsu-dachi*** and block with right hand.

Step forward into left ***kokutsu-dachi*** and block with left hand.

Triple punch
(sanbon-zuki)

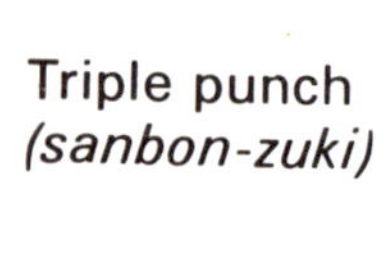

Reverse punch
(gyaku-zuki)

From ***gedan barai,*** step forward into right ***zenkutsu-dachi,*** punching with left ***chudan gyaku-zuki.*** Step forward into left ***zenkutsu-dachi*** and punch with right hand.

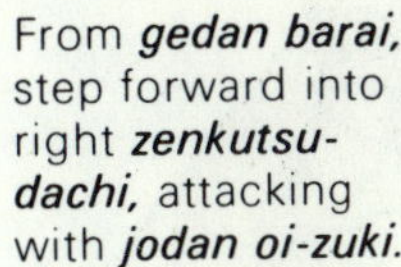

From ***gedan barai,*** step forward into right ***zenkutsu-dachi,*** attacking with ***jodan oi-zuki.***

Then, in same stance, punch with left ***chudan gyaku-zuki,*** followed by ***chudan choku-zuki.***

Knife-hand block spearhead *(shuto-uke nukite)*

From right ***kokutsu-dachi,*** step forward into left ***kokutsu-dachi*** and block with left hand. Without stepping forward, shift to left ***zenkutsu-dachi,*** and attack with right ***chudan nukite.***

Snap punch, lunge punch
(kisami-zuki oi-zuki)

From ***ju-dachi,*** without stepping forward, execute left ***jodan kisami-zuki.*** Step forward and punch with ***chudan oi-zuki.***

Sidethrust kick
(yoko-geri kekomi)

From ***kiba-dachi,*** step across with left foot, raise right knee, kick directly to side with right leg with forceful thrusting motion. Immediately snap kicking foot back to knee of supporting leg and step into right ***kiba-dachi.***

Back kick
(ushiro-geri)

From ***gedan barai*** in ***zenkutsu-dachi,*** turn back to target. Raise knee of kicking leg and turn head to look at target. Thrust kicking leg directly backward, immediately retract kicking leg and pivot to front. Step into opposite ***zenkutsu-dachi.***

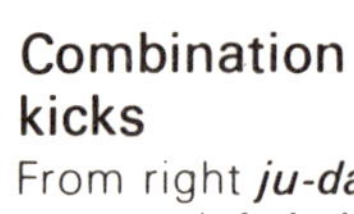

Combination kicks

From right *ju-dachi* execute left *jodan mawashi-geri.* Step

forward into left *ju-dachi* and follow with right *chudan mawashi-geri.*

From *zenkutsu-dachi,* and without changing stance,

execute *jodan mae-geri,* snap kicking foot back to knee

of supporting leg, immediately

From left *ju-dachi* execute *chudan mae-geri.* Step forward into right *ju-dachi,*

immediately follow with left *jodan mawashi-geri* Step

execute ***jodan yoko-geri,*** again snap kicking leg back

and continue with ***jodan ushiro-geri.***

into left ***ju dachi*** and execute ***jodan yoko-geri.***

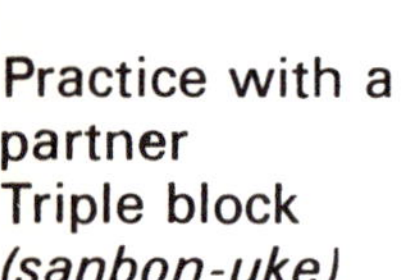

Practice with a partner Triple block *(sanbon-uke)*

Facing each other in natural stance, ***a*** punches with right hand ***jodan, b*** blocks with left ***age-uke, b*** then punches ***jodan*** with right hand and ***a*** blocks with left ***age-uke, a*** then

punches ***chudan*** with right hand and ***b*** blocks with left ***chudan soto-ude-uke, b*** in turn punches with right ***chudan-zuki*** and ***a*** blocks with left ***chudan soto-ude-uke. a*** then

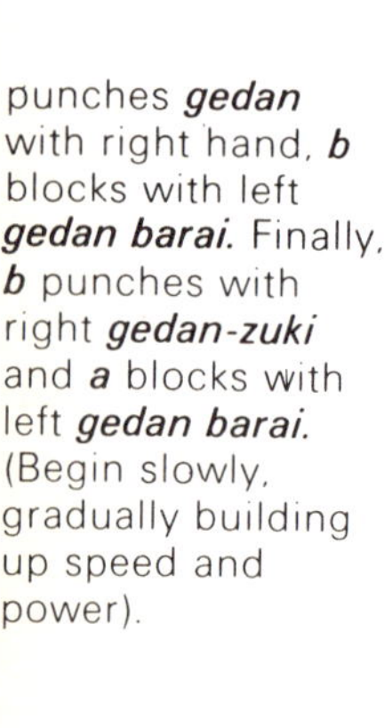

punches ***gedan*** with right hand, ***b*** blocks with left ***gedan barai.*** Finally, ***b*** punches with right ***gedan-zuki*** and ***a*** blocks with left ***gedan barai.*** (Begin slowly, gradually building up speed and power).

In modern karate, little emphasis is placed upon throwing techniques. This is unfortunate, since there are occasions when they would constitute a response more appropriate than the potentially dangerous striking techniques.

Many traditional grappling techniques of the ***ju-jutsu*** systems were incorporated into karate-***jutsu,*** and in essence they resemble some modern judo throws, but with the important difference that they do not depend upon grasping the opponent's clothing to obtain leverage. Indeed, to do this is to place the thrower in great danger of being struck before he is able to apply the technique.

Most of the body throws (as opposed to the leg throws) follow from a blocking technique, which has created an opening or disturbed the opponent's balance. Even so, the type of throw popular in judo, where the thrower turns his back on his opponent, is not recommended.

Leg throws, which normally leave the hands free for defence, are excellent as initial attacking moves. Even if unsuccessful, they often leave the opponent unbalanced and open to a follow-up technique, and thus are often utilized in combination attacks.

NB: When practising throwing techniques, always try to maintain control of your opponent and follow through immediately with the final blow. Do not let him roll away or recover the initiative.

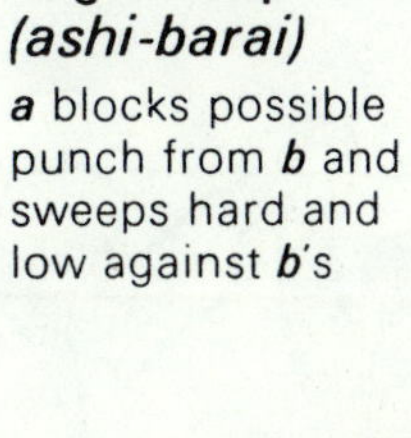

Leg sweep
(ashi-barai)

a blocks possible punch from ***b*** and sweeps hard and low against ***b***'s

front leg, knocking it from under him and follows up with punch to face.

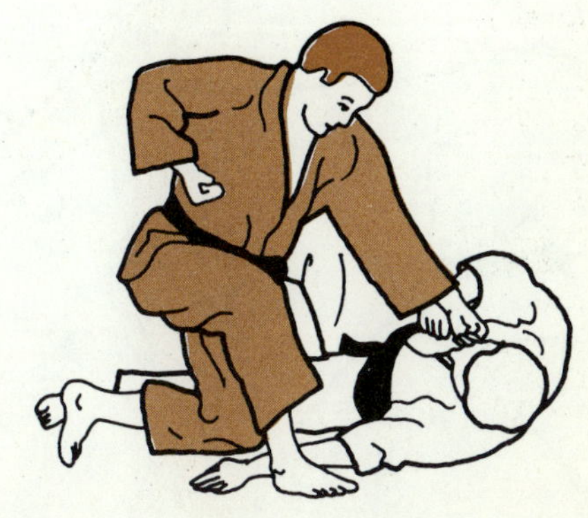

Minor outer reap
(ko-soto-gari)

b blocks and grasps ***a***'s kicking leg and counters with right reverse punch to head.

Grasping ***a***'s shoulder, he swings his right leg hard at back of ***a***'s heel. Lifting the leg

One-leg throw
(kata-ashi-tori)

a blocks ***b***'s punch with ***age-uke.*** He then slides left foot behind ***b***'s front leg, swings blocking arm in knife-hand strike across ***b***'s throat, and grasps his front leg. Lifting front leg, ***a*** continues to drive

Major outer reap
(o-soto-gari)

b blocks punch with ***shuto-uchi*** and counters with ***teisho*** to jaw.

Grasping punching arm, ***b*** swings his right leg behind ***a***'s front leg and drives it backward behind knee. ***b*** follows through with

and pushing down with other hand, ***a*** is swung forcefully up and

over onto his back. ***b*** then follows up with punch to face.

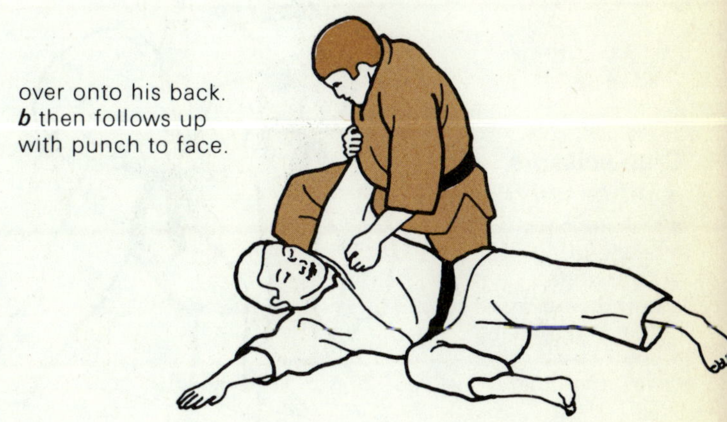

b backwards with left hand , throwing him to ground.

shuto-uchi and straight arm lock.

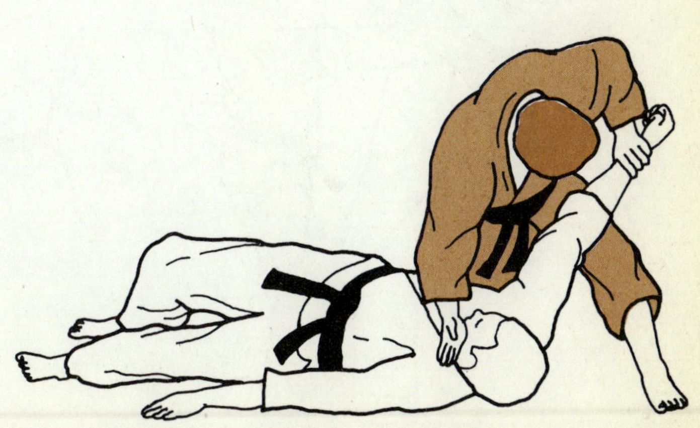

Wheel reap
(kaiten-gari)

b feints open-hand stride at ***a***'s head, forcing him to keep his guard high, and

Crab scissors
(kani-basami)
a sidesteps ***b***'s attack and, grasping attacking arm throws himself bodily at ***b***, one leg going behind the knees, the other

across stomach or chest. With scissor-like action, ***a*** knocks ***b*** to ground. Follow-up technique is generally heel strike to abdomen or face.

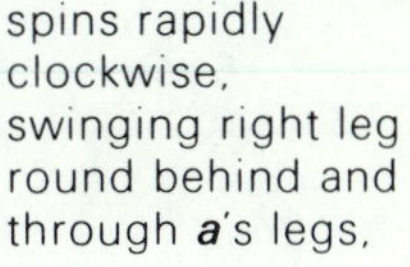

spins rapidly clockwise, swinging right leg round behind and through ***a***'s legs,

knocking him to ground and following through with punch to ribs.

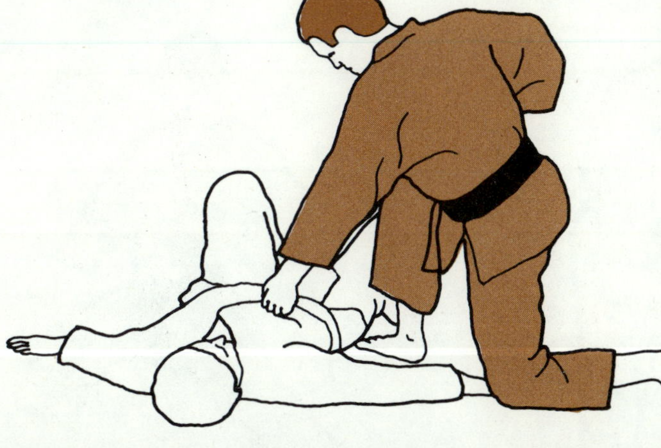

CHAPTER 17. PRE-ARRANGED SPARRING - YAKUSOKU KUMITE

PART 4 - KUMITE AND KATA

Kumite ('an encounter with the hands') describes a method of practising karate techniques with the help of a partner.

There are two main types of ***kumite,*** pre-arranged ***(yakusoku)*** and free ***(ju).*** Here, we are concerned with the former, which is subdivided into four categories: basic one-step sparring ***(kihon ippon kumite),*** three-step sparring ***(sanbon kumite),*** five-step sparring ***(gohon kumite)*** and semi-free one-step sparring ***(ju-ippon kumite).*** Free sparring (also called free-style) is dealt with in the following chapter.

Sparring itself began in the 1920s' to give karate-ka the opportunity to refine basic skills by putting them to use in a combat-like situation; and to aid the development of certain other skills - timing, body shifting, anticipation, courage, etc. - which ***kata*** alone fail to instil. Only the relative uncertainty of physical confrontation can lead to a speeding-up of response to stimulus. Equally, fighting spirit cannot be tested by ***kata,*** nor do ***kata*** indicate to the student the degree of effectiveness of his techniques. Ideally, ***kata*** and ***kumite*** should go hand in hand.

The advantages of ***kumite,*** particularly ***yakusoku kumite,*** are many and varied. Many karate-ka believe that ***kumite*** is by far the most effective way of teaching the wide range of karate techniques, many of which are too dangerous to be practised in ***ju kumite*** and are banned from competition karate.

Points to remember in kumite

Unless otherwise specified always attack your partner hard; a soft technique will lead him either to react half-heartedly, or overvalue the power of his block.

When blocking, always have your counter-attack uppermost in mind, and use your defence as a part of the counter.

Never be content to retreat and block passively; cultivate an aggressive defence.

Keep your eyes on your partner at all times.

Do not tense up in anticipation of an attack.

Practise *tai sabaki* (body shifting) to avoid retreating in a straight line. Always be full of spirit, and *kiai* strongly.

Always bow *(rei)* correctly at the beginning and conclusion of practice with a new partner.

Five-step sparring (gohon kumite)

The most basic form of sparring in karate, ***gohon*** incorporates only hand techniques; specifically, two punches – lunge punch ***(oi-zuki)*** and reverse punch ***(gyaku-zuki)*** – and two blocks – upward rising block ***(jodan age-uke)*** and middle level forearm block ***(chudan soto ude-uke)***. The practice was devised to develop strong blocks and punches, and fast forward and backward changes of stance.

Partners face each other and bow. Attacker then assumes left front-stance ***(zenkutsu-dachi)*** by moving his right leg back, and at the same time executes a left downward block ***(gedan barai)***. Defender remains upright in natural stance ***(hachiji-dachi)***. Attacker says loudly 'jodan' or 'chudan', to indicate predetermined area of attack; then (initially by count) attacks five times with the relevent technique (i.e., lunge punch to upper or middle level). Defender steps back with right

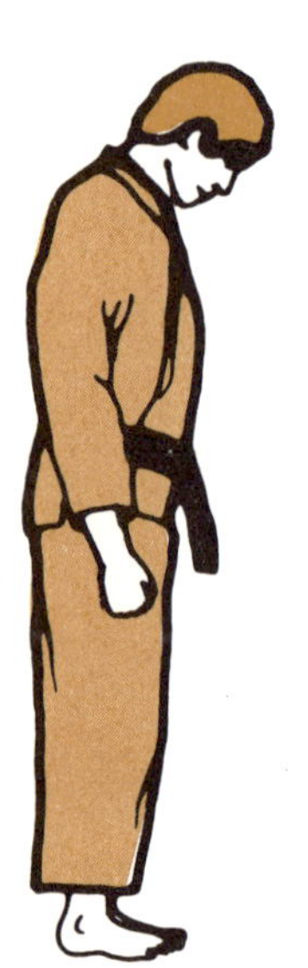

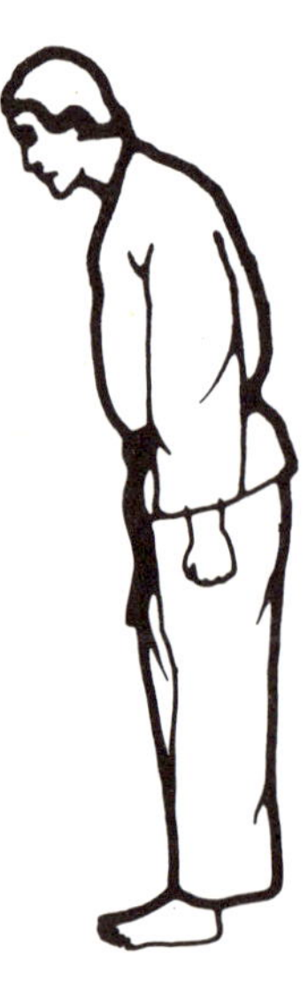

foot at the first attack, and defends with the appropriate block (i.e., ***jodan*** or ***chudan***). This process is repeated left and right alternately in sequence with the attacks, and after the fifth block the defender counter-punches with a middle-level reverse punch ***(chudan gyaku-zuki)*** and gives a loud ***kiai.*** Both then return slowly and smoothly to the ready ***(yoi)*** position; the former defender assumes the attacking role, and the process is repeated.

Generally, ***gohon kumite*** is carried out with the class lined up facing each other, so that after every completed sequence (usually five ***jodan*** attacks for both partners, followed by five ***chudan*** each), at the teacher's command, one side moves one place to either left or right so that each karate-ka faces a new partner. The sequence then begins again. Practised in this fashion, ***gohon kumite*** can be an extreme test of physical and mental stamina.

Basic one-step sparring (kihon ippon kumite)

Partners stand facing each other and take turns in attacking and defending with predetermined attacks and defences against agreed targets.

The attacker assumes a stance appropriate to the form of attack being practised (generally ***zenkutsu-dachi,*** front stance), whilst defender remains erect, usually in the natural stance (***shizentai*** or ***hachiji-dachi***). On command of the ***sensei,*** attacker strongly executes the pre-arranged technique, and defender blocks and counters as agreed. At the end of the sequence, both karate-ka return smoothly to the starting position.

Defender blocks ***oi-zuki*** (lunge punch) attack with ***age-uke*** (upper rising block) and counters with ***jodan-mawashi-zuki*** (roundhouse punch to head).

Defender blocks ***oi-zuki*** (lunge punch) attack with ***age-uke*** (upper rising block) but counters with ***gyaku-zuki*** (reverse punch).

In this sequence the ***oi-zuki*** (lunge punch) attack is blocked by ***age-uke*** (upper rising block) and countered with ***jodan uraken*** (backfist to the face).

Kihon ippon kumite is basically used to 'groove' a technique into the subconscious. It is equally effective for hand or foot techniques and should be practised over and over again, on both sides (i.e., from right and left stances). This is most important, even though some karate-ka dislike practising on their weaker side; because research into movement and motor-learning indicates a transference in the part of the brain that deals with motor function, which leads to improvement in the skill of the strong side.

In these two sequences, the kicking attacks – one of ***mae-geri*** (front kick) and one of ***yoko-geri*** (side kick) – are blocked by ***gedan-barai*** (downward sweeping block) and then countered by ***gyaku-zuki*** (reverse punch).

Three-step sparring (sanbon kumite)

This is similar to basic one-step sparring, except that the attacker, instead of allowing the defender to block and counter unhindered, is himself supposed to assume the role of defender and in turn block the counter technique and thrust home his own predetermined counter-attack.

To make this practice effective, all the techniques must be performed with power and commitment, or the attacker will find himself beaten to the punch by a resolute defender who has maintained a firm position because he was unconvinced of the need to dodge, duck or block the initial technique.

Karate-ka find these fierce but controlled clashes - practised properly, with strong spirit and loud ***kiai*** - not only extremely exhilarating but also greatly beneficial to their basic technique, timing ability and fighting spirit.

Any techniques can be practised in ***sanbon kumite,*** and the pre-arranged sequences can be all hand or all foot techniques, or a mixture of both.

Semi-free one-step sparring (ju-ippon kumite)

This type of sparring is midway between basic and free-style. As in the basic forms, attacker and defender are predetermined and target area and mode of attack pre-arranged. In ***ju-ippon kumite,*** however, both partners are free to move about the ***dojo*** in any appropriate stance (usually ***ju-dachi***). When the attacker closes to a proper distance for a successful attack, and either finds or creates an opening in his partner's defence, he immediately drives in with a powerful controlled attack which his partner must evade or block and instantly counter.

Initially, the attacker holds the final position at the completion of his attack, to allow his partner practice in getting home his counter. The next stage is for the attacker instantly to assume a defensive position instead, and attempt to block or evade the counter-attack. This is similar to ***sanbon kumite,*** except that the techniques of ***ju-ippon*** are not pre-arranged to the same extent.

Advance karate-ka practice a variation of ***ju-ippon kumite*** in which only the attacker and defender are predetermined, the choice of target and technique depending on whatever is appropriate at the moment an opportunity for attack is presented.

A further variation is sometimes used to instil into the higher grades the importance of maintaining a proper distance ***(ma-ai)*** from one's opponent. If the attacker comes too close, the defender is allowed to pre-empt the attacking role and himself drive in a controlled attack before the attacker has realized his danger.

Both partners must be at pains to ensure that semi-free sparring does not degenerate into free-style sparring. The spirit of ***ju-ippon kumite*** should be one of co-operation rather than competition. If it does develop into a free exchange of techniques, the tendency is that both karate-ka, in sheer self-defence, will rely upon techniques they know to be effective for them. This is fine in its place; but will not allow the practice of a wide range of techniques, which is the purpose of semi-free one-step sparring.

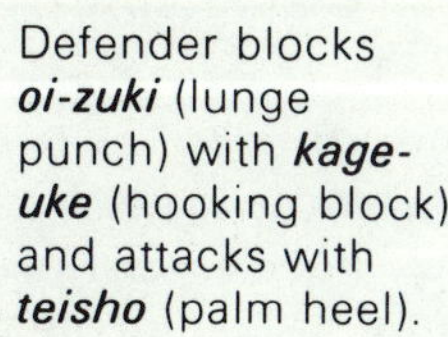

Defender blocks *oi-zuki* (lunge punch) with *kage-uke* (hooking block) and attacks with *teisho* (palm heel).

In this completely unrehearsed form of practice, sometimes called 'free-style' or 'free-fighting', both karate-ka are free to deliver any technique or combination of techniques except those deemed too dangerous. ***Ju kumite*** is similar to boxing, except that the attacks are not delivered with full force but are stopped or 'pulled', either at skin level or just short of contact. Indeed, one of the tests of a karate-ka's skill is the ability to execute a powerful technique with a degree of control that places his partner beyond danger.

Many students cannot wait to begin free-sparring, which they erroneously see as the culmination of karate training. In fact, allowing beginners to practise free-sparring too soon could impede their progress in acquiring a proper level of skill. Some masters go so far as to prohibit their students from engaging in free-style practice, maintaining not only that ***ju-ippon*** (semi-free) ***kumite*** is more beneficial for the mastering of the techniques of karate but also that it does not foster that undesirable spirit of competition and desire for victory which is a frequent result of the casual practice of free-style.

In protecting students from the pitfalls of pride and egoism, however, one also denies them the opportunity of practising and developing spontaneous reaction to attack. This difficulty could perhaps be overcome if students were made aware of the different categories of free-style: limited; unlimited soft; and unlimited hard.

LIMITED FREE-SPARRING

This category includes all methods of sparring in which there is a degree of pre-arrangement. The ***sensei*** might, for example, wish to concentrate upon the practice of ***tai sabaki*** (body shifting): if so, he will specify one partner as the attacker, allowed to attack with either predetermined techniques or those of his choice, while the other defends by blocking and evading the techniques, offering no counter-attack. This type of practice can be extremely effective: the attacker knows he runs no risk of being thrown or countered, and therefore can deliver his techniques with total commitment; at the same time, the defender knows that his only priority is to practice his defence.

Naturally, this type of training begins slowly, and becomes faster as experience is gained. A further step is to make the defender not only shift position to evade an attack but also slide, jump or turn immediately, so that his body is brought into a strong counter-attack position, again without executing a counter technique.

Either partner attacking whenever an opportunity is presented, with attacking techniques predetermined, provides another example. If the teacher wants to emphasize leg techniques, he might restrict attacks to perhaps ***chudan mae-geri*** (middle-level front kick) and ***jodan mawashi-geri*** (upper-level roundhouse kick).

Another type of limited free-sparring very effective in building up rhythm in combination techniques is exemplified by one partner's attacking continuously, either with a pre-arranged combination of techniques or with any of his choice, while the other simply defends, with or without countering. After a predetermined period (from 10 to 60 seconds), the roles are reversed. (This is more difficult than it might appear, and is a tremendous strain on stamina).

What has to be emphasized is that sparring should be co-operation, not contest. In practice, however, it takes a firm ***sensei*** to ensure that antagonism and competition do not creep in. If the students begin to fight against, rather than co-operate with, each other, they will find it impossible to practise minor techniques, or any that might, owing to a lack of expertise, leave an opening in their defence. This is a particular danger in the next category we shall consider.

UNLIMITED SOFT

In this practice, both partners attack and defend completely spontaneously, with very fast but very lightly focused techniques. Knowing that the blows and blocks will be very light, each karate-ka is able to take chances and practise secondary techniques without running the risk of injury. It is in this type of practice that the wearing of pads and protectors can be extremely helpful. Some teachers feel that it is somehow a betrayal of the martial spirit to wear pads; but I believe they can be useful if used with discrimination.

Practice in unlimited soft free-sparring cultivates skill in both attacking and defending, in body shifting, correct distancing, timing, balance, tactics, control and spirit.

UNLIMITED HARD

This differs greatly from the other categories, in that the techniques, although stopped short of full contact, are executed with full speed and power. Some styles (e.g., Shotokan, Kyokushinkai) also encourage a marked degree of strong body contact in this practice. Generally, neither pads nor protectors are worn in this practice which comes as close as possible to the 'one chance' concept of total commitment. The pace is usually slower than that of the preceding categories; the karate-ka circle each other warily, awaiting the opportunity of executing a decisive technique. It is very similar to competition or sport karate, except that its criterion is not which blow lands first, but which is judged the more effective. As soon as a technique is delivered to a vital point with power and control, from a strong and stable stance, the 'defeated' partner acknowledges the blow, and the practice continues.

It is vital that, even in this fiercely combative type of sparring, both partners continue to work together. This means being honest in acknowledging when a blow strikes the target, and not immediately thrusting home a retaliatory technique to 'even up' the score (which would be nonsensical, for if the first blow had not been controlled the opportunity for retaliation would not occur).

On occasion, however, students are encouraged to continue to fight at close quarters, if they honestly believe that the opponent's blow lacked the power and accuracy to make them, in reality, unable to continue. This gives invaluable opportunity to practise the close-range strikes and throws all too often neglected. Again, as soon as an undeniably effective blow is delivered, the practice is brought to an immediate halt.

It does sometimes happen – although thankfully very rarely – that one meets an opponent in the proper sense of the word: one who appears to be ignorant of the true aims of karate practice and seems intent on striking hard, with little or no control. Paradoxically, such an encounter can be turned to the student's advantage, since it allows the opportunity to test mental control and physical skill against an element of real danger.

Ju kumite, used properly, is an invaluable part of karate-do training. It aids the development of both the mental and the physical aspects of the art; and reinforces the lesson that 'spirit is more important than physical power'.

Free-style – ***ju-kumite:*** P Mead (1978 SKI Open Champion) blocks a side thrust attack from D Hague.

For a number of reasons, many Western karate-ka question the need for ***kata*** training. One argument put forward is that karate is a fighting art, and that time spent practising ***kata*** would be better employed perfecting techniques of self-defence against possible attack by muggers or the like.

But such statements demonstrate a very superficial understanding of the nature of ***kata,*** their purpose and practice.

In pre-medieval Europe, because the arts of reading and writing were not widespread, the transmission of knowledge - of historical events, folklore, philosophy, medicine, etc. - from generation to generation and from place to place was often accomplished by the work of the Scōps, or wandering poet-minstrels. The Scōps weaved their acquired knowledge into new songs and stories, which they then sang and recited at courts and

1. *Yoi.* Feet together, open left hand on left hip, pressing against closed right vertical fist.

2. Pivot 90° anti-clockwise on right foot, assuming kneeling position with right knee on floor, heel of left foot in line with right knee. Right arm is swung into downward blocking position, left is placed across chest with clenched fist, knuckles downward. Face continues to point in original direction.

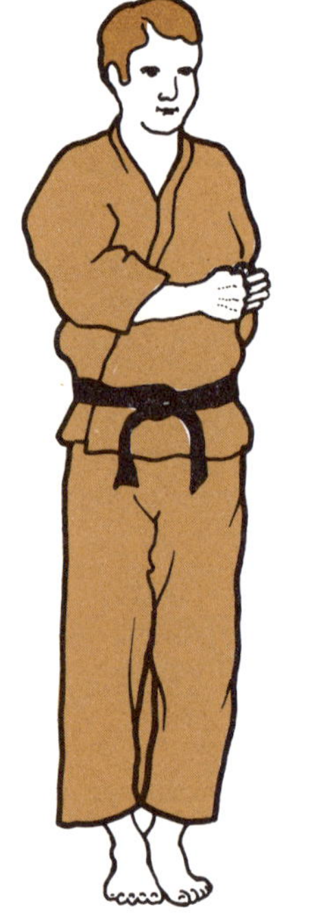

SHORIN-RYU AND SHOREI-RYU KATA

Examples of two advanced Shotokan ***kata*** - one typifying the Shorin-***ryu*** category, the other the Shorei-***ryu*** - are presented in detail here.

EMPI: A Shorin-*ryu kata.* Light, fast movements dominate.

6. Keeping right foot in position, step forward into left front stance and execute downward sweeping block.

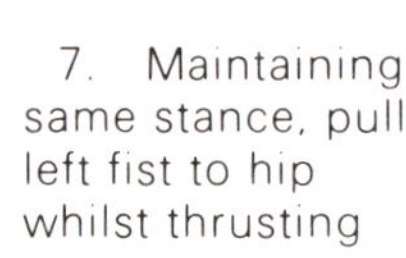

7. Maintaining same stance, pull left fist to hip whilst thrusting right fist in upward arc directly to the front in upward rising punch ***(age-zuki).***

gatherings throughout their travels. Poetically enshrined, the substance of the songs proved relatively easy to remember.

In just the same manner were the techniques that comprised the repertoire of the various fighting arts transmitted, except of course that instead of learning songs students learned series of physical movements. Again, since literacy was an attribute possessed by only a favoured few, there was little point in writing down the techniques: few would be able to read them; and there was always the chance that, written down, they could fall into the wrong hands.

Later, when literacy became more common, some of the techniques were indeed committed to paper; and with the foundation of the ***ryu*** (each with its own 'headmaster') these scrolls ***(makimono)*** became closely guarded secrets. But learning physical skills from the

3. Resume upright position, left fist placed on left hip with knuckles downward, right fist placed on it 'cup and saucer' fashion, knuckles to front. Whilst rising the body returns to front-facing position.

4. Facing 90° clockwise, now execute downward sweeping block ***(gedan-barai)*** whilst dropping the body into front stance ***(zenkutsu-dachi)***.

5. Keeping right foot where it is, turn body 90° anti-clockwise whilst drawing left foot into line with right, assuming straddle ***(kiba-dachi)*** stance. Left fist is thrust sharply across lower chest in hook punch ***(kage-zuki)***. Right fist is drawn back to right hip, knuckles downward.

8. Open right hand, and, keeping hips low, jump forward onto right foot. In this movement, right knee is raised high. Upon landing, left foot is drawn up behind right, with toes only on the floor. Both knees are bent. As you jump, re-clench right fist and draw it towards your left shoulder as if pulling an opponent closer. At the same time, punch forward and downward with left fist.

written word alone was next to impossible; and students were faced also with the problems of ensuring that they continued to practise correct technique if their teacher was ever absent, or if they themselves had to move to another area.

It was in answer to such problems as these that the *kata* were devised.

WHAT ARE KATA?

Essentially, ***kata*** are fixed sequences of techniques, designed as effective defences against attacks by several opponents from different directions.

The onlooker watching a karate-ka practising ***kata*** might think he was witnessing a type of dance. In many instances, he would unfortunately be correct, for very few karate-ka progress in technique and understanding to the point where they are able to exhibit the true nature of ***kata,*** wherein the performer actually 'sees' his attackers in his mind's eye and reacts accordingly. In this stage, there

9. Keeping right foot in place, turn 180° anti-clockwise and assume left front stance. Body is leant forward over left knee, forming a straight-line extension of rear leg; the head, however, still faces direction of 8 (i.e., now to the rear). In this position, execute downward sweeping block with right hand to the rear, ending over right buttock. Left fist is pulled to the hip.

10. Maintaining left forward stance, body is jerked upright whilst head is now turned in direction in which body is facing. Left hand performs downward sweeping block, right hand going to hip.

13. Keeping right foot in place, turn 180° anti-clockwise and in left forward stance, with body leaning forward, repeat the techniques exactly as in 9, with right arm blocking to rear with downward sweeping block, ending with fist over right buttock.

14. Keeping same stance, quickly straighten back so that body is erect, look to front and execute left downward sweeping block.

is no 'What comes next?'; techniques flow smoothly and powerfully from the trained subconscious. The mind itself is calm and 'unstopping', seeing all and troubled by nothing. As Takagi ***sensei*** (renowned instructor and director of the JKA) put it: 'Karate is moving Zen, and it is the Zen state that you must strive for.'

The novice understands ***kata*** to be a sequence of blocking and countering techniques, to be performed time and again in order that the pattern of movements becomes ingrained. At the same time, he gains practice in control of body movement, balance, different stances, punches, kicks, strikes, tension and relaxation, and correct breathing.

As he becomes more competent, the student learns progressively more difficult and complex ***kata,*** which must be practised incessantly. Each ***kata*** now acquires a different significance. Some he will 'like',

11. Still maintaining body position, left hand is withdrawn to hip while right hand is thrust forward in upward rising punch. (This is a similar movement to 7.)

12. Body jumps forward onto right foot, and the same techniques are performed as in 8.

15. With right foot remaining in position, swing left foot and opened left hand in parallel arc across front of body. Left foot is placed in line with right, in straddle stance. Left hand with palm towards face is stopped diagonally to left front at head height. Throughout this movement, the gaze is fixed on the hand.

16. Keeping left hand and foot in place, simultaneously strike hand with

others he will 'hate', but, although they are extremely tiring, the karate-ka will find that he has to spend less time on correcting basic technique and more upon the perfecting or 'polishing' of each technique. The rudiments of balance, form and execution have been learned and now the student struggles to 'put it together' under the ***sensei's*** cold gaze. At this point, most students begin to realize that the ***kata*** have a function beyond that of merely training the body and the memory.

Now, imaginary opponents enter the conceptualization of the ***kata,*** and techniques performed previously to the teacher's command take on an extra quality as they become reactions to invisible attacks. Soon, the karate-ka finds that he has done a complete ***kata*** without once thinking of the sequence. At this stage, ***kata*** graduate from imitation fights to very real encounters with,

outside edge of right forearm and place instep of right foot behind left knee. Whilst doing this, the eyes look to the front. At the moment of impact, *kiai.*

17. Return right foot to its former position and re-assume straddle stance. Right hand swings back across face in a circular movement to right hip whilst left hand, palm downwards, brushes underneath it towards right armpit as if pushing up a kimono sleeve.

19. Pivoting on right foot, turn 90° anti-clockwise and perform left downward sweeping block in left front stance. Right fist comes to rest on right hip.

albeit imaginary, foes; and each technique is performed with speed, power and focus, as required.

There is yet a further stage to master, in which the Zen state of complete awareness is evident. Nothing distracts from the master's ***zanshin,*** his perceptive and intuitive understanding of the one-ness of both his actions and those of his opponents. Here, spirit and body are unified and each encounter is one of life or death; although, having once accepted this notion, the karate-ka must discard it as being of no consequence. In this state, karate-do is Zen, and Zen is karate-do. The karate-ka tests and strengthens his resolution in moments of crisis; indeed, perhaps in the face of the supreme crisis - death.

The Hagakure (see Chapter 4) reminds us that we tend to think of moments of crisis as being somehow different from our everyday existence, so that

It then is thrust slowly to front until arm is fully extended in open-hand block position, fingers towards ceiling.

18. Still in straddle stance, execute first right middle-level punch and then left middle-level punch.

20. Keeping same stance, twist hips further anti-clockwise, withdraw left fist to hips and thrust right fist forward in upward rising punch (as 7 and 11).

21. Keeping left foot in same place, step forwards into right back stance ***(kokutsu-dachi)*** and perform middle-level knife-hand block ***(shuto-uke)*** with the right hand.

22. Bring front foot (right) back level with rear foot,

when the moment comes we are unprepared for it. In fact, the time is now – that is, whenever it happens will be the 'now' – and it is better to act than to anticipate.

On a more mundane level, it is obvious that, if practised properly, ***kata*** afford the opportunity to practise full-power blows to weak points and prohibited areas in a manner absolutely impossible in free-style practice. No techniques are 'pulled', the most dangerous and deadly 'foul' combinations are freely utilized.

At the highest level, ***kata*** train the mind and spirit to be unfearing and indomitable. The purely physical is transcended; the expert does not 'do' karate, he 'is' karate. To reiterate, in the face of this, that time spent practising ***kata*** would be better employed on perfecting techniques of self-defence, would be foolish in the extreme.

and place left foot in position vacated by right. Stance is now reversed. At the same time, execute left middle-level knife-hand block.

23. Keeping in left back stance, thrust right fist forward in middle-level punch, simultaneously withdrawing left hand to hip.

24. Step forward with right foot into back stance and execute right middle-level knife-hand block.

27. Raising right knee, open right hand and jump forward onto right foot, re-clenching hand and drawing it to left shoulder. Left foot comes up to touch back of right heel, toes only on floor. At the same time, thrust left fist forward in a lower-level punch (same as 8 and 12).

28. With right foot in same position, turn 180° anti-clockwise and step into left front stance. Head

It is interesting to note how very many of the world's most successful competition fighters are also champions in ***kata.*** The list would be far too long to include here! Certainly, if practised assiduously, ***kata*** give the karate-ka practice in the use of techniques he may well not favour, even, in general non-***kata*** training, tend to avoid. Avoiding a particular technique may lead to the habit of depending upon only one or two favourite techniques, which might not be suitable in all instances. To combat such a tendency, and to ensure that the karate-ka acquires all-round skill, Funakoshi recommended that ***kata*** practice be emphasized, and that sparring should be only secondary to ***kata.***

To the karata-ka who believes that he has achieved mastery of ***kata,*** one question should be posed. So you have the ability to perform a complex ***kata*** fluently, powerfully, and with

25. Keeping front (right) foot in same place, turn 180° anti-clockwise into left front stance, executing left downward sweeping block.

26. Maintain this stance, pull left hand to hip and thrust right fist forward in upward rising punch (same as 7, 11 and 19)

continues to look in original direction of 26. Body leans forward and while left fist comes to hip, right arm executes downward sweeping block to rear (same as 9 and 13).

29. Keeping same stance, body quickly assumes upright position and head jerks round to face forward. Simultaneously perform left downward sweeping block (same as 10 and 14).

30. In same stance, withdraw left fist to hip. At the same time, head faces diagonally 45° to front right and right hand, palm upwards, open with fingers bent, performs middle-level block diagonally to right front ***(teisho-uke).***

proper *zanshin.* But how is your *zanshin* when *sensei* says 'Once more', and then, 'Once more',' and then, 'Once more' . . . ?

To the female karate-ka, it should be emphasized that gender is no excuse for sloppy, unfocused, carelessly executed *kata.* Indeed, this is the main area in karate-do practice in which men and women are on equal terms. *Kata* makes no sexual discrimination, neither does Zen – and nor does life.

KARATE KATA

Though all styles of karate have *kata,* some have more than others, and some emphasize their importance more than others. In many instances, the *kata* practised by the various styles are very similar, because they originate from a common source.

In general terms, *kata* can be divided into the two basic types designated by Funakoshi: Shorin-*ryu* and Shorei-*ryu;* the former, emphasizing fast, light movements, more suited to the

31. Bring right foot to left and rotate body 90° clockwise, then step forward smoothly into right front stance. At the same time, in a scissor-like circular motion push right hand in palm-heel block position *(teisho)* forward and upward to shoulder height, and left hand, also in palm-heel block position, downward until arm is fully extended.

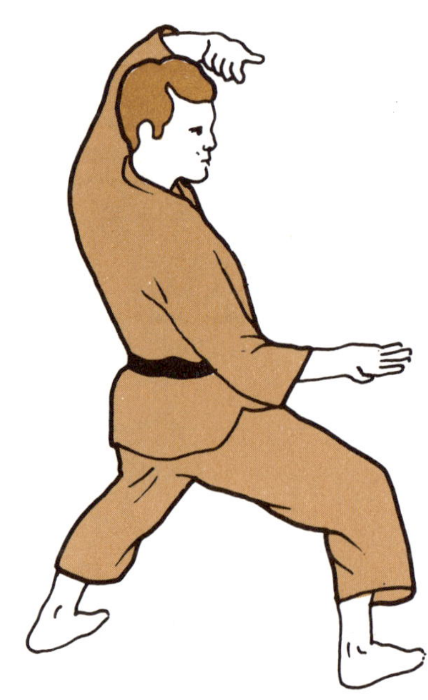

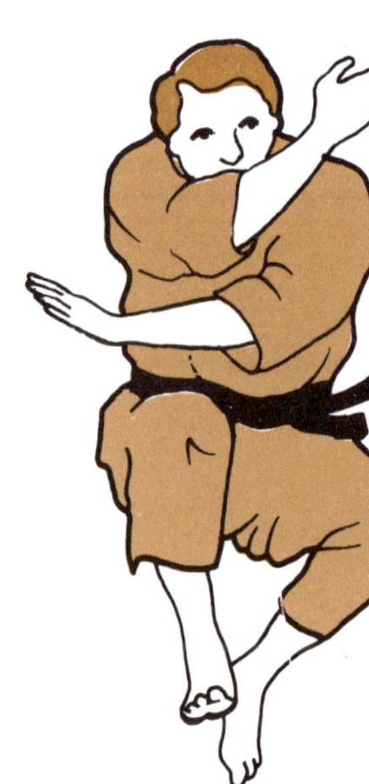

stance. Open both hands. Right hand, palm upward, is placed level with lower abdomen. Left hand, rotated clockwise with palm upward, is place just above eye level about 9 inches in front of forehead.

36. Maintaining straddle stance, swing both hands in arc (as in a throwing motion) over head into a similar position on left-hand side. Immediately jump off ground with both knees high in the air, as if jumping over the body of a thrown opponent. Turn 360° anti-clockwise in the air, and land in right back stance. Simultaneously perform right middle-level hand block and *kiai.* (The object of this technique is to block an upper-level attack with

smaller karate-ka, the latter, stressing strength and power, more befitting the heavier, less agile exponent. Funakoshi points out that each has its weaknesses as well as its strengths, all of which must be well understood by the student.

In the Shorin-*ryu* category he includes:

The five ***heian*** (peaceful mind) ***kata*** whose name suggests that the karate-ka who has mastered these five forms can be confident in his ability to defend himself.

bassai ('to penetrate a fortress' which implies the need to inculcate a will strong enough to break through any defence).

kanku (named after Ku Shanku, its Chinese originator; now meaning 'to look at the sky', referring to the opening movements).

empi ('flying swallow', referring to the similarity between some of the movements and the erratic up-and-down flight of the swallow).

32. Stepping forward with hips kept low into left front stance, hands reverse their positions, both kept in palm-heel block form.

33. Stepping forward in a similar manner into right front stance, hands are again reversed. This is the last of a right-left-right sequence of identical moves, which are performed slowly with focus *(kime).*

35. Sliding both feet forward, change into right-facing straddle

the left hand whilst thrusting the right between the opponent's legs. He is then pulled in and thrown across the shoulders in the manner of the judo shoulder-wheel throw *(kata garuma).*

37. Step directly backwards with right foot into left back stance and execute left middle-level knife-hand block.

38. ***Yame.*** Smoothly withdraw left foot and assume same ready position as in 1. NB. When moving from one hand technique to another, particularly when blocking, practise the full movement with both hands. Do not just move the blocking hand while allowing the other to remain on the hip or in its former position.

gankaku ('crane on a rock', so named because the ***kata*** includes repeated use of a one-legged stance prior to kicking).

In the Shorei-***ryu*** group, he includes:

The three ***tekki*** ('horse riding') ***kata*** (which use the ***kiba-dachi,*** or horse/straddle stance).

jutte ('ten hands': implying that the karate-ka who has mastered this ***kata*** is as effective as a group of men).

hangetsu ('half-moon': derived from the semi-circular hand and foot movements employed).

jion (whose originator was identified with the temple of Jion, a Buddhist saint).

This list, of course, represents only a selection of ***kata*** available.

KATA PRACTICE: Points and Suggestions

(a) Formerly, it was considered that it would take at least three years of practice to master one ***kata,*** and that even an expert would only know up

HANGETSU: A Shorei-*ryu kata.* Strong powerful movements. The first half of the *kata* smooth and slow, showing focus and relaxation; second half explosive, with fast and powerful techniques.

1. ***Yoi.*** Natural stance ***(hachiji-dachi).***

2. Keeping right foot where it is, slide left foot forwards slowly in semi-circular motion into left half-moon stance ***(hangetsu-dachi).*** At the same time, execute a middle-level inside block with left fist ***(chudan uchi-uke)***

5. Keeping same stance, withdraw right fist to hip and execute middle-level punch with left fist. This is an exact mirror image of 3

6. Step forward with left foot in a semi-circular motion into left half-moon stance. Simultaneously execute left middle-level inside block while withdrawing right hand to hip. This is an exact copy of 2.

to half-a-dozen. Nowadays, karate-ka tend to have a much wider knowledge - in breadth if not in depth - of the various ***kata.*** Generally, however, ***dan*** grades - as well as practising a wide range of ***kata*** - spend a great deal of time on their ***tokui*** (favourite) ***kata*** in order to gain more than a superficial knowledge.

(b) Students often say: I like this ***kata,*** but I don't like that one.' This usually means that they find one easier to perform than another. Beware the pitfalls that this attitude implies.

(c) Remember that ***kata*** training, as well as being an exercise in ***zanshin*** and technique, is also a vehicle for the practice of correct breath control. Remember that successful focus is accompanied by an abrupt exhalation of breath. This naturally can only be done if inspiration (breathing in) has occurred. Beginners often find that while executing a

while right is withdrawn to hip. All movements are slow and deliberate and must demonstrate correct tensing and relaxing of muscles.

3. Maintaining same stance, withdraw left fist to hip while slowly thrusting right fist forward in middle-level punch.

4. Step forward with right foot in semi-circular motion into right half-moon stance. At the same time, right fist performs a middle-level inside block. This is an exact mirror image of 2.

7. Maintaining same stance, withdraw left fist to hip while thrusting right fist forward in middle-level punch. This is an exact copy of 3.

8. Keeping same stance, form both hands into forefinger single-knuckle fist *(ippon-ken).* Left hand is slowly thrust forward parallel with extended right arm, until fist reaches a position approximately level with right wrist. At this point, both fists are drawn slowly back to points just level with or slightly below nipples, with elbows out.

sequence of techniques they have held their breath; this means that the correct rhythm of breathing has not been attained and therefore the techniques will lack power.Concentrate on breath control, until it becomes instinctive. Generally speaking, inspiration takes place as limbs are retracted from an extended position, and exhalation occurs as limbs are thrust out from the body. In breathing, take pains to ensure that the chest and shoulders do not rise; air should be drawn in by strong diaphragmatic movement, and should feel as though it is pushed into the lower belly.

Practise this assiduously in ***kata*** training and it will carry over into pre-arranged ***kumite*** and free-style, with the effect that an opponent will get no clue from heaving chest and shoulders as to your state of exhaustion, or as to whether you are inhaling or exhaling, which might serve to give him

9. Still keeping same stance, slowly extend both fists – still in single-knuckle form – to a position directly in front of nipples.

10. Again maintaining same stance, open both hands, forming four-finger knife-hands, palms facing inward. In a slow, large movement, cross arms in front of face, initially keeping them as straight as

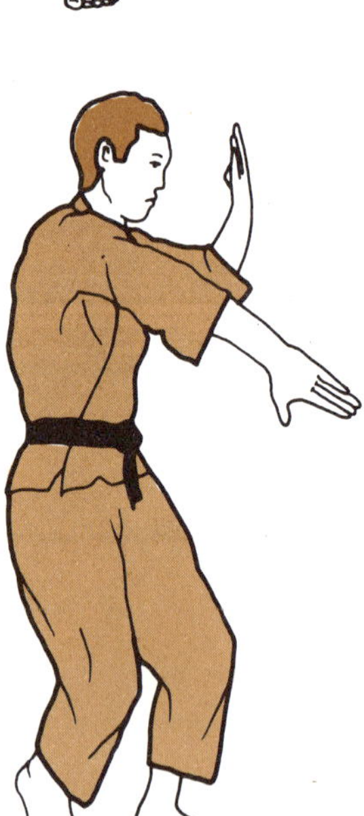

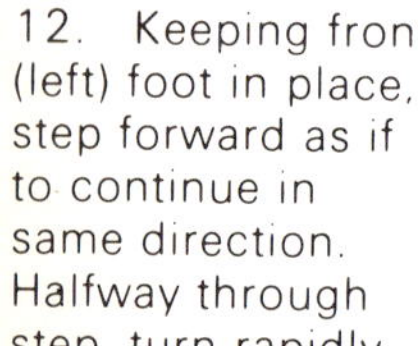

12. Keeping front (left) foot in place, step forward as if to continue in same direction. Halfway through step, turn rapidly on left foot 180° anti-clockwise, so that you face directly opposite original direction. While turning, perform left open-hand downward sweeping block with left hand and right middle-level inside block with open right hand. In this technique, arms cross in a scissor-like motion. Change of stance and double block are to be executed extremely quickly and are accompanied by a ***kiai.*** Final position is left half-moon stance, with right open hand – palm inward – level with right shoulder, and left open hand – palm inward – level with and in front of left thigh.

an opening for attack.

(d) It is usual to break down a new ***kata*** into several segments and learn each sequence separately. When each is mastered, the segments are joined once more. Masters Funakoshi and Egami stressed that the three most essential points of ***kata*** practice are: (1) light and heavy application of strength, (2) expansion (relaxation) and contraction of the body, and (3) fast and slow movements in techniques. Basically, they meant that speed, in itself, is of no merit, nor is indiscriminate use of tension and power. To understand a ***kata*** properly is to understand the relationship between fast and slow movements, relaxed and tensed muscles, and to be able to apply the correct degree of strength at the decisive moment. In order to facilitate this understanding the various techniques and sequences of the ***kata*** should be practised

possible. When fully extended over head, allow elbows to bend until right angle is formed between upper and lower arms. At this stage, palms of the hands are still facing inward, approximately level with the ears, and upper arms are level with the shoulders.

11. Keeping same stance, straighten arms again, cross them in front of face (reverse of movements in number 10) and bring them down across body and out to sides. In final position, palms still face inward.

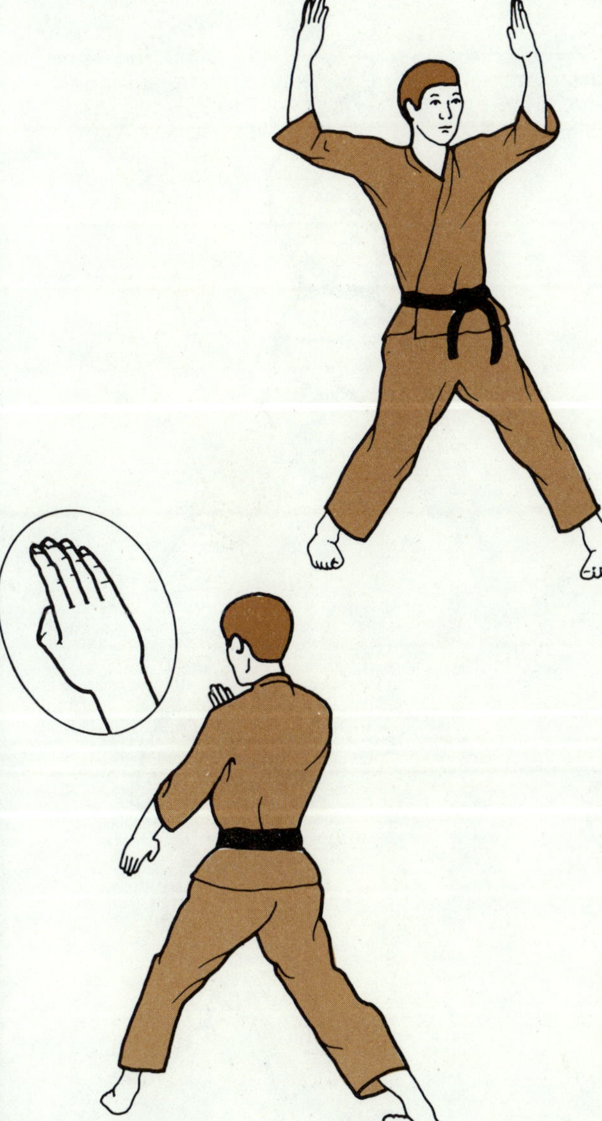

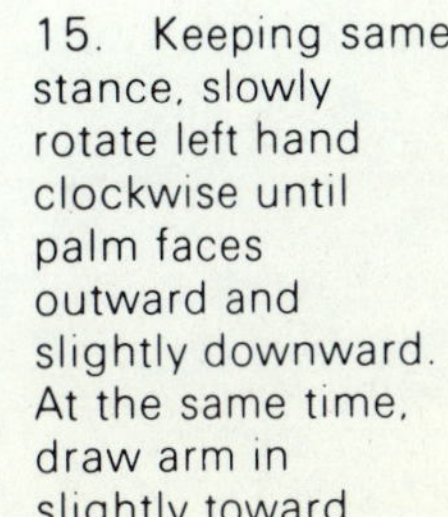

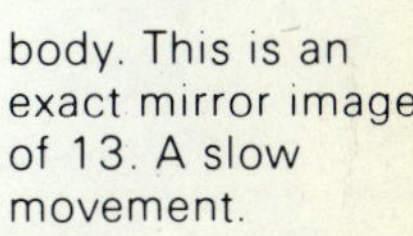

13. Maintaining same stance, slowly rotate right hand anti-clockwise until palm faces outwards and slightly downwards. At the same time, draw arm a little inward toward body. This is a movement designed to block an opponent's punch and then grasp his arm and draw him in range for counter-attack. A slow movement.

14. Keeping left foot in place, step forward with semi-circular motion into right half-moon stance. Right hand performs open-hand middle-level downward sweeping block. Left hand executes open-hand middle-level inside block. This is a mirror image of the hand techniques in 12. A fast movement.

15. Keeping same stance, slowly rotate left hand clockwise until palm faces outward and slightly downward. At the same time, draw arm in slightly toward body. This is an exact mirror image of 13. A slow movement.

with a partner in ***yakusoku***.

(e) ***Kata*** should be practised initially at a rhythm dictated by the ***sensei's*** count. This will help to give an appreciation of the fast and slow sequences, etc. When the full ***kata*** is practised, it is usual to do it first to count, slowly and lightly. Then it is done again, still to count, with proper speed and power. At intermediate level, this is followed by its being done again at slow speed, emphasizing correct breathing and focus, and then yet once more at full speed and power. At advanced level, this alternating sequence of practice is continued until the karate-ka is totally exhausted, at which point the will-power and spirit come into play. It is not at all unusual for the high grades to do all five ***heian kata, bassai dai, empi, gankaku, jutte, hangetsu, jion, tekki shodan, tekki nidan, bassai sho, chinte, kanku dai, kanku sho,*** etc., all performed first slowly and then

16. Keeping right foot in place, step forward with semi-circular motion into left half-moon stance. Left hand performs open-hand downward sweeping block while right hand performs open-hand middle-level inside block. Stance and techniques are identical to those of 12. A fast movement.

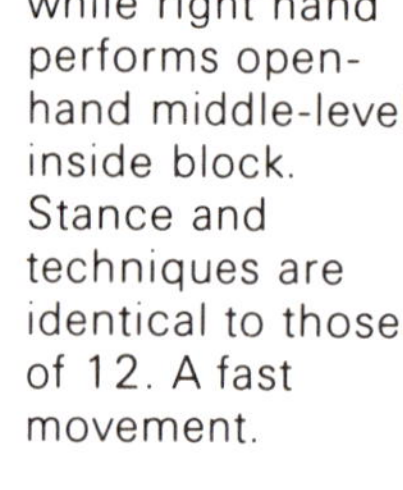

17. Maintaining same stance, slowly rotate right hand anti-clockwise until palm faces outwards and slightly downwards. At the same time, draw arm in slightly towards body. This is identical to 13. A slow movement. You should now have executed identical techniques in left, right and again left, half-moon stances.

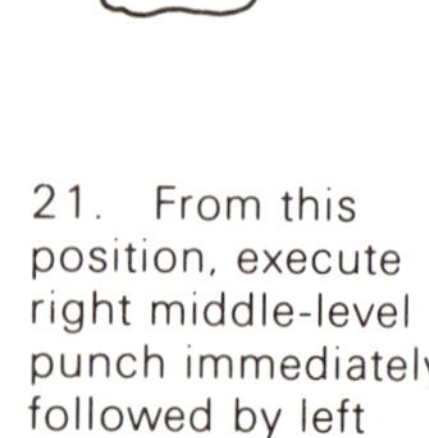

20. Keeping front foot in position, quickly pivot 180° anti-clockwise to face opposite direction. Left foot moves slightly, to facilitate left front stance. While turning, left hand executes a middle-level inside block. Right fist is withdrawn to hip and both fists are closed. This is a mirror image of 18. A fast movement. (Some karate-ka include a slight forward-sliding motion *(yori-ashi)* in this movement).

21. From this position, execute right middle-level punch immediately followed by left middle-level punch, a mirror image of 19. A fast movement.

with speed and power, with no rest at all between them. By this stage, everybody is swaying with exhaustion – some cannot even keep their eyes open – but nobody ever stops or drops out! And here is where karate's indomitable spirit is forged. (Naturally, this severe type of training cannot be applied indiscriminately; it needs a good ***sensei*** to know just how far to push, and when.)

(f) It is useful sometimes to practise ***kata*** in the opposite direction to normal.

(g) Remember at all times to maintain ***zanshin,*** concentrated but calm awareness and attention to the matter in hand.

(h) Do not set preconceived limits to your performance. Probably no one is fully aware of his potential. Remember that in karate-do you are fighting a battle with yourself.

KATA COMPETITION

A summary of the requirements and criteria of ***kata*** competition can be found in Chapter 21.

18. Turning 90° clockwise, pivot on front (left) foot and step into right front stance ***(zenkutsu-dachi),*** simultaneously perform right middle-level inside block with closed right fist. Left closed fist is withdrawn to hip. This is a very fast movement.

19. From this position, execute left middle-level punch immediately followed by right middle-level punch. The two punches are to be considered as one technique ***(ren-zuki).*** A fast movement.

22. Keeping left foot in position, turn 90° clockwise, and step into right front stance while performing right middle-level inside block, with left fist going to hip. An exact copy of 18. A fast movement.

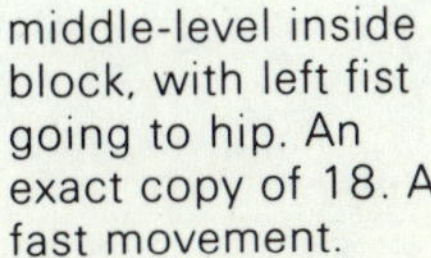

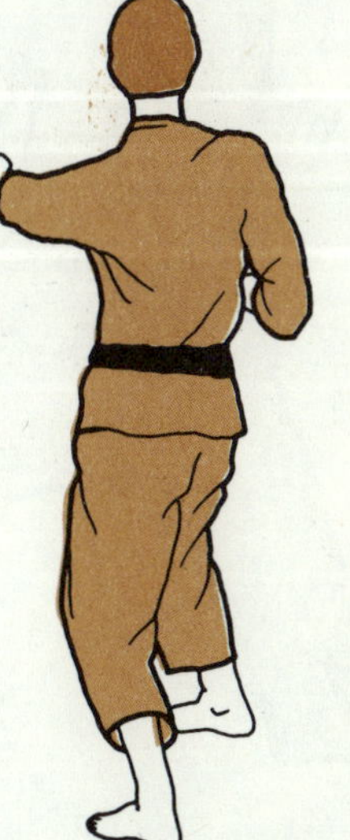

23. From this position, execute left middle-level punch immediately followed by right middle-level punch. An exact copy of 19. A fast movement.

24. In a slow, controlled movement, turn 180° anti-clockwise on front (right) foot. Left foot is first drawn in towards right, and then, lifted off the ground in an arc, is placed slowly in line with right foot almost back on spot it just vacated, except that now it faces opposite direction. Slowly move into left back stance *(kokutsu-dachi)*. At the same time, left fist is drawn in towards right, and then in large movement over head, in arc parallel with foot, execute slow backfist strike *(uraken-uchi)*, coming to rest at a point level with left shoulder. Throughout the technique, gaze is to be fixed upon left fist. Aim is to strike opponent's fist. A slow movement.

27. Maintaining left front stance, execute left lower-level sweeping block. Immediately following this, thrust right fist forward in middle-level punch, with-drawing left fist to hip. Following this, straight away execute upper-level rising block *(jodan age-uke)* with left arm, right fist retracting to hip. A fast movement. (The techniques of 26 and 27 form a continuous rapid sequence.)

25. Keeping body in same position, slowly step forward with right foot until it just crosses the left, and place toes down gently. It is assumed here that your opponent has grasped your left arm and you have reacted to his pull by moving in closer in a balanced position. A slow movement.

26. Keep right foot where it is and snatch left hand in towards right shoulder. Simultaneously kick directly forward with left front kick *(mae-geri).* Aim here is to jerk your arm from your opponent's grasp and at the same time to attack his gripping arm with a front kick. Immediately after kicking, step forward with left foot into front stance. A fast movement.

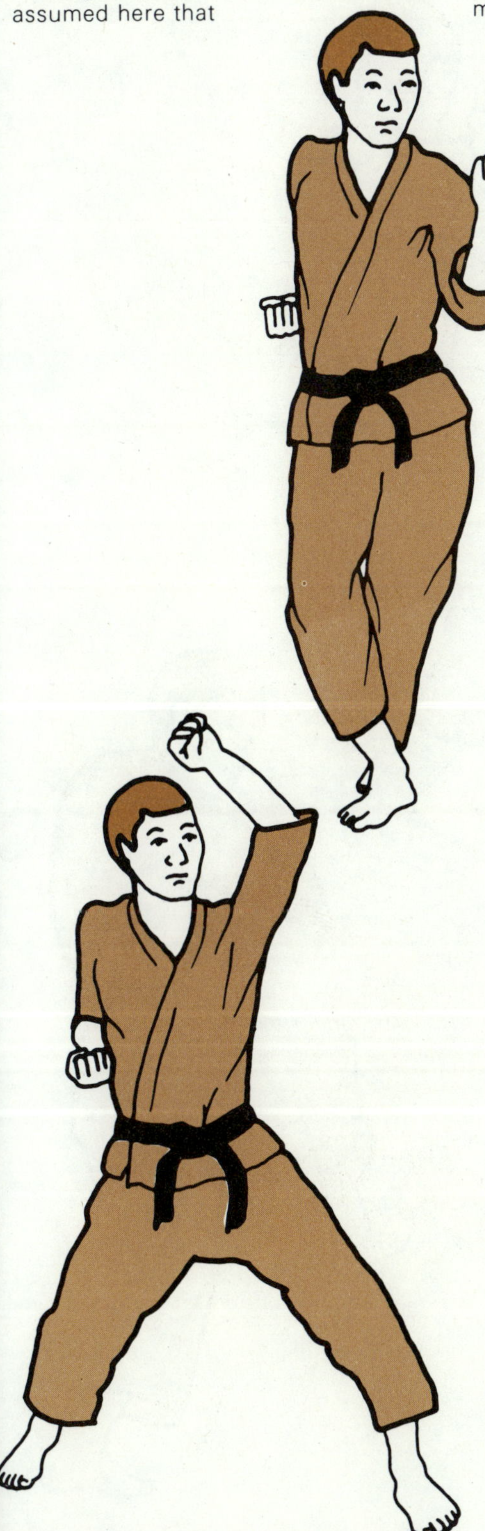

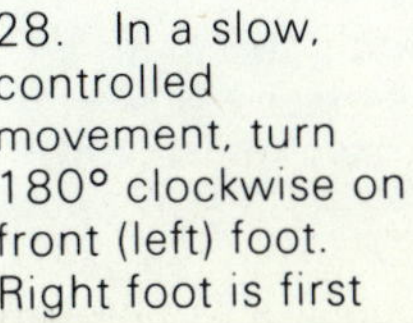

28. In a slow, controlled movement, turn 180° clockwise on front (left) foot. Right foot is first drawn in towards the left and then lifted off ground in an arc, is placed slowly in line with left foot almost back on the same spot that it just vacated, except it now faces the opposite direction. Slowly move into right back stance. Simultaneously reverse in a large arc parallel with the foot, over the head, into a slow middle-level back-fist strike, coming to rest in line with right shoulder. Throughout the movement, the eyes are fixed upon the right fist. This is an exact mirror image of 24.

29. Keeping body in the same position, slowly step forward with left foot until it just crosses the right and place the toes down gently. A slow movement.

30. Keep left foot where it is and snatch right fist in toward left shoulder. Simultaneously kick directly forward with right front kick. Immediately after kicking, step forward with kicking leg (right) into front stance. An exact mirror image of 26. A fast movement.

this, straight away execute upper-level rising block with right arm, left fist retracting to hip. An exact mirror image of 27. A fast movement. (The techniques of 30 and 31 form a continuous rapid sequence.)

32. In a slow controlled movement turn 180° anti-clockwise on the front (right) foot. The left foot is first drawn in towards the right and then raised from the floor and in an arc is placed slowly down in line with the right foot, almost in the same position as before,

31. Maintaining right front stance, execute rght lower-level sweeping block. Immediately following this, thrust left fist forward in middle-level punch, with-drawing right fist to hip. Following

except that now it faces the opposite direction. Slowly move into left back stance. Simultaneously, left fist is drawn in towards right, then in a large movement over the head it follows an arc parallel with the left foot, executing a slow backfist strike, coming to rest at a point level with the left shoulder.
This is an identical movement to 24. A slow movement.

33. Keeping same back stance, open left fist and straighten fingers into horizontal knife-hand, and straighten arm to shoulder level.

34. Keeping front (left) foot in position, swing right foot in semi-circular motion to kick extended left palm. This is the crescent-moon kick ***(mikazuki-geri)***. A fast movement.

35. Still keeping front (left) foot in position, lower right foot behind left into a front stance position. (Right foot is placed parallel with but to the right of the spot it just vacated in order to perform the kick). At this point, twist hips anti-clockwise, withdraw left hand to hip and execute right lower-level punch, and ***kiai.*** (Movements 34 and 35 form a continuous rapid sequence.)

36. Right foot remains in position while left is drawn slowly in towards it on the toes. Knees are bent, front (left) knee being flexed slightly inward.

This is the left cat stance ***(nekoashi-dachi).*** Simultaneously bring both hands together at wrists to form double palm-heel block, at knee height, just in front of bent left knee. Keep body as erect as posible.

37. ***Yame.*** Resume original stance as in 1.
NB: Since one of the functions of this kata is to teach the correct application of tension and relaxation, breath control is of paramount importance. In general, the breathing sequence follows the normal pattern: inspiration prior to executing a technique, exhalation during execution.

A contest between two karate-ka (often termed ***shiai,*** a 'test meeting'; but more correctly ***shobu: sho,*** victory, ***bu,*** defeat) is by no means a modern innovation. Originally, two men who wished to test their acquired martial skills in actual combat did so without the restriction of rules; which often resulted in the death of one or both of the participants. ***'Shinken shobu',*** as such contests were termed, took place on the Chinese mainland as recently as the 19th century.

In course of time, fights to the death came to be frowned on by the more responsible masters, and it became usual to agree to a basic set of rules: the ***shiai*** must take place in a specific area, and would end when one of the combatants was knocked out or signified his inability or unwillingness to continue by going beyond the marked-off area. While blows were still delivered with full power and full contact, the more lethal blows were normally withheld; though it would seem that, more often than not, it was rather by luck than by judgement that fewer deaths occured.

As karate developed in Okinawa, the concept of it as a martial art continued to prevail, and no real attempts were made to devise rules that would allow it to be practised as a sport. Some Okinawan styles maintain this attitude to date.

With the proliferation of schools of karate in Japan, however, and the development of different styles, certain groups began to introduce into the training free-sparring ***(ju kumite),*** in which each karate-ka was free to attack or defend as he saw fit, with prescribed techniques.

This development was initially strongly opposed by some of the leading karate-do masters. In 1927, for example, some students at Shichi-Tokudo decided to introduce free-sparring with protective helmets and padding. Instructors Funakoshi and Otsuka heard of this, and attempted to discourage the practice. When their attempts met with no success, neither taught at that ***dojo*** again.

Despite such strong opposition, the popularity of sparring continued to increase. First, pre-arranged sparring was instituted, followed shortly by free-sparring.

In practice, the free-sparring in some ***dojo*** paid scant respect to the rules. Taiji Kase (7th ***dan*** JKA) has described in graphic detail the ferocity of the fighting in ***dojo*** just after World War II, when students from different karate styles met to train in groups. Basically, the training sessions comprised one-step sparring, three-step sparring and free-sparring. In the last, no attempt was made to hold back or 'pull' the blows, and senior grades would have to jump in to separate the combatants when the ***kumite*** degenerated into brawling. Kase ***sensei*** recalls that during one of these sessions, all his front teeth were knocked out and some ribs broken. His revenge was to break his opponent's ribs and nose. (He came out of these events comparatively lightly; many received much more severe injuries, including loss of eyesight).

This type of competition - in truth, real ***shobu,*** without co-operation between partners or restriction of potentially dangerous techniques - was not allowed to continue. Nevertheless, it became apparent to some of the leading karate masters of the time that a compromise was necessary, to allow karate-ka to test the efficiency of their techniques in the immediacy and uncertainty of combat and at the same time ensure their safety. To this end discussions began with the aim of formulating rules and procedures for competition karate.

Most styles of karate-do agreed on the basic selection of allowed and prohibited techniques, and on the criteria for judging their efficiency. This ensured a ban on the use of full-power contact, and restriction of the target area to the trunk above the waist, and the head. Certain techniques - such as ***nukite*** (spear hand), ***kin-geri*** (kick to the testicles) and ***fumikomi*** (stamping kicks to lower limbs, etc) - were classed as too dangerous to be used in competition. This provoked a strong reaction from certain ***sensei,*** who strongly condemned the restrictions on the grounds that they changed karate from a martial art into a sport. As such, they claimed it could no longer be considered ***budo,*** nor could it concur with the original precepts of karate-do.

In the event, while the mainstream of karate continued to develop the concept and practice of competition karate along the lines agreed above, a distinct divergence took place (see Chapter 3)

In 1964 the Federation of All Japan Karate-do Organizations (FAJKO) was formed to bring the many karate groups and styles together and to enable a set of rules to be devised which would allow competitions to be held among and between the different groups. FAJKO was officially recognized by the Japanese Government and the rules for competition agreed upon followed closely the criteria established and accepted by the mainstream karate groups. In 1969, the first All Japan Karate-do Championship was held under FAJKO rules. By this time, karate-do had begun to spread to many countries throughout the world. ***Budo*** purists would say that, in the main, only the technical and sporting aspects had survived the migration, to give rise to emphasis on the sporting element of karate.

Whatever the truth of this

view, it soon became apparent that there was a need for the creation of a world body, which would establish agreed rules and regulations for national, international and world championships. To this end, delegates from 33 countries came together in Tokyo in 1970 and formed the World Union of Karate-do Organizations (WUKO), whose inaugural declaration stated its intention to utilize karate-do as 'an effective means whereby to advocate the sound union of body and mind and to help enhance peace and progress for mankind'. To mark the inauguration of WUKO, the first karate-do world championship tournament took place in Tokyo, under agreed internationally standardized rules of judging and procedure.

Great Britain was one of the 33 founder members of WUKO, and has taken part in all subsequent world championships. For the British team, the greatest moment came at the 1975 world championship in Long Beach, California, when they took on and defeated the Japanese national team, and by so doing became world karate champions.

Since the establishment of WUKO and FAJKO, the JKA has withdrawn and attempted to set up a European organization to rival the officially recognized European Karate Union (EKU) and also a world championship to rival the official WUKO event, through its strong connections with the International Amateur Karate Federation (IAKF).

Despite political manoeuvring by the IAKF, however, WUKO has been confirmed as the officially recognized international governing body for karate-do by the General Assembly of International Federations (GAIF). This is seen as a step towards the acceptance of karate as an Olympic sport under the auspices of WUKO, the IAKF's application to the International Olympic Committee having also been rejected.

This display of political ambition has had a detrimental effect on the strength of the British team, since WUKO has banned participants in IAKF events from taking part in the official championships. Because the KUGB is part of the JKA in Great Britain none of its excellent karate-ka are eligible for selection for WUKO events. In 1975, for example, Billy Higgins and Terry O'Neill took part in the IAKF competition and so were banned from taking part in the official world championship. As

Author (2nd left) and 1977 Open SKI British Championship team being congratulated by Asano ***sensei***.

it happened, long negotiations between WUKO officials and the chairman and secretary of the British Karate Control Commission (BKCC) were successful in obtaining special permission for them to compete on the understanding that the circumstances would not arise again. Unfortunately, KUGB members again took part in the 1977 IAKF championship and therefore once more made themselves ineligible for places on the British team at the official world championships in December 1977 – where Great Britain, in spite of once again defeating the Japanese team, lost to West Germany in the quarter finals, the eventual winners being the Netherlands.

In the face of such difficulties, WUKO has continued to expand and now embraces more than 70 member countries. Like any other major international concern, it has its problems; but it continues to work for the establishment of, in the words of Ryoichi Sasakawa, its president: 'The world of karate-do . . (in which) there is no discrimination of colour, age or sex . . (and in which) all are united in a single family as brothers and sisters.'

CHAPTER 21. COMPETITIONS

Basically, there are two types of competition: ***kumite*** and ***kata.*** We will begin by looking at the former.

THE KUMITE COMPETITION

Under the generally accepted WUKO rules (of which a brief summary is given in the Appendices), a karate ***kumite*** contest takes place on a flat, unobstructed surface, 8m.sq. Three metres apart, in the centre of the square, two parallel lines are drawn, and the two contestants face each other from these marks. The only other person allowed in the square is the referee, who is in direct control of the fighters. At each of the four corners of the square sits a judge, with a red-and-white flag and a whistle, whose function is to draw the attention of the referee to points scored by either man, or to any infringement of the rules that may have escaped the referee's notice. In addition to the referee and four corner judges, there is also an arbitrator, who ensures the fairness of the contests and the decisions.

Normally, contests last for two minutes. Extensions can be ordered, however, in case of draws, and some matches – often finals – are over a longer period, generally three or five minutes.

To begin a contest, the referee calls the participants to the centre lines, whereupon they face each other and bow ***(rei)***. He ensures that the fighters are in a ready ***(yoi)*** position, then calls 'start' ***(hajime)***.

From this moment until the referee calls 'stop' ***(yame)***, each fighter attempts to pierce the other's guard with fully focused blows and kicks to a designated target area. If this happens, and the technique is executed with correct form – i.e., is delivered from a good stable stance, is fast, accurate and focused, and delivered with spirit – the referee will stop the match and award a full point ***(ippon)*** to the successful fighter. This indicates that the blow would have been sufficiently powerful, if not 'pulled', to stop the fight there and then. If the technique did not fulfil all the above criteria but is still considered to have been effective, the referee will halt the match and award a near-point ***(waza-ari)***. Two near-points constitute a full point; and under one-point contest ***ippon shobu*** rules the first contestant to reach one full point wins the match.

Should no clear winner emerge on points, the referee can ask the judges to make a decision, based on certain criteria (see Appendices), as to which contestant should be adjudged the winner. It is also possible to win by default, by the opponent's disqualification for committing certain prohibited acts (see Appendices).

THE TARGET AREAS

Under WUKO rules, there are six designated target areas: head, face, neck, chest, abdomen and back.

It will be immediately apparent that many of the extremely effective but dangerous techniques and target areas utilized in karate-do are not included in this list. Many, in fact, appear on the list of prohibited techniques and acts. A contestant making use of any of these will be warned by the referee and is open to disqualification.

INDIVIDUAL AND TEAM COMPETITION

There are two types of ***kumite*** competition, the individual and the team. In the former, two contestants fight to decide who will proceed to the next round, and this process continues until one karate-ka is adjudged overall champion. In former days, no differentiation was made between large and small competitors; now, however, the trend is towards specific weight categories.

Teams can be made up of any odd number of competitors, usually five but occasionally seven. Normally, each member fights in predetermined order against his opposite number in the opposing team. The winning team is the one that gains the greater number of wins; or, in the case of a draw, has accrued the greater number of points as opposed to near-points. Should the result still be a draw, a representative from each team is selected to fight a deciding contest (see Appendices). As in the individual competition, the winning team goes through to face another team in the next round, and the process continues until one team emerges as the overall winner.

There is another, though little used, method of team competition, in which the winner of a match between individual team members continues to fight the next in line on the opposing team, and continues to do so until defeated. By this method, the winning team is the one whose member defeats the last man on the opposing team (for further details, see Appendices).

One problem of the karate ***kumite*** contest is that it is sometimes very difficult for the referee to determine the relative efficiency of the techniques delivered. It was with this in mind that the system of having four corner judges was instituted. Nevertheless, given the nature and speed of karate, complaints are often levelled about the poor standard of refereeing and judging in competition. To remedy this, WUKO holds regular referees' and judges' 'clinics', and the EKU and the EKB hold regular courses of instruction to promote and maintain a high standard.

Given that there are rules laid down for competition, and for scoring, it is inevitable that bad decisions will occur; any karate-ka entering a competition should fully realize that no one is infallible. On the other hand, one can but agree with the competition fighters who maintain that referees and judges should themselves have had experience of competition fighting, since only people with background knowledge are really competent to judge whether or not a technique should score.

As noted earlier, in ***shobu ippon kumite*** the first contestant to score one full point - even if through two near-points - wins the match. This system, although closer to the original concept of one conclusive blow, gives an advantage to the karate-ka who specializes in basic techniques; in particular, in counter-punching with reverse punch ***(gyaku-zuki),*** or front kick ***(mae-geri).*** Of course, certain combinations are also utilized; but in the main, with just one point at stake, there is a tendency for both competitors to adopt a cautious, conservative approach to the match, unwilling to give an opening by making use of - from the spectator's point of view - a more interesting or exciting technique.

In some instances - in championship finals, for example - a three-point match is held ***(shobu sanbon kumite),*** in which the winner is the first to gain three full points (new WUKO rules allow ***sanbon*** to be interpreted as 'best of three full points', with or without ***waza-ari*** awarded). This leads to the competitors' making adventurous use of a greater variety of techniques, since they are not open to instant defeat by a single counter-attack.

OTHER TYPES OF KUMITE COMPETITION

In view of the difficulties that arise in the judging of contests under WUKO rules, some organizations experiment with different sets of rules. The Kyokushinkai organization (not affiliated to FAJKO), for example, organizes competitions under what it terms 'knock-down' rules, which it holds to be more realistic and closer to the ***budo*** concept than the 'no contact' or 'controlled contact' rules.

Briefly, knock-down rules allow full contact to be made to head and body with kicks, and full contact to the body with punches. (Punches to the head are not allowed, nor are kicks to the knee joints or strikes to the groin and throat.) So, while indeed allowing the karate-ka who trains to withstand punishment to carry on fighting even if hit with a technique that may have scored under WUKO rules, the Kyokushinkai competition again imposes rigid restrictions on karate-do technique, and is therefore just as much a 'sport' as are WUKO competitions. (The problem is, of course, that there will always be the need for rules in competition, unless we are prepared to accept free-for-all, anything-goes matches; and these, by their very nature, would also be against the ultimate aim of karate-do, which is 'to subdue the enemy without fighting'.) Before being allowed to take part in 'knock-down' contests, competitors have to break a determined number of wooden boards with karate techniques.

To determine the winner in the case of a draw, Kyokushinkai rules hold that the contestant who is more than 3 to 5 kilos the lighter shall be adjudged the winner. Should the weights be more or less equal, the match is awarded to the contestant who has broken the most boards. These two rules may be felt to be of little value in assessing fighting skill; for the ability of one contestant to break more boards than the other has manifestly done him no good in combat! Likewise, the fact that one karate-ka weighs more or less than his opponent has had no effect on the outcome of the match. On the other hand, one must applaud the Kyokushinkai's concern to keep ***kumite*** and ***shiai*** as close to ***budo*** as a sport form could possibly be.

Another method of judging a contest is to allow the match to run more or less uninterrupted for its designated time, each scoring technique being scored on machines carried by the

Jumping side kick: Kanazawa *sensei* (8th *dan*) executing *yoko tobi-geri*.

judges. This 'clicker' system, or a very similar method, from the spectator's point of view certainly leads to more exciting exchanges of a much greater variety of techniques. Conversely, the system moves even further from the 'one chance, moment of truth', which lies at the heart of karate-do.

CONTACT KARATE

To many concerned with the values of traditional or authentic karate-do, particularly in Great Britain, contact karate is distinct from sport karate, and should more properly be termed 'kick boxing'. It is considered to have many faults, and the piercing attacking techniques of true karate are nullified by boxing gloves and foot protectors; it appeals to a technically unsophisticated public little concerned with technique and control.
But it does have some commercial potential in Great Britain, and has long been 'big business' in America, where these commercial pressures have created the momentum for progress (see Karate in America).

ATTITUDES TO SHIAI

Anyone entering a match naturally should do so with the correct frame of mind. This is basically a determination to win – but not at all costs. The true object of competition is not the gratification of the ego; it properly allows the karate-ka to test the efficiency of his techniques and to practise ***zanshin*** in strictly regulated encounters that are not pre-arranged. Competition karate should never be regarded as a combat situation, and succes in competition is just that, no more.

Fast-moving competition – the fighter on the left successfully blocks the kick and prepares to counter with a reverse punch.

In my experience in competition fighting – as competitor, judge and referee – I have witnessed all manner of disgraceful conduct. Some contestants behave arrogantly, show little regard for courtesy and demonstrate no respect for referees or decisions. Many exhibit to the world that they have never considered anything but the physical aspect of karate; so determined are they to win that control is swiftly discarded; and should they be scored on, their temper is as quickly lost. One should ***never*** put one's opponent in danger; and to keep control of your temper and yet lose the match to what you believe to be a bad decision is a major victory for YOU! He who believes there will ever be a perfect system of judging the result of a karate match is not a realist.

If you win in ***shiai,*** you are very good at competition karate; but never forget that there are many other spokes to the karate-do wheel, and that there will come a time when you are too old for ***shiai.*** If you place too much emphasis on winning matches in your youth, you may find that your ego has been fed to the extent that it cannot face the future without regrets. If you manage to be a winner in ***shiai*** and still be aware of the transient nature of such success, then you have a true understanding of karate-do.

Another point: given the nature of the rules of ***shiai,*** a 'bad' competition result is not necessarily what it would have been if the encounter had taken place without rules. In Asano ***sensei's*** words: 'In ***shiai*** if you hit me and I stand up, then probably you will win. If, on the other hand, I fall down, then I win! How is this karate?' In other words, apart from the artificial nature of sport karate, there is the problem of one's opponent 'taking a dive'. This type of 'sportsmanship' can only be strongly condemned

NB: Remember at all times, the referee ***must*** be obeyed instantly to avoid danger.

THE KATA COMPETITION

Individual kata

An individual competition usually begins with the names of all the competitors being pooled, and drawn in pairs. The two karate-ka are then given a ***kata*** to perform simultaneously, drawn at random from an agreed and defined list.

The two contestants begin the ***kata*** in a marked-off, flat and unobstructed area similar to the ***kumite shiai-jo*** (contest area), facing the chief judge or referee. The area is surrounded by a number of judges with red-and-white flags, whose job it is to indicate, by raising the relevant flag, which of the contestants has, in their opinion, best performed the ***kata.*** The chief judge or referee then announces the winner, who goes on to compete in further rounds.

When the number of contestants has been whittled down to a predetermined number (usually eight or ten), a different method is utilized, in which each karate-ka is allowed to perform his favourite ***kata.*** The number of judges for this type of event is generally increased to seven, each of whom, instead of using flags to indicate the winner, has a box of cards numbered 0.0 to 10.0 (whole numbers and tenths) from which he selects an appropriate score. The competitor's top score and bottom score are generally deleted; the remainder are added together to form his final score. The winner is the karate-ka who scores the highest points, and places are awarded in like manner.

The fourth World Karate-do Championship, held in Tokyo in December 1977, included for the first time a ***kata*** competition in addition to the ***kumite*** contest, in response to worldwide requests and because, as Mr Eiichi Eriguchi, general secretary of WUKO and chairman of FAJKO, stated in the UK ***Combat*** magazine: '***Kata*** is of great importance in the tradition of karate, the survival of which it has helped to make possible. The increase in the popularity of ***kumite*** matches, however, has often led to ***kata*** being neglected. This trend is unacceptable to most serious karate students'.

TEAM KATA

A ***kata*** team consists of three karate-ka, who perform a ***kata*** in unison.

Because of the number of contestants involved, there are no flag eliminations in team ***kata;*** instead, the points system is used to decide which teams go through to the finals. In the finals, the teams perform their favourite ***kata,*** and again marks are awarded out of ten by the judges. As in the individual scoring, highest score and lowest score are discarded, the remainder being added together to form the final mark. The team with the highest final score are adjudged the winners.

CRITERIA FOR JUDGING KATA CONTESTS

The judging of a team event resembles that of an individual ***kata*** match, except that each member has to move in complete unison with his or her partners; failure to do so will naturally result in a lower score.

The overall execution of a ***kata*** is judged basically by its salient features, which can be categorized as:

(1) concentration *(zanshin).*

(2) correct form (correct application of techniques in correct order).

(3) speed and power (appropriate to the nature of the techniques).

(4) breath control.

(5) correct direction of movements.

(6) general attitude and manners.

It is generally unwise for the karate-ka to enter more than three, possibly four, competitions a year, for the serious preparation necessary can interfere with his regular important training.

Having decided on the competition to enter, he must familiarize himself with the rules (which may vary, depending on the organization promoting the event).

It is a good idea to design a plan of approach to training for the weeks leading up to the event. This programme should entail mental and psychological training as well as physical.

PHYSICAL PREPARATION

Since competitions last sometimes as long as 12 hours or more, and entail an indeterminate number of matches, often with long periods of inactivity between them, a prerequisite for the successful competitor is a high degree of stamina, both muscular and circulo-respiratory. This becomes even more vital if the karate-ka is involved in a number of drawn matches with their consequent extensions. At this point, the contestant who is still capable of delivering rapid, well-controlled and accurate techniques has a marked advantage over his weary opponent. Knowing oneself to be still strong has an extremely beneficial psychological effect, too. An appreciable amount of preparation time, therefore, should be set apart for stamina training.

An excellent method of improving stamina is to increase the frequency of running a set distance within a set time. If you dislike long-distance running, simply measure out a course of, say, two miles and run round it comfortably, making note of the time it takes you. Then set yourself a programme of regular runs over this distance, each time attempting to better the time of your previous run. This is superb all round conditioning training. If you can, ensure that the last lap of the course is uphill. If this is not possible, make sure that – no matter how tired you feel – you always sprint the final 500 yard stretch. This practice reinforces the knowledge that, despite your body's protestations, your spirit can always 'pull something out of the bag'.

Running (or jogging) should ideally form a regular part of karate training; but if it doesn't, do begin at least six weeks before a competition, and start slowly and sensibly. (With proper caution, this programme is emphatically recommended, even to karate-ka who suffer breathing disabilities. The results of a regular programme are staggering!)

A drawback of jogging and running is that one develops a regular rhythmical breathing pattern over a relatively long period of time, whereas a match involves rapid interchange of fast and slow movements, often with a broken rhythm, over a relatively short period of time. To combat this problem, I devised a system of training that would afford practice in karate technique and yet still develop physical and circulo-respiratory endurance. The exercises themselves are not new, being either common to most sports (such as sit-ups) or specific karate techniques themselves. What I did, however, was to establish a karate circuit-training programme.

Briefly (fuller details are given in Chapter 26), this sets out a number of exercises, whose object is for the karate-ka to see how many he can perform in two minutes. Then follows a 90-second rest period, during which the score is entered on his score-card, to give him each time a target to beat. An important feature of this circuit is that the karate-ka competes with himself, which also builds up determination and spirit. The programme itself is extremely exhausting, and in the weeks before a competition should only be used once or twice a week at the most. One of its advantages over ordinary running and regular circuits is that local muscular endurance, as well as overall circulo-respiratory capacity, is enhanced, which ensures more efficient circulation of blood through the muscles, enabling them to store a greater amount of energy ready for release upon demand.

As for the techniques themselves, the karate-ka should concentrate on repeatedly practising those that work most effectively for him; usually, the simpler these are the better. In WUKO competitions, the most successful techniques in general are: reverse punch ***(gyaku-zuki)***, lunge punch ***(oi-zuki)***, and front kick ***(mae-geri)***. Occasionally, combinations are successful, but these too tend to be relatively direct, such as leg-sweep ***(ashi-barai)*** followed by lunge-punch. An opponent can sometimes be surprised by an attack or counter with an unexpected technique such as roundhouse kick ***(mawashi-geri)*** or jumping hammer fist strike ***(tobi-tetsui-uchi)***, but these are more open to counter-attack, and are best attempted only when the opponent is at a distinct disadvantage (unbalanced, or in rapid retreat, etc.).

But, no matter what the technique or combination of techniques, practise it time and again until it becomes instinctive. Needless to say, knowing there are certain specific techniques likely to be employed against you, it is important to practise appropriate blocking and countering movements just as seriously and wholeheartedly as the offensive techniques.

METHODS OF TRAINING WITH A PARTNER

(i) Your partner should move freely around the ***dojo*** or contest area, using only light blocking techniques, while you attack with your best techniques from a variety of positions, concentrating on developing precision and speed enough to pierce your partner's block. All the blocks must be extremely light, and self-discipline maintained to ensure that the karate-ka co-operate and the practice does not degenerate into free-style. To this end, the receiver uses only blocks; no counter-attacks.

Then the roles are reversed; your partner becomes the attacker, you the defender.

(ii) The next stage is basically the same, except that the defender now introduces counter-attacks to the blocking techniques.

When practising these two stages, it is a good idea to alternate timing training with stamina training. In other words, first try moving slowly and smoothly into a good attacking distance, and then attack as fast as humanly possible. The next time, still using only the limited techniques which suit you best, try to keep up a continual attack throughout the time period.

If you become well known in competition circles for a specific technique, it is a good idea at this stage to begin work on 'grooving' a surprise technique into your armoury. Tyrone Whyte, for example, a member of the British team, at one time gained a reputation for being a counter-puncher, particularly with reverse punch ***(gyaku-zuki).*** Knowing this, his opponents began to take steps

Karate self-defence demonstration: escape from hair grab and counter, by the author and wife Evi.

to ensure that he found few openings for this technique. In answer to this, Tyrone practised hard to develop other techniques, making more use of kicks and sweeps, until he had enlarged his repertoire, and he is now one of the foremost competition karate-ka.

(iii) In this practice it must be well understood that it is vital to maintain a high degree of control, as there is a degree of danger present.

The karate-ka face each other, exactly as if in competition. One is designated attacker; the other, defender, who is allowed to counter-attack as hard and as fast as possible.

On the word of 'begin' ***(hajime)***, when the contestants move into attacking range, the attacker must immediately attack forcefully with a fast, focused technique – but one technique only. The defender can (a) block and counter, if the attacking technique is unsuccessful, or (b) defend by attacking (that is, if the attacker moves into range but is too slow in attacking, the defender takes the initiative and launches his own attack).

This is excellent contest training, and develops tremendous spirit and sense of timing and distance.

By reversing the roles in the above training methods you gain expertise in both attacking and defending.

MENTAL PREPARATION

Practically every contestant at a championship suffers to some extent from 'nerves' or 'tension'. Knowing this, and being aware of the likely effects of this condition, can help the karate-ka to come to terms with the effects and perhaps alleviate them.

Basically, the physical sensations are caused by nervous anticipation. Mental excitement is transferred into muscular tension, which affects people in different ways. The anticipation, however, usually turns out to be worse than the event itself, and generally the degree of tension diminishes once the competition is under way.

Before the day of the competition, nervous stress can show itself in various ways. Some top-class karate-ka find that they are prone to heartburn or digestive disorders; if this is the case, experience will naturally dictate the sort of food to be eaten during the run-up period. Others find it practically impossible to sleep on the night before a contest.

It is important to realize that, since most competitors suffer these or similar problems, learning to accept them and taking steps to overcome them is far more sensible than worrying about them. Do not be fooled by the confident tones and cheerful demeanour of many karate-ka; inside, they are probably just as nervous as you. Competitors are rarely nervous about the possibility of losing in itself; their concern stems rather from the desire not to let ***sensei*** or club down. And the more successful a fighter becomes, the more pressure he is under from the audience's expectations of his performance.

Once the first fight is won, however, the confidence gained usually dispels most of the tension; though long waits between bouts can build it up again. To counteract this, some people become quiet and introspective, others become more extrovert and 'bouncy'. Each karate-ka should try to find what works best for him; though it does seem that muscular recovery from fatigue is speeded up if the athlete keeps the muscles moving lightly.

In preparing himself psychologically for the contest, the karate-ka should cultivate a positive, determined attitude. This is necessary because the body's response – as well as speeding up the heart-rate, releasing adrenalin into the bloodstream, and causing the mouth to become dry and the palms to moisten – can also inculcate a negative attitude, which forms a very real barrier to success.

THE 'FIGHT-OR-FLIGHT' RESPONSE

First defined by Walter Cannon, a physiologist at Harvard University in the 1920's, this response is a basic pattern of reactions to stress situations, which will vary in intensity according to the strength of the challenge.

Primitive man, confronted with a dangerous situation, had either to stay and face it or to run for safety. That basic response to threat, although subject to evolutionary changes and modifications, is still present in modern man, and it has a definable sequence of effects on the human body.

The 'fight-or-flight' response is centred in the hypothalamus, a small nerve-cell cluster in the centre of the brain, which controls the autonomic nervous system (regulator of the body's involuntary functions) and sets the pituitary gland into operation to order the release of hormones into the bloodstream.

The effects of these activities are various. Many of the body's muscles become tense; breathing becomes quicker and deeper, blood vessels smaller; heart-rate speeds up. This closes off the surface blood vessels and raises the blood pressure. The autonomic nerves command the spleen to release more red corpuscles, which help the blood to clot more quickly and carry the oxygen required for the production of energy; they also ensure that the bone marrow produces more white corpuscles, which counteract infection; and cause the adrenal glands to release the hormones associated with fear and rage.

All these reponses serve to prepare the body for rapid action in defence of a physical threat:

The eyesight becomes more acute, owing to dilation of the pupils.

Because the breathing rate is increased, more oxygen is introduced into the body (this is further facilitated by the mucous membranes in the nose and throat becoming smaller).

The increased heart-rate ensures an extra supply of blood-borne fuel and oxygen to the brain and muscles, which provides a boost of extra energy.

Because the surface blood vessels constrict, less blood is lost if the skin is cut, and the increased number of red corpuscles ensures that bleeding stops more quickly. At the same time, proliferation of white cells acts as a greater preventative to infection.

The body temporarily halts such operations as digestion and salivation, which are not vital to combat the immediate threat. The muscles of bowels and bladder also relax, possibly to ensure that the body jettisons as much as possible, to allow fractionally faster movement.

Clearly then, the feelings of nervous anticipation experienced by practically every competitor in ***shiai*** owe much to well-understood physical processes designed to ensure he is in top-class condition for an encounter. Realizing this should allay any apprehensions that 'nerves' are a sign of weakness. On the contrary, they indicate that everything is functioning just as it should be.

The more experience one gains, the better one is able to accept and accomodate the 'butterflies in the stomach'; and in ***shiai,*** particularly in the early rounds, the karate-ka who can relax and demonstrate confidence and a strong, positive, fighting spirit is at a distinct advantage over a more tense, less flexible opponent. It is much more difficult to fight a person who shows no emotion.

In this connection, it is a very good idea to practise keeping a 'stone face'. Make a conscious attempt to keep your face expressionless at all times, so as not to betray your emotions or intentions. Many fighters have little mannerisms - a move of the head, a narrowing of the eyes, a tightening of the throat muscles - that tend to give slight advance warning of an attack. It is usual to take a breath before executing a technique; but doing this by allowing the chest and shoulders to rise is yet another indication of the state of readiness or unreadiness for attack. In circumstances where split seconds can mean the difference between success and failure, it is only sensible to eliminate facial or bodily movements that might give warning.

Many karate-ka, when bringing their preparatory training to an end, stop their intensive training perhaps a week before the competition, and maintain peak condition by running and by light stretching calisthenics. It is advisable to try and get as much physical rest and mental diversion as possible, so that on the day you will be uninjured and in first-class health.

TRAINING FOR KATA COMPETITION

There is really only one way of training for a ***kata*** competition, and that is to practise the prescribed ***kata*** and the favourite ***kata*** again and again, until they have become instinctive. One point worth bearing in mind, however, is that you will be expected to perform the ***kata*** in a place unfamiliar to you, which can sometimes be unnerving. You will also be the centre of attention for hundreds of pairs of eyes.

For the latter problem there is little remedy, beyond a reminder that true ***kata*** practice inculcates a calm, detached concentration, upon which awareness of an audience may impinge but should not disturb. The more practice you get, the less this aspect will bother you.

To guard against the loss of orientation unfamiliar surroundings sometimes cause, it is a good idea to vary the direction in which you practise ***kata*** in your own ***dojo***, so as not to become too accustomed to beginning and ending facing the same direction or object. You might also like to practise the ***kata*** with your eyes closed - having first taken sensible precautions, of course. This develops an acute sense of spatial awareness, sense of balance, and sense of direction as dictated by the ***kata*** rather than by such external considerations as size and layout of ***dojo.***

PSYCHOLOGICAL

Throughout the history of the martial arts, exponents have been told always to watch the opponent's eyes. It is said that the pupils dilate immediately before an attack. Even if this be true, however, it is unrealistic to concentrate attention wholly on this point. One should ***look*** at the eyes rather than at the body; but one must try to ***see*** the whole, not the part. If you look at the body you may be distracted by feints, which leave you unprepared for the real danger. Thus, many top competition fighters cultivate a stare that seems to look right through their opponent.

Karate-ka who find it difficult to look at their opponent's eyes in competition (because they have not practised it continually in ***yakusoku*** and ***ju-kumite***) can be placed at a considerable psychological disadvantage. Faced with an opponent who looks directly into his eyes and forces him to look away (thereby demonstrating a degree of superiority), such a karate-ka can be completely unnerved.

It is a good idea to try to establish psychological domination. In addition to mastering the opponent's gaze, remember never, under any circumstances (except as a tactic to make him commit an unwise move), allow him to feel you are at all intimidated by him. If he attacks with a strong ***kiai,*** counter with an even stronger one. Remember, the battle is as much mental as physical.

PHYSICAL

There are two broad categories of fighter: those who prefer to attack whenever possible, and those who prefer to await an attack and then counter. Ideally, of course, one should be equally proficient at both attacking and counter-attacking; whichever group you happen to be in, it is imperative that you practise techniques from the other group for use should the opportunity arise. A famous example of the success of such a stratagem occurred in the 1963 JKA All-Japan Championship and concerned two renowned instructors, H Shirai and Keinosuke Enoeda 8th ***dan.***

The year before, these two had also met in the final. In that 1962 final, because Enoeda was known to be a strong attacking fighter, Shirai (who basically is a very fast counter-attacker) had only to await the

R Harrison (2nd ***dan***) winner of the SKI Open Championship in 1976, attacking with roundhouse kick (***mawashi geri***).

moment – as Enoeda began the expected attack, he met him with a tremendously fast front kick to win the match.

But Enoeda was determined not to be caught in the same way again. In the 1963 final, when the two met once again, he changed his tactics completely; although he feinted several attacks, he never followed them through. Consequently, Shirai was forced to take the offensive – and immediately found Enoeda's front kick flash in for a full point score.

Since the match was judged by the three-point system, Shirai was forced to continue to attack if he wanted to be in with a chance. Enoeda, on the other hand, refused to change his tactics and remained on the defensive – and once again, as Shirai leapt in, Enoeda countered with a powerful reverse punch. Enoeda had gained his revenge.

If you are basically an attacker, remember that whenever you do attack you must do it with as much speed and controlled power as possible. A half-hearted attack will give an immediate psychological and physical advantage to the opponent. Naturally, your technique will not score, and he will be confirmed in his assessment of the strength and efficiency of his blocking and countering. There is an old ***samurai*** saying: 'If you must fail, then fail magnificently!'

In any match, distinct opportunities for attacking arise, and these must be made use of absolutely immediately. Of course, this is easier said than done: but the first thing to make sure of is that you maintain a good attacking distance (***ma-ai***), close enough to be able to attack effectively but not so close that you allow the opponent to snatch the initiative and attack first.

In general, you should try to attack:

(i) just at the instant your opponent begins to attack.

(ii) just at the moment he moves.

(iii) immediately he has completed an unsuccessful attack, before he can regain his mental and physical composure.

(iv) just as he begins to breathe in after exhaling.

(v) immediately you sense a weakening of his spirit (e.g. after being strongly blocked).

E de Roek scoring on P Videan to win the SKI Open Championship, 1975 – front kick to the stomach – ***chudan mae-geri***.

Against a strong karate-ka with a good defence, you will almost certainly need to employ combination techniques, and these are more successful against a moving opponent than against a static, well-balanced one. Most successful are combinations involving foot-sweeps and follow-up punching techniques, or initial attacks which are meant to cause the opponent to block and thus leave an opening for the main attack. This latter sometimes fails simply because the first technique is not strong enough to be considered a major threat, therefore the opponent is not unbalanced or forced to commit himself to the desired block.

For those who prefer countering to attacking, the best opportunities usually occur when

(i) immediately your opponent begins to attack, you beat him to it.

(ii) waiting for him to attack; when he does, at the last moment you sidestep and counter.

(iii) you block his attack strongly and counter immediately before he regains mental and physical equilibrium.

In many cases, the distinction between attacking and countering is a very fine one; often, as the Japanese phrase ***go no sen o toru*** has it, 'defence equals offence'. A useful stratagem for the counter-attack is deliberately to let your opponent see an opening that will tempt him into launching an attack for which you are ready and which leads him into position open for your counter.

Essentially, this is the strategy employed in the JKA All-Japan Championship 1957 by the karate master whom many consider one of the world's greatest exponents, Hirokazu Kanazawa, 8th ***dan,*** chief instructor to the SKI.

In the intensive training just before the championship Kanazawa broke a bone in his hand and considered withdrawing. In the end, he entered one match, which he promptly won; and at the end of the day he stepped forward onto the rostrum to be acclaimed All-Japan Champion!

Knowing he could not make full use of his injured hand, Kanazawa used his left hand to block with, and to feint attacking techniques; and deliberately enticed his opponents into actions that caused gaps in their defences. He then made use of these split-second chances to drive home the right hand, to score the winning point.

It is of course necessary to practise incessantly to gain the speed required to capitalize on manufactured openings; and it is sensible not to give an opponent an opening for his favourite technique, if he really is a master of it. He might still get it in. It is often better to offer him opportunities for punching techniques if he is known to be a kicker, or openings for kicking techniques if he is a puncher, to tempt him to commit himself to attack with a technique which is not as polished as his favourite.

As the martial-arts proverb has it:

If you know neither your enemy nor yourself, you stand in great peril in every battle.

If you know yourself but not your enemy, your chances of success or failure are equal.

When you know yourself and your enemy, you will never be in danger.

In an unofficial survey conducted by Al Weiss and Alan Vasquez of ***Official Karate*** magazine in America, it was noted that more than 75% of all matches won at tournaments on the East Coast of the United States were won with points scored with basic, straight-forward techniques learned early in training. The reverse punch is by far the major point-winner, followed by the straight punch, backfist, side kick and roundhouse kick. The spinning kicks, most often used by Korean stylists, are exciting to watch, but they are rarely effective in US competition. It is obvious then that emphasis in training on the basics that are the foundation of karate can help, if not ensure, success in competition.

It is a good idea to investigate the strengths and weaknesses of your forth-coming opponents. Try to analyse their style and overall pattern of fighting; watch particularly for the favourite technique and watch out for the preliminary 'setting-up' manoeuvres. In the hustle and bustle of a large open event, this is not so easy in the early rounds, but is is often possible when the number of fighters still competing diminishes. In international matches, the team coach and his assistants become invaluable in this respect, for they are free to study the opposition and formulate tactics and advice to pass on to their own team members.

It is also important in big events that the coach is on hand during the course of a match, to relay last-minute advice to the fighter and to tell him how much time he has, either to score or to force a draw, or even to maintain the appearance of aggression while protecting a winning margin.

Naturally, a good coach will know his team individually; the character, foibles, style, strengths and weaknesses of each. This is vital knowledge for advice given during the course of the match can be only a reminder. There is no point in yelling, 'Catch him with front-roundhouse as he attacks', to a fighter who does not use that particular technique well. At best, this sort of advice distracts his attention, and instils a sense of inferiority if the karate-ka knows full well he cannot do what his coach is demanding. At worst, he will try to carry out the advice and probably lose at once to the inevitable counter.

Unless the advice is in code (which need not be at all difficult), it can also work against the desired effect by forewarning the opponent that an opening in his defence has been noticed; for he will, of course, straight away rectify this.

This chapter on strategy and tactics cannot be closed without reference to the Zen mind approach to combat. In Chapter 4, the concept of a 'mind like water' (***mizu no kokoro***) or, as it is otherwise termed, 'mind like the moon' (***zuki no korkoro***), was considered as an essential requisite in combat.

I have for a number of years now been a member of an SKI 'A' team that has figured in the finals of numerous events, including the last three SKI All-Style open championship. My performance in previous years had been reasonable; I had won more matches than I had lost. Conversely, I had never really been comfortable in competition - always worried about letting my team down. I was also very conscious of the shouts from the crowd, and of the great tension, particularly in the finals. In the year before the 1977 championship, I had found myself concentrating more and more upon the Zen aspects of karate-do, but had never achieved much success.

On the day of the 1977 event, for one reason or another, the team did not think we would do as well as in previous years, so we all entered every round more or less as an end in itself. Perhaps that attitude is significant - for I found that I was relaxed and calm. Suddenly, all of my opponents seemed to be moving in slow-motion. I was very much aware of the crowds and of the atmosphere; but all was relegated to the periphery of my mind. Aware intuitively of my opponent's intentions, I was hardly aware of having scored at all - until the referee shouted, and the flags went up. This calm but intense heightening of perception continued throughout the whole day, and in fact this turned out to be my most successful championship - I lost not a single match.

Having once experienced ***satori,*** I have at least a clear objective in front of me in training; and perhaps my experience will draw others to consider the philosophical teachings as well as the physical instructions of the ***budo*** masters.

The concept stresses that you should visualize your opponent as a part of yourself, so that when he moves you react smoothly and instantaneously with him. In order to achieve this degree of perception, it is important that you have no concern for the outcome of the match; otherwise, tension may create slight hesitation in executing techniques, which could cost you dearly. It is vital also not to fix your attention on any specific aspect of your opponent or his movements, or you may well find yourself surprised from an unexpected direction. Rather concentrate calmly upon the wholeness of the situation, as if you really are an uninvolved, detached observer.

Frankly, few karate-ka ever achieve this state, mainly because most are not taught of its existence, let alone of its desirability; and therefore, to many people in karate, it may sound a little 'hard to swallow'. For my part, I know it exists. I know, too, if only in the smallest degree, just what a marvellous sensation it is. And if I have achieved it, if only on one occasion, then so can you.

It would be dishonest of me to say that I now always fight with this attitude, because I do not; but, having once experienced it, I know full well that I must keep striving until it becomes second nature to me.

CHAPTER 24. HEALTH AND DIET

Good health is not always essential to the acquisition of skills in sport; nor is physical fitness the answer to all life's problems. But being physically fit does enable one better to cope with the stresses of daily life - and to protect oneself against degenerative disease.

The disturbing and indisputable fact is that, for men in the prime of life, cardiovascular disease (coronary thrombosis, high blood pressure, strokes, etc.) is the biggest single cause of death. Now, evidence strongly suggests that if you undertake regular physical exercise, involving a programme for improving circulo-respiratory capacity, you will effectively reduce your chances of suffering coronary heart disease. Evidence further suggests that if you do suffer a heart attack, it is likely to occur later, is less likely to be fatal, and your chance of making a complete recovery is much better - if you have taken regular exercise.

Viewed in this light, regular karate training, combined with supplementary training (jogging, swimming, etc), would seem to be an effective method of adding positively to the value of life, particularly of the later years.

As we grow older, we lose the flexibility of youth. Regular exercise, in helping to maintain muscular endurance, strength and joint flexibility, will ensure that impairment of physical abilities is largely reduced and its effects alleviated. Science and the medical profession are generally agreed that the changes brought about by ageing owe much to – and certainly are exacerbated by – a lack of sufficient physical activity. This, surely, is a cogent reason for beginning early a regime of controlled training like that of karate, which promotes flexibility in all the major joints.

There is another practical benefit to be gained from a thorough training in karate-do. The 100% effort, both physical and mental, which it demands ensures that the student leaves his worries – whatever their nature – behind when he enters the ***dojo.*** His problems remain, of course, and have to be faced; but training sessions at the very least afford him relief from continual worry. And as he advances, the student comes to view life's problems in a truer perspective. By continued practice in meeting and solving the physical and mental crises that arise during training, he finds himself more able to deal confidently with his external problems. In short, he begins to carry his karate-do training out of the confines of the ***dojo*** and into his daily life.

Many people hesitate to join a karate club because they suffer from some physical disability. In most instances, however, the practice of karate techniques, which involve the whole body (including, of course, the major joints and muscles), can be of help to anyone as long as a sensible approach is maintained; though, naturally, any aspiring karate student who does suffer a disability should first consult his or her doctor to gain medical approval.

If the desire is there, almost anyone can improve his or her fitness, regardless of handicap. One problem that can arise with disabled students, however, is that they may feel compelled to compare their own performance with that of karate-ka who do not share their handicap. But such students should realize that this is not a problem exclusive to them. Many students suffer the same compulsion. Indeed, if such comparison is made in the right frame of mind – with a view to setting oneself standards – all well and good. In the main, however, it is better not to do so.

The student should have only one desire in his heart: to do as well as he humanly can. Only with this true aim can he consider himself, regardless of grade or capability, the equal of any karate-ka.

SMOKING AND KARATE-DO

Cigarette-smoking is an addiction, a drug dependency; and as such has no place in ***budo.*** The ***budo-ka*** should be self-reliant and not dependent upon external aids to function adequately in times of stress. To continue to smoke, in the face of the overwhelming medical evidence for tobacco's harmful effects, is positively foolish.

DIET

The karate-ka, through his daily training, becomes more aware of his body's functions, capabilities and limitations. It is true that, at some time during the years of training, each individual, by a process of trial and error, arrives at the diet that best suits him or her; but the following section, which explains briefly the basic facts of nutrition, should lead the karate-ka to further understand the bodily processes and perhaps even to consider experiments in dietary combinations.

THE CALORIE

The energy required by the human body to carry out its functions, internal (digestion, heart action, etc.) and external (physical movements), is measured in calories (one calorie being the quantity of heat required to raise by 1°C the temperature of one gram of water).

All food – protein, fat and carbohydrate – contains a given number of usable calories:

1 gram (g) of protein gives 4 calories.

1 g of fat gives 9 calories.

1 g of carbohydrate gives 4 calories.

From this table, it would appear that fats are the best energy producers. This is misleading, however; for, although they provide a higher number of usable calories than protein or carbohydrate, they are less economical since they use up greater quantities of oxygen in releasing the energy. Fats, therefore, though essential as a long-term energy source, are mainly a secondary source of energy.

From the athletes point of view, carbohydrate provides the quickest and most efficient source of energy; it supplies glucose, which is stored in the liver, where it remains ready to enter the bloodstream immediately the demand for increased energy is made. In the form of sugar, carbohydrate passes via the liver into the circulation, and thence into the tissues and the muscles, providing energy and heat.

Under normal circumstances, protein provides very little energy. Its main function is to create and maintain the body tissues, however, which is naturally a very important part of a healthy diet.

Generally speaking, a normal diet – one that provides all the necessary fats, proteins,

A fine example of ***kiba-dachi*** (straddle-leg) stance in ***tekki nidan kata.***

carbohydrates, vitamins, minerals and water – is quite adequate for the long-term karate training schedule. Research has shown, however, that, for basic fitness and optimum body weight, it is far better to be a 'nibbler' than a 'scoffer'. There is strong evidence to suggest that people who consume their calorie intake in one or two big meals a day put on more fat than those who eat more frequent but smaller meals.

Mild exercise is not harmful to digestion, though as a rule karate training or competition (which involves emotional stress) should not be undertaken until at least three hours have elapsed since eating. Digestion is a relatively slow process, so eating immediately before training or competition would be of little direct benefit in terms of energy gain; most of the energy used will already be stored in the body in one form or another. Remember, too, that the process of digestion, particularly of protein-rich foods like meat, is itself energy-consuming, and therefore diverts some of the energy away from the muscles.

It has been estimated that one fifth of the body's basic utilization of energy takes place in the brain. Now the brain cannot store energy itself; it derives its 'food' from the sugar in the bloodstream. If the brain is hyperactive, displaying signs of stress and worry, it consumes a larger amount of energy, thus depleting the reserves available for use by the muscles: yet another reason for seeking the calm 'mind like water' of the advanced ***budo-ka.***

At times of high energy requirement, it is best to have liquid or semi-solid foods, rich in carbohydrates. Honey is a very rich and easily digestible source of energy; and some specially enriched glucose-like drinks are now available.

The well-trained, fit karate-ka with optimum body weight and no physical impairment might like to experiment (with caution) with the following regime, which has been shown to improve performance in events that demand muscular endurance.

First, in the seven to ten days preceding the event, severely restrict the intake of carbohydrates; then, two to three days before the event, train very hard in order to exhaust the muscles and burn up the remaining carbohydrate-derived energy. The time remaining should be spent comparatively quietly while following a high carbohydrate diet. It must be emphasized, however, that this is only for fit people, and only for the 'special event'. It is ***not*** suitable as a long-term diet.

Vitamins, minerals and water are also needed to meet the body's requirements. As a rule, though, it is unlikely that anyone following an average Western diet will be deficient in any of these. Nevertheless, it is perhaps worth noting that to consume excessive quantities of certain vitamins (A and D, for example) can be harmful.

KARATE AND WEIGHT CONTROL

Regular exercise contributes directly towards weight maintenance or reduction in the following ways:

(a) If strenuous, it will lower the percentage of body fat; thus, of two people of similar stature who weigh the same, the one who takes regular exercise will tend to have more lean muscle.

(b) It regulates (to a degree varying with the individual that part of the brain – the appestat – which controls the body's desire for food.

(c) Perhaps most importantly, vigorous exercise dramatically increases calorie expenditure, not only during the exercise but for several hours after it has finished.

Assuming that a base hourly calorie expenditure of 67 for men and 56 for women (average height and build) is needed to keep the body and its organs functioning, it has been estimated that, even sleeping all day, a man would burn up about 1,600 calories, while the average woman would consume approximately 1,300. Even allowing for considerable variation between individuals, it is possible to chart the approximate increased calorie expenditure on exertion.

ACTIVITY	PERCENTAGE INCREASE OVER RESTING RATE
Slow walk 2.7 mph	+ 137%
Swim 20-25 yds/min	+ 270%
Cycle, level ground	+ 310%
Walk 4.5 mph	+ 400%
Swim 40-45 yds/min	+ 625%
Brisk walk, 5-8 mph	+ 860%
Jogging, 8 mph	+1170%
Walking up stairs	+1360%
Sprinting	+1870%

RESTING RATE

0 1 2 3 4 5

Calories per pound of body weight for thirty minutes

Having discussed what goes into the body, we must also mention waste products. The karate-ka would be well advised to make sure that his diet includes a certain amount of vegetable or cereal fibre (roughage). This can be found in bran, wholemeal bread, raw fruit and vegetables; and in some cooked vegetables, such as carrots, cabbages, potatoes, cauliflowers, etc., provided that they are not over-cooked.

Fibre has the effect of speeding up the passage of the food through the digestive system, which leads to regularity of bowel movements, which in turn helps to prevent the problems of constipation, diverticulitis (a disorder of the colon) and haemorrhoids. It seems also that inclusion of vegetable fibre in the diet helps to decrease the level of cholesterol in the blood, which may decrease the risk of coronary heart disease. The simplest way of ensuring consumption of sufficient roughage is to add one or two tablespoonsful of All-Bran or the like to your breakfast cereal. Regularity in the bodily functions is a sign of health, and thus should be sought by the karate-ka.

A final point: it is wise to empty the bladder, and the bowels if possible, before competition or strenuous prolonged exercise.

CHAPTER 25. TRAINING FOR FITNESS

The importance of improving the circulo-respiratory capacity has already been stressed (Chapter 22). This chapter explains why such improvement is important, and gives further information about the types of exercise that are most beneficial when combined with regular karate training in the ***dojo.***

The term 'circulo-respiratory capacity' (CRC) refers to the ability of heart and lungs to cope with the demands made by the mental and physical processes of the body. Also referred to as 'aerobic power', this capacity largely determines the ability of the body to maintain reasonably vigorous levels of physical activity for an extended period. In simple, terms, we call it 'stamina'. It is not, however, related to muscular endurance, the quality that determines the ability of localized muscle groups to function over an extended period.

In general terms, CRC is an important factor, probably the most important factor, in any activity that involves the large muscle-groups of the body. It is simple to determine which activities are largely dependent upon CRC; they are the ones that have to be stopped not because of muscle fatigue but because of shortness of breath and a pounding heart.

In the initial stages of karate training, the beginner will find that, owing largely to the unfamiliarity of the required movements and the need to perform them frequently to achieve mastery, muscular endurance is more of a limiting factor than lack of aerobic power. For the higher grades, however, there comes need for a vastly greater CRC. Now that the basic techniques are performed unconsciously (or at least with a markedly higher degree of efficiency), the requirement now is a greater ability to perform them in rapid succession, with no loss of speed, power or focus over extended periods.

Effective karate techniques depend very greatly upon the karate-ka's ability to deliver them with great speed and accuracy. The more relaxed the body in the initial stages, the faster the 'snap' of the technique, and the greater the power generated. The focus (***kime***) of the technique is dependent upon the forceful contraction of all the muscles of the body directly or indirectly concerned with delivery of the technique, for one split-second at the moment of completion. The relaxed state of body and mind, plus the breath control necessary to unite spirit, power and delivery, is simply not possible if the lungs are straining for air, the shoulders and chest heaving, and the mind distracted by the sheer physical effort required.

The advanced karate-ka will, of course, often reach this state in the course of training, with the aim of increasing stamina and endurance. There is no doubt, however, that techniques 'lose their edge' at this point, and understandably so. At this stage, the spirit is being trained. Nonetheless, the greater the CRC the longer the karate-ka will be able to deliver powerful, fast and accurate techniques, with full focus.

Exercise based upon aerobic principles is a cyclical process: as the CRC increases, so does the degree of endurance of the muscle-groups utilized in the aerobic exercises. If we take running: when we first start jogging (or walking, if medically unfit), we find it necessary to stop frequently for breath. Then the rest intervals become fewer, and eventually we can step up the rate until the jog becomes a run. During this progression, the leg muscles find they have to work harder as stamina increases; muscular endurance is built up, allowing the runs to be longer or faster, and so the process continues.

Isometric exercise – static exercise, such as pushing one hand against the other with maximum force – does not increase strength through the complete range of movement of the joint involved. This type of exercise can be dangerous to people with high blood pressure or a heart condition Isotonic exercise is that in which a muscle-group overcomes a resistance by moving it through the full range of joint action, such as doing armcurls with a bar-bell. In both cases, the strength involved is essentially specific to the muscle-groups involved in the exercise; for overall fitness, therefore, neither type of exercise is as beneficial as those exercises which improve CRC.

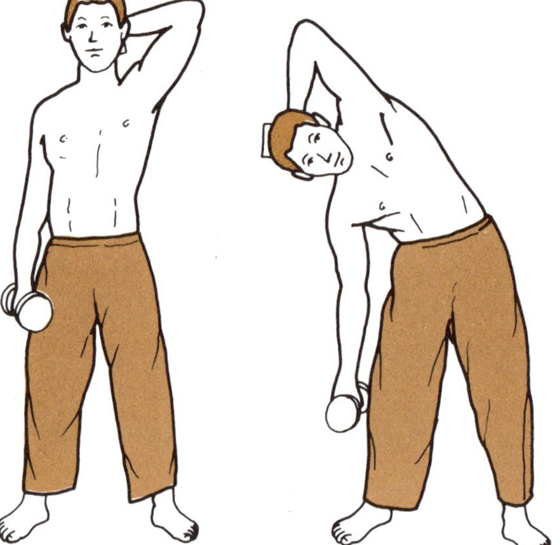

WEIGHT-TRAINING AND KARATE

Many Okinawan karate masters acknowledge that, for one reason or another, it will occasionally be impossible for the karate-ka to utilize his techniques with maximum efficiency; and that, in some circumstances, it is necessary for him to withstand a blow in order to deliver a counter. With these points in mind, they advise the desirability of developing extra power and muscular strength to facilitate the forceful delivery of effective blocks and counters whatever the limitations imposed upon the defender by a specific situation.

With the aim of producing this greater physical power, Okinawan karate has traditionally included the use of weight-training equipment in its programme. In the past this equipment was rudimentary, consisting only of readily available articles (weighted jars - ***kame*** - for example). In the last few years, however, modern weight-training equipment (such as barbells and dumb-bells) has been added to augment the traditional equipment.

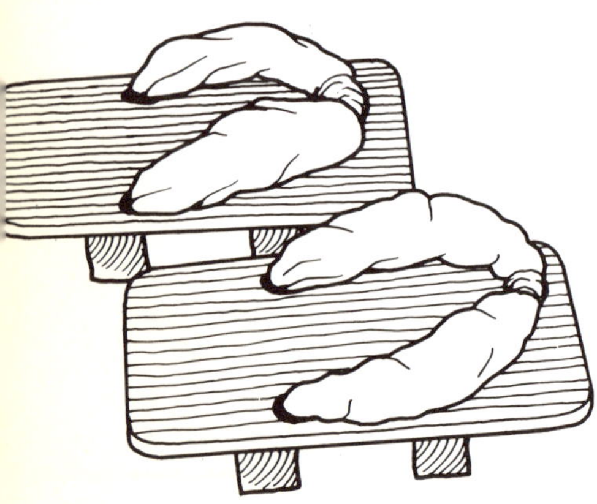

Japanese karate has, in the main, tended to relegate the use of weight-training equipment to a position of minor importance in its training methods, relying essentially on the repetition of techniques to build up power and improve endurance. Nevertheless, elementary weight training methods have always been a feature of more advanced karate training, regardless of style. Tatsuo Suzuki, Hanshi (8th ***dan*** Wado-**ryu**), for example, trains regularly with weights. He emphasizes that they should be light weights, which allow a high degree of repetition; and recommends the holding of light dumb-bells for trunk-stretching and punching exercises, and the wearing of iron boots (***geta***) for practising kicking techniques. He also constantly practises squat-jumping, sit-ups and press-ups as overall strengthening exercises, and stresses the importance of including running in the training schedule.

What are the benefits, then, that can accrue from weight training as an adjunct to karate, and which exercises are most beneficial? To comprehend fully the advantages of weight-training (and to dispel for ever the myth that it will make you slow and 'muscle-bound'!), it is necessary first to understand what muscles are, and how exercise affects them.

THE MUSCLES

Muscle is made up of small bundles of fibres wrapped in sheath-like tissue. The bundles themselves are wrapped in similar sheaths of tissue connected to tendons, which are in turn attached to the bones. When relaxed, muscle is quite soft and pliable; upon contraction, it becomes hard, tense and stretch-resistant. The nourishment it requires in order to function is carried by the bloodstream.

As the temperature of a muscle is raised, it becomes possible to make it contract more quickly. On the other hand, heated muscle is quickly fatigued. One of the benefits, therefore, of 'warming up' thoroughly before training or a contest (*shiai*) is that by heating the muscles and taking advantage of the increased contraction speed it is possible to speed up the performance of techniques. Research has indicated that a rise in muscle temperature/body heat of two degrees can speed up muscular action by up to 20%.

Such a rise, however, is gained only by drastic methods; the karate-ka should content himself with vigorous preparatory exercises, which effectively raise body temperature but are not so energetic that they induce fatigue.

Basically, muscles work in pairs, one contracting, the other extending. For example, when bending the arm to a right angle at the elbow joint, the 'prime movers' are the biceps, while the 'antagonists' are the triceps. (This example is an extreme simplification, of course, since many other muscle-groups are also called into play in order to hold the body in a position which allows the 'prime movers' and 'antagonists' to bring about the desired movement. Yet more groups come into action to aid the elimination of subsidiary muscle action, which may adversely affect the successful operation of the more important muscles.) Thus, it becomes important to exercise muscles through their full range of movements, so as to avoid uneven development.

With this in mind, the karate-ka should approach weight training with a set plan; a plan based upon the desire to strengthen basic karate technique, increase overall muscular strength and endurance, and, if possible, enlarge CRC.

Weight training is not to be confused with body-building (although it may well be that the combination of regular karate training and weight training will to some extent rid the body of surplus fat, and give better muscle definition). Cultivating the body for its own sake is simply a way of 'feeding the ego', which, as we noted in the section dealing with Zen and the philosophy of karate-do, can have only a detrimental effect on the karate-ka's progress along the 'way'.

All things considered, it would seem that the most effective plan for the karate-ka would be a system of weight-training exercises that have an overall effect on the musculature of the body. And in this category of exercises I include those which, although utilizing no extra equipment, entail the movement of the muscle-groups against the resistance provided by body weight itself: i.e., sit-ups, press-ups, squat-jumps, etc.

From the outset, it is important to remember that the exercises should be balanced; they should provide equally distributed exercise to muscle-groups, and not be 'one-sided'. It must also be stressed that common sense should rule. Sensible precautions must be taken at all times, and this includes setting realistic limits to the exercises, especially in the early stages.

Effective weight training is a progressive exercise in that the best results are obtained by either (a) ***increasing*** the number of repetitions with a ***constant*** weight (press-ups with body weight), or (b) ***maintaining*** the number of repetitions with ***increasing*** weights (bench-press with added poundage).

A combination of both systems is perhaps more interesting; though for the karate-ka who anyway spends most of his available time in practising technique, the former method may be more advantageous, for the following reasons:

(i) the student does not need to rely upon the availability of expensive equipment, and

(ii) more importantly, it is possible to combine a gain in muscular strength with an increase in aerobic power (CRC), since the greater possible number of repetitions places a lighter but longer demand on the heart and lungs.

To reap the full benefits of a sensible regime of weight training as a complement to karate training, the body must be given time to rest and recover from its exertions; and a sensible and nutritious diet must be followed, to allow the muscles to replenish their stores of fuel.

The benefits of such a system can be summed up as:

(i) an increase in physical strength and muscular endurance, allowing stronger techniques to be delivered and enabling the body to withstand a greater degree of impact shock.

(ii) an increase in the speed of muscle contraction, resulting in the faster execution of karate techniques.

(iii) the combination of (i) and (ii), enabling the body to speed up the rapid changes of stance and body movements (***tai sabaki***) necessary in karate.

(iv) if the system of light weights and many repetitions is followed, it is probable that CRC will be increased - though it must be stressed that, for this purpose, other exercises (running, swimming, cycling, etc.) would be far more efficacious.

EXERCISE SYSTEMS

Suggestions for specific exercise systems are included in Chapter 26.

To make the best use of a weight-training programme, given that the majority of a karate-ka's time will be devoted to the practice of technique, it is important to have a clear plan of approach, and specific aims in view.

This means that the karate-ka be selective: he must decide which specific muscle groups require strengthening and select the appropriate exercise. For karate purposes initial concentration on leg, arm and stomach exercises is advisable; as is a pre-weight-training session of jogging or brisk calisthenics. The programme should end with further stretching and twisting exercises; indeed, many authorities advise that all punching and kicking exercises with weights be followed by the same techniques done at speed without weights. As a general rule, half-an-hour of weight training should be balanced by one hour of techniques proper.

In selecting the exercises, try to ensure that they are spaced out so that two or three of the same type do not follow each other consecutively. The usual sequence is to have an arm-and-shoulder exercise, followed by an abdominal exercise, followed by a leg exercise. Thus, all the major groups receive proportionate exercise. This general all-over conditioning can form the basis of the programme, and should be maintained at every session. Specific exercises in addition to these can be added as required.

PROGRAMME 1. BEGINNERS
After warm-up:

1 **Press-ups** on fingers and knuckles. 10 repetitions. 3 sets.
2 **Sit-ups,** legs straight, fingers locked behind head. 10–15 repetitions. 3 sets.
3 **Half-squats** Barbell (60–80lb) across shoulders, heels supported ½ in off floor. Keep head erect and lower body smoothly into seated position on a bench or hard chair placed just behind knees. Do not place weight on bench but push smoothly with legs until body is upright again. Purpose of the bench or chair is to ensure that legs do not bend beyond about 90°, thus preventing any possibility of injury to knee joint in the untrained person. 8–10 repetitions, 3 sets.
In general, breathe in before beginning any repetition and exhale upon approaching completed position.
4 **Leg-supported press-ups** Same as basic press-ups but with feet supported 2–3ft off floor. 10 repetitions. 3 sets.
5 **Bench sit-ups** As normal sit-ups, but with buttocks supported off floor and feet restrained; thus increasing range of body movement. 10–15 repetitions. 3 sets.

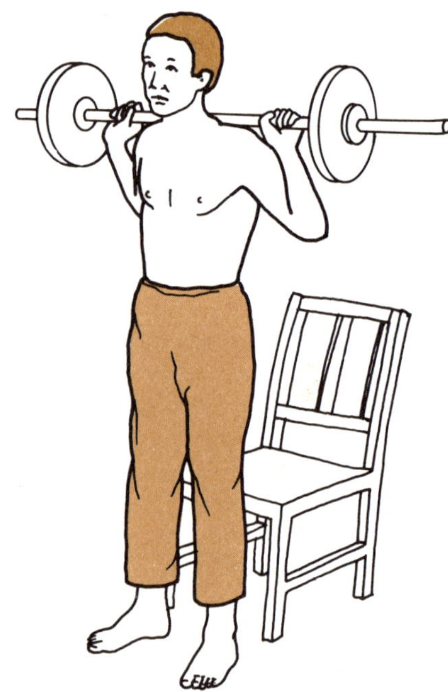

6 **Jefferson lift (straddle lift)** Stand astride barbell, lower body (keeping it as erect as possible), grasp bar and smoothly return to standing position, holding breath on way down and exhaling on approach to upright position. Weight 60–80lb. 10 repetitions. 3 sets.
7 **Loosen off** Calisthenics.

PROGRAMME II. ADVANCED

After warm up:

1 **Press-ups and/or bench press** Lying flat on secure bench, raise and lower barbell, inhaling as it is lowered, exhaling as it is pressed upward.
NB: With heavier weights, use weight stands or have companion ready to take weight if necessary.
60-100lb. 8-10 repetitions. 3 sets.

2 **Straight-leg lift on flat or inclined bench** Can be done with or without weights on the feet; excellent abdominal exercise. Keeping legs straight, slowly lift into approximately 80^{0} angle, hold, then return. For greater severity, do not allow feet to rest on floor at any time during repetitions. Body weight or light foot weights. 10 repetitions. 3 sets.

3 **Jumping** from full-squat position into the air with knees pulled up to touch chest, dropping smoothly back into full-squat position. This is one repetition. Movement must be carried out explosively but rhythmically. Breathe out on the jump, inhale on descent. Body weight. 10-15 repetitions. 3 sets.

4 **Loosen off** Calisthenics.

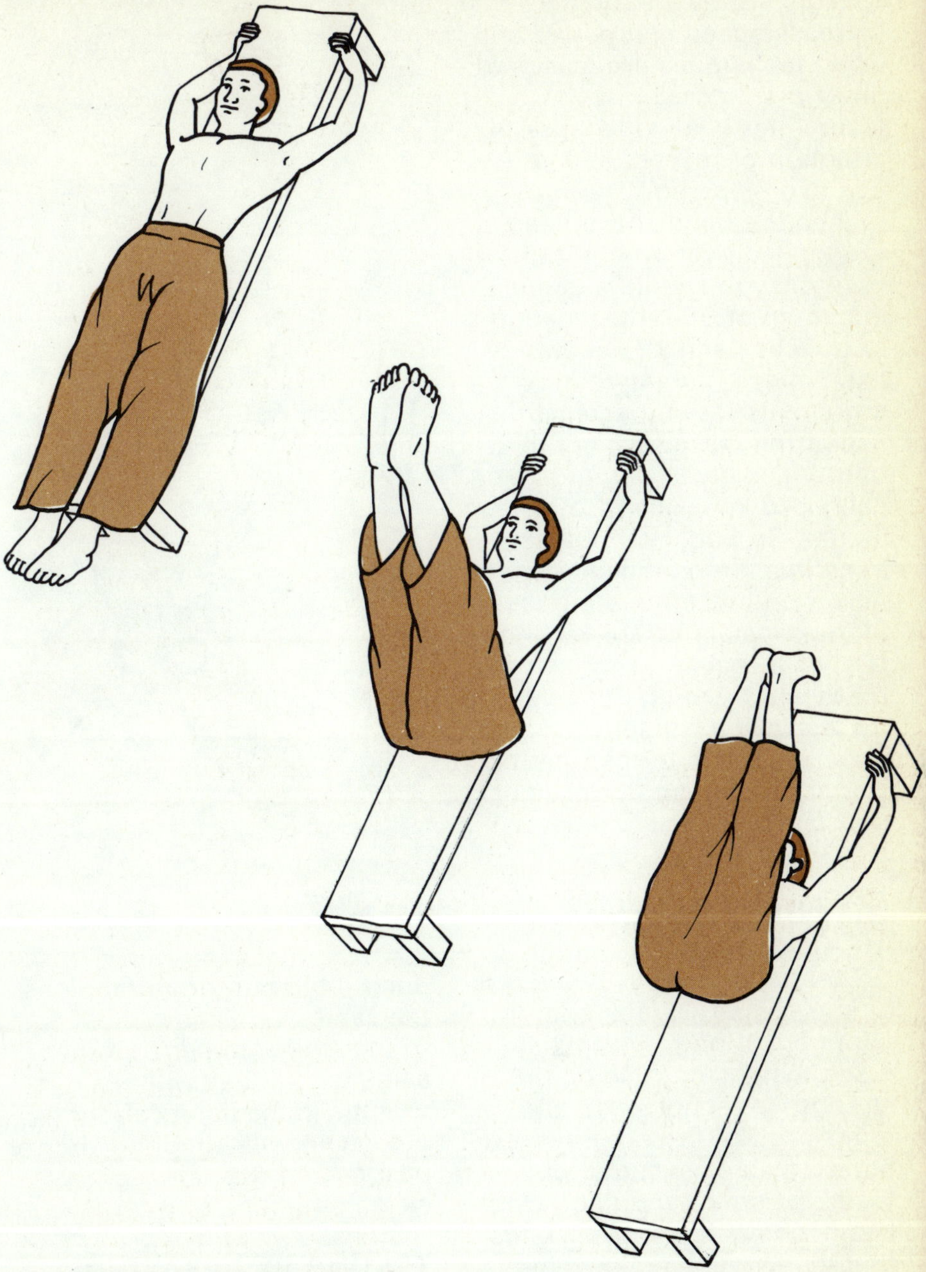

MAKIWARA TRAINING

The *makiwara*, an apparatus unique to karate training, is essentially a padded board used as a target for strikes and punches. It gives practice in the 'feel' of applying a technique with power to an object, rather than in 'pulling' it, or striking the empty air. It serves to toughen the striking weapons, and indicates faults in technique (bent weak wrists, etc.) that could go unnoticed in general practice. It also aids concentration, ***kime,*** breath control and confidence.

Generally, the *makiwara* best suits the practice of hand techniques, but kicks can also be practised. Normally, however, it is considered that kicks can be more usefully practised against a bag.

When punching or striking the *makiwara*, aim two inches beyond the surface and make sure that fist is tightly clenched, or, in knife-hand techniques, that fingers are firmly held together. As usual, breathe out sharply at moment of impact and inhale as you withdraw to ready position. Ensure full hip movement.

Begin slowly and gently. Increase speed and power only when techniques are mastered; never practice 'sloppy' techniques. Only one lapse of attention or respect and you can injure yourself.

When the hands have been toughened over a period of training, you should aim at a minimum of 80–100 repetitions of punches and strikes with each hand. There are arguments for and against the use of the ***makiwara,*** but to utilize it solely to demonstrate calloused knuckles is to pervert its use. Probably its greatest benefit is the confidence in power and technique it builds in the sensible karate-ka who follows a regular programme of ***makiwara*** training. Remember, the ***makiwara*** will let you know in no uncertain terms whether you are punching correctly or not. The empty air will never tell.

THE PUNCHING AND KICKING BAG

There are normally two sizes of bag used in karate: one about 3 ft long, 1½ ft thick (used mainly for building up strength in techniques); and one about 1 ft long, 8in thick hung on an elasticated rope (used for timing training). Once again, common sense dictates that the karate-ka begins his practice with caution, building up speed and power with experience. Do not stuff the bags with sawdust; this can settle into a concrete-like density that can easily damage toes and fingers. The best filling consists of leather or rubber waste, packed in tightly.

One of the traditional methods of strengthening karate techniques is to strap a small weight to the feet or to hold a light weight in the hand whilst practising basic kicks and punches. A modern innovation is the weighted ankle or wrist strap, which takes the place of the traditional iron clog (***geta***) and dumb-bell; but the principle is the same.

Remember to perform the same techniques without weights immediately after practising with weights, and for best results use only light weights (5–8lb).

TESTING BY BREAKING—TAMESHIWARI

For the more advanced student, breaking techniques are used to test the degree of skill and power developed by training in karate techniques. Normally wood, tiles and bricks are utilised; but, to forestall any possibility of injury, expert guidance should be sought before breaking practice is undertaken. Remember at all times that ***tameshiwari*** is a test of skill, not an end in itself.

PROGRAMME III. THE KARATE CIRCUIT

As explained in Chapter 22, this karate circuit was devised as a means of utilizing karate techniques and general strengtheners to promote muscular and circulo-respiratory endurance. It has the added effect of increasing proficiency in the karate techniques themselves.

Naturally, each karate-ka or instructor can design a specific circuit to suit his requirements. The one given below, however, has been found to be extremely beneficial.

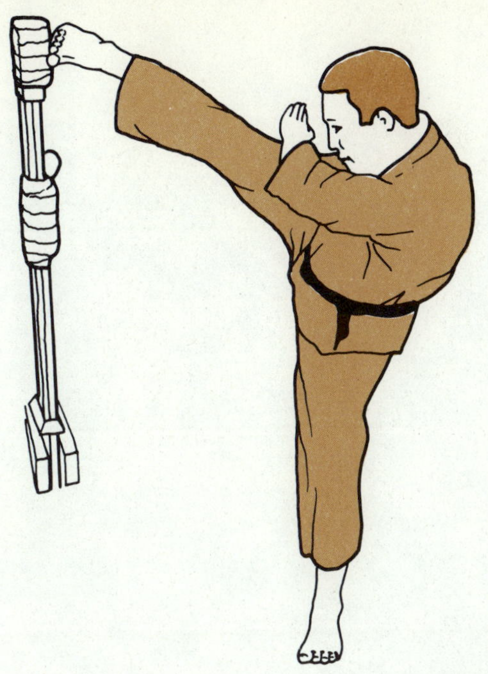

1. Knuckle press-ups.
2. Sit-ups.
3. Front kicks rising from full squat position, alternate legs.
4. *Sanbon-zuki.* Three punches moving forward across the *dojo* and back.
5. Roundhouse kicks, moving to and from across the *dojo.*
6. Front-leg snap kick, rear-leg snap kick, moving forward across the *dojo* and back.

Each exercise is timed and two minutes are allotted for each person to see how many *good* (not sloppy) techniques and exercises he can do within the time. A 90-second rest is given between exercises, during which each karate-ka marks down his score on his personal card; thus, he sets his own targets and is able to chart a regular improvement. Because the student competes only with himself, this circuit builds up great determination; also he sees the futility of 'cheating' in karate, since the only person he can cheat is himself.

In normal circumstances, once a week or fortnight is sufficient for this practice; though it can be undertaken more frequently in training for a special occasion. Serious students can follow the circuit in their own time once a week for optimum results.

NAME DATE	PRESS-UPS	SIT-UPS	SQUAT KICKS	SANBON ZUKI	ROUND-HOUSE KICKS	FR. FOOT BKK FOOT KICKS
2 January	54	48	40	80	80	84
3 February	58	52	42	82	86	78
4 March	61	54	46	84	84	84

Student's personal circuit score-card.

Ice-breaking: not all styles of karate practise destruction techniques. When practised, however, they serve to show the force generated in the technique. Here, a member of the Kyokushinkai (Ultimate Truth) school breaks three large ice blocks with knife hand (***shuto-uchi***).

Since karate practice involves physical contact, it is inevitable that bodily injury will occasionally occur. Serious injury is fortunately rare; much more common are sprains and strains, and impact injuries.

SPRAINS AND STRAINS

Muscles, tendons and ligaments can be sprained or strained by sharp over-extension of a limb around a joint, or by rapid contraction of a muscle in a disadvantageous body posture. It is thought that a brisk, thorough session of calisthenics prior to training or competition helps to prevent this type of injury. Strains and sprains may also be caused by a blow, as in the case of a 'sprained' ankle resulting from an unsuccessful foot sweep (***ashi-barai***).

In most cases, the most effective treatment is to immobilize or support with elasticated or crepe bandages the injured limb or joint. When the injury occurs to the large musculature of the body, however, little can be done except to rest; to continue to train with a 'pulled' muscle serves only to aggravate the condition.

Some long-lasting injuries, such as those to knee or elbow joints, can be greatly helped by the wearing of an elasticated support. This may be particularly effective in the treatment of the so-called 'tennis elbow', a painful and occasionally chronic injury caused by rapid over-extension of the arm, often combined with rotation. This is a quite common injury in karate, owing to the methods of delivering punches and strikes.

Other common injuries, particularly among lower grades, are sprains and dislocations of the fingers and thumbs (often caused by attempts to block or parry kicking attacks with an open hand). Reduction of dislocations should be carried out as quickly as possible, but only by a trained person. The digit(s) should then be immobilized by bandaging and strapping. In the case of damage to an individual finger or toe, it is sometimes helpful to 'splint' it to its neighbour with tape.

If there is any reason to suspect a fracture, or a complete tearing of a muscle or tendon (as occasionally happens with the Achilles' tendon in the leg), it is important to seek proper medical attention so that the correct treatment can be obtained.

IMPACT INJURIES

These form by far the largest groups of injuries in karate, affecting mainly the hands and feet, forearms and shins.

The most common injury is bruising of the soft tissue at the point of collision between attacking and defending limb. It seems, however, that the body develops a certain tolerance to slight contusions (many karate-ka seem to take a delight in inspecting their bruises and judge a training session by the number and variety of discolorations on the shins and forearms!); though if the injury is more severe, it can inhibit further use of the limb. Occasionally, a nerve is damaged by the impact, causing a tingling sensation and some loss of motor function. Recovery usually follows of its own accord.

The application of cold compresses will usually serve to reduce swelling and deaden pain. Recovery will then take its natural course. Should the skin over an injury be broken, care must be taken to guard against infection.

For fractures of the fingers or toes (often the result of badly executed technique) proper medical attention must be sought immediately, since X-rays will be needed to determine accurately the nature and position of the injury, and it will probably be necessary to splint or plaster the digit(s).

Fractures to arms and legs (generally the result of a fall, or a powerful blocking technique) are rare. Should a fracture be suspected, however, proper medical attention should be obtained at once. If it is absolutely necessary to move the patient before help arrives, great care must be taken to avoid causing further damage: the limb should be immobilized by splinting or bandaging, if possible under the guidance of a club member with first-aid training.

Potentially more serious impact injuries are those to the head, neck and trunk; though the majority, which occur to the face, generally involve only simple cuts and bruises.

The Head

It has been estimated that about 80 in 1,000 karate injuries occur to the head and face; and that of those 80 injuries, at least 72 will be minor.

Nose-bleeds can usually be stemmed by the application of external pressure to the sides of the bridge of the nose, the head being tilted back. In severe cases, however, medical help may be required. Cuts should be cleaned and covered with a plaster; if serious, they should be sutured. Ice-packs may be applied to reduce swelling around the eyes.

More severe injuries generally involve damage to bones and teeth. In the case of a nasal fracture, or of loss of or damage to teeth, only proper medical treatment will ensure maximum recovery. In the latter case, the wearing of a suitable gumshield is strongly advocated; dentistry can be expensive, and the loss of teeth is, to say the least, a great inconvenience. (Should you be so unfortunate as to lose a complete tooth, find it and take it with you to the dentist; provided that it is in good condition, it may well be possible to have it re-inserted.)

Malar (cheekbone) and mandibular (lower jaw) fractures are rare. Should either be suspected, however, it is imperative that a correct diagnosis be made and re-alignment carried out as soon as possible.

The Neck

In general, damage to the trachea (windpipe) is best left to heal itself unless it is serious, in which case medical treatment must be obtained immediately, since surgery may be required.

The Trunk

The most common trunk injury is caused by a blow to the solar plexus; less frequent are injuries to the ribs and groin.

Blows to the solar plexus cause a momentary loss of function of the diaphragm, which prevents the inspiration of breath. In practically all instances, breathing will be resumed spontaneously.

Damage to the ribs is potentially more dangerous. If there is any suspicion at all of a fracture, the area should be X-rayed and medical diagnosis made. Evidence of a fracture is given by a sharp pain upon taking a deep breath, and by short and shallow breathing. If the lower right ribs are broken, the liver may be injured; fracture of the lower left ribs may have damaged the spleen. If there is damage to the lungs, blood – bright red and frothy – may be coughed up.

If there is suspicion of damage to internal organs, DO NOT apply bandaging to the chest; promptly remove the patient to hospital, taking care not to exacerbate the injury. If possible, a trained first-aider should take charge of conveyance of the patient.

Kicks to the groin are prohibited techniques in competition, but in practice they occur, by accident, fairly frequently. A hard blow in this area can cause severe pain, loss of motor function, disruption of the breathing processes; even, very rarely, unconsciousness and death. Normally, however, recovery is rapid and complete. The patient should be kept calm. It may help to bounce him on his buttocks, or on stiff legs, to facilitate the dropping of the testicles, which may have been forced into the lower abdomen.

TRAINING AND MYOCARDITIS

Myocarditis – inflammation of the heart muscle – is a condition as yet little understood. A common factor in the recent much-publicized deaths from myocarditis of several active and apparently fit sportsmen, however, is that each victim had attempted to continue strenuous training while suffering, or barely recovered from, the effects of a viral infection.

MOUTH-TO-MOUTH RESUSCITATION

If breathing stops, for any reason, mouth-to-mouth resuscitation should be started at once.

(a) Remove any foreign substances from the patient's mouth (vomit, false teeth, etc) and keep the tongue pulled forward. This must take seconds only.

(b) Tilt the patient's head back, to keep the air passage open.

(c) Open the patient's mouth with one hand, pinch his nostrils shut with the other.

(d) Take a fairly deep breath, place your mouth over the patient's and blow forcefully into it.

(e) At the end of a normal-length exhalation, remove your mouth and take another breath.

(f) Whilst doing this (e), you should see the patient's chest fall as he exhales automatically.

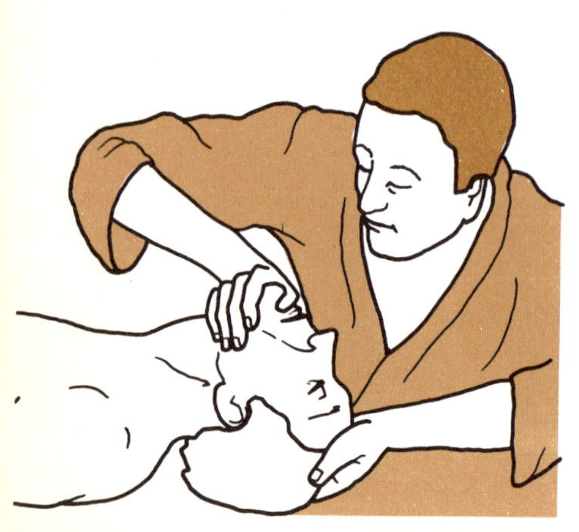

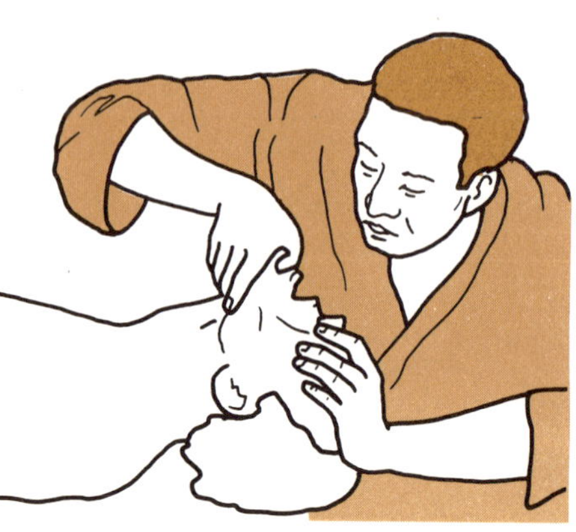

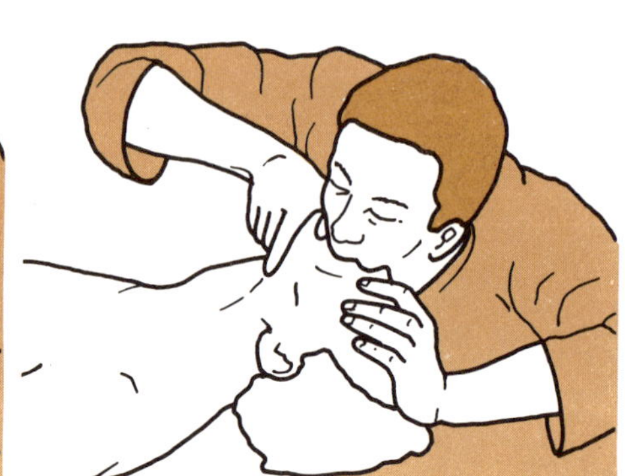

It must be appreciated that the number of such cases has in fact been very small. Nevertheless, as a general safeguard, the old adage that you should 'sweat out' a cold should be firmly ignored. Severe exertion following or during a feverish illness ***is*** potentially dangerous. Better to allow the body to use its energy in combating the infection, and then work up gradually to former training levels. Many viral infections inflame the muscles (which is why we feel aches and pains when we have 'flu'); this being so, you will not be doing them any good by subjecting them to further stress. Remember, the heart itself is just a muscle – and you would certainly be foolish to place it under unnecessary stress.

CONCLUSION

Karate, when practised in a controlled manner, is not as dangerous as it might appear. The potential dangers can be obviated by both tangible and intangible means. The former include gum-shields, protective pads, 'boxes', sparring mittens, shin pads and instep protectors (thought not all karate organizations approve the use of all of these). Intangible means of protection include proper spirit, self-control, good technique; and, in competition, a first-class referee.

Statistics reveal that competition injuries are much more common among grades below brown belt, which might suggest that competition should be restricted to karate-ka with a greater degree of experience and expertise; also that injuries occur more frequently in the opening hour of competition, which may well be the result of nervous tension and not being properly warmed up.

It is absolutely vital that a doctor be present at competitions. The UK Martial Arts Commission (MAC) has compiled a list of medical practitioners willing to attend competitions; organizers can obtain the name and address of the nearest such doctor by writing directly to the secretary of the MAC.

It is advisable to call on the services of the Red Cross, the St John's Ambulance Brigade or a similar organization for supplementary medical assistance.

In the United States, medical assistance is generally provided by ***sensei*** with some knowledge of Oriental medicine (katsu) or, at best, paramedics. All too often, minor injuries are treated by ***sensei*** serving as officials. And on those occasions when a major injury does occur, the injured competitor is taken to a nearby medical facility or, if it is decided that he should not be moved (by those generally not competent to make such a decision), an ambulance is called. This practice is under attack by many concerned ***sensei*** and leaders of the karate community who believe the judgement of how an injury should be treated . . . and whether or not it is major or minor . . . should not be left in the hands of untrained karate-ka or even semi-professionals. Nearly all of the major tournaments provide full, professional medical aid, but the directors of small local events are still reluctant to spend the money necessary to provide proper care.

(g) When this occurs, repeat the inflation process

(h) Continue until the normal breathing process is re-established, or until a medically qualified person takes charge of the patient.

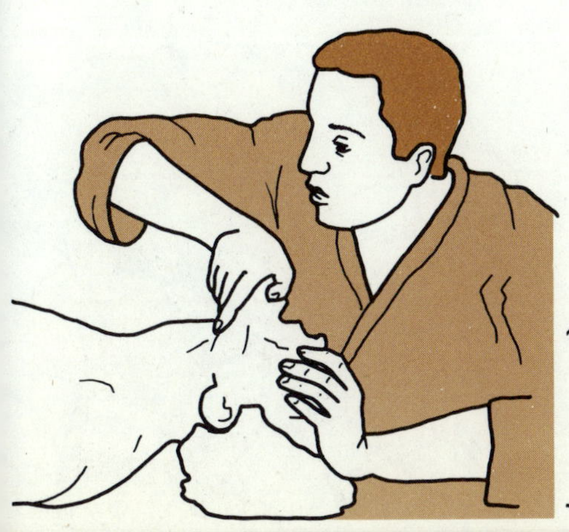

(i) If natural breathing *is* safely re-established, turn the patient into the recovery position and watch him carefully until trained help arrives.

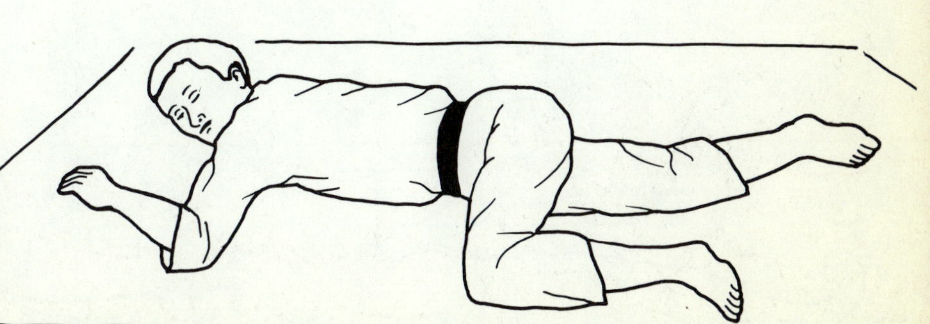

EXTERNAL CARDIAC MASSAGE

In cardiac arrest, the pupils of the eyes are widely dilated, skin colour turns blue-grey, and no carotid (neck) pulse is discernible. Operation of the heart may be restored by rhythmic and firm application of pressure to the breastbone.

(a) Place the patient on his back on a firm, flat surface (e.g., floor).

(b) Strike the chest smartly over the heart; this may restart it.

(c) If this fails, kneel at right angles to the patient's chest.

(d) Place the heel of your hand on the lower part of his breastbone, your fingers and palms raised off his chest.

(e) Place the heel of your hand on hand on top of the first, rock forward with your arms straight and press down smoothly but firmly. The forward movement should be quicker than the backwards rocking movement. Depress the sternum about 1½ in.

(f) Repeat the pressure once every second.

NB. Cardiac massage without respiratory resuscitation is likely to prove useless, so have somebody administer mouth-to-mouth resuscitation. If no-one else is available, stop the cardiac massage after every 6-8 compressions and inflate the lungs yourself.

(g) Repeat the process until the patient recovers or until medical help arrives.

NB The above applies to adult patients only. Children require much less pressure on the sternum, and not such a hard breath into the mouth.

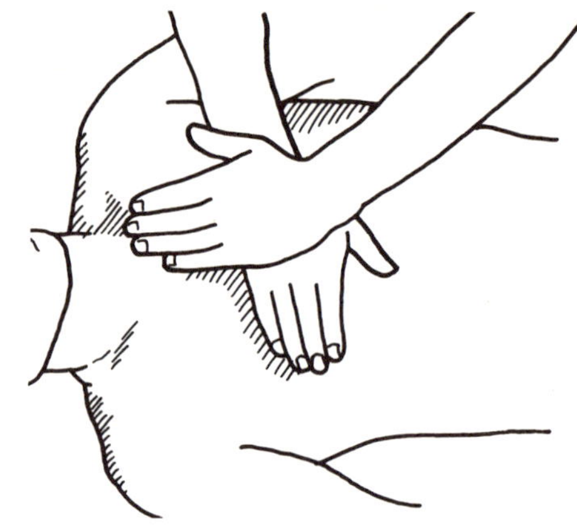

KATSU OR KAPPO

Katsu and ***kappo*** are names given to the first-aid techniques traditionally taught in the Japanese martial arts. There is very little evidence in the Western world regarding their medical efficiency; but their long history, and the testimony of Western experts who have witnessed them in practice, tends to confirm their usefulness.

In an emergency, and if there is no alternative at hand, the following ***katsu*** may be used to revive an unconscious patient:

(a) First, stroke the patient lightly from chest to abdomen ten times.

(b) Sit the patient up and rest your knee behind his heart; not in the centre of the spine, but close to it.

(c) Place your right hand under the patient's right armpit, your left hand on top of his left shoulder.

(d) Thrust your knee repeatedly against his back, simultaneously pulling his shoulder inward and upward with your right hand, and pressing downward on his other shoulder with your left hand.

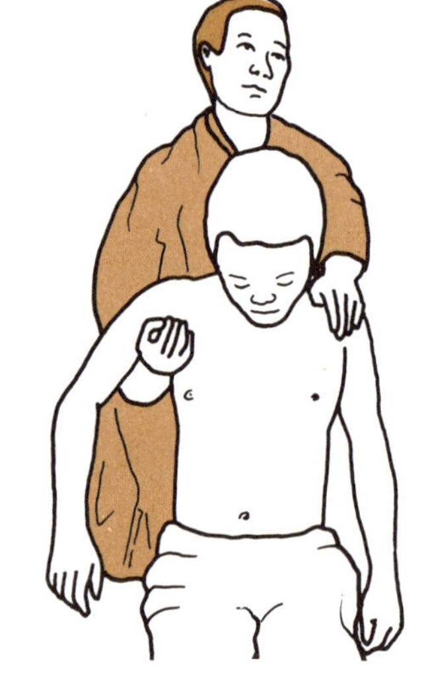

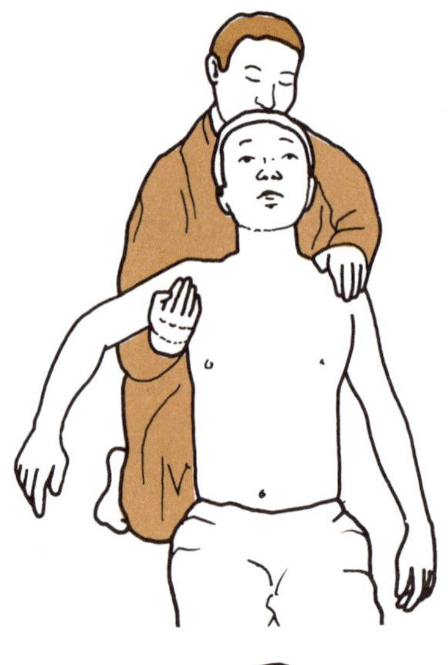

The vital points *(kyusho)* are the most vulnerable areas of the body, damage to which can cause severe pain, unconsciousness, and occasionally death. Much depends, however, upon the severity of the blow, the physical condition of the recipient, and the speed with which resuscitation techniques are applied.

Many of the vital points will be recognized as coinciding with the acupuncture points utilized in Oriental medicine. Others such as the eyes and the point of the chin, are peculiar to the martial arts.

In general, ***kyusho*** are those points of the body least protected by bone or muscle, where the nerve-centres are most accessible. The following list describes the main ***kyusho.***

Head

1. Top of head
2. Frontal area, between coronal suture and forehead
3. Temple
4. Base of nose, between eyes
5. Bridge of nose
6. Eyes
7. Upper lip, beneath nose
8. Lower edge of jaw
9. Articulation of lower jaw, below and in front of ears

As well as inflicting local damage, a blow to the head can cause trauma to any of the 12 cranial nerves, which may result in concussion, loss of co-ordination and unconsciousness.

Front of Body

10. Cavity below ears
11. Side of neck: jugular vein or carotid artery, vagus nerve
12. Adam's apple
13. Top of sternum
14. Bottom of sternum
15. Solar plexus
16. Lower abdomen
17. Rib cage, below armpits
18. Rib cage, below nipples
19. Rib cage, either side of abdomen
20. Testicles
21. Side of stomach
22. Inner part of upper thigh
23. Outside of thigh
24. Knee cap and joint
25. Shin
26. Top of foot, just beneath ankle
27. Elbow
28. Back of hand

Attacks to ***kyusho*** of chest and abdomen impart shock to the internal organs, and can result in disruption of the sympathetic nervous system, which in turn can induce trauma of the cranial nerves.

Back of Body

29. Spine
30. Back of head
31. Back of neck
32. Kidneys
33. Tip of spine
34. Back of upper thigh
35. Lower calf
36. Back of knee
37. Ankle (below ankle bone)

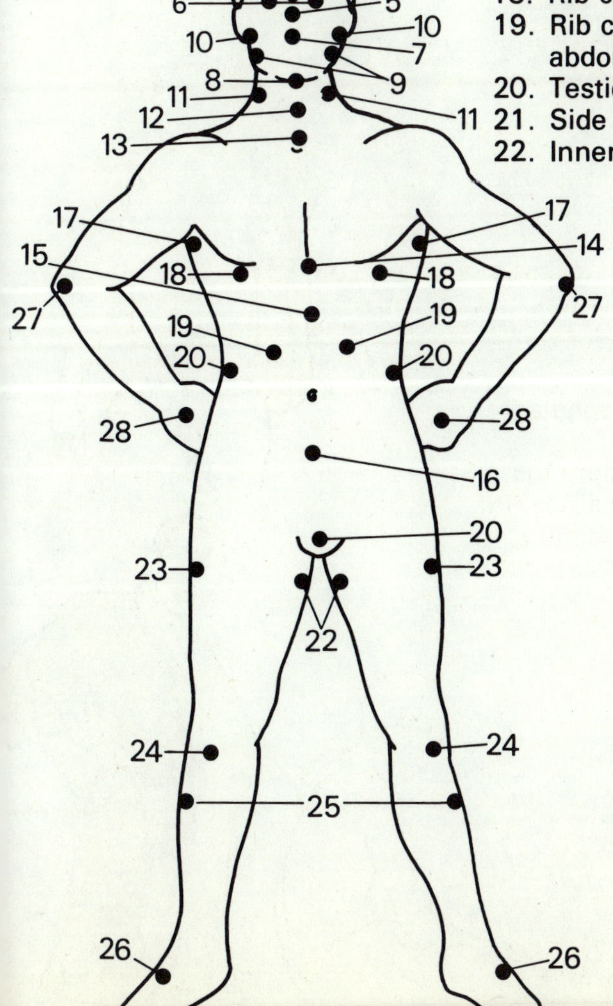

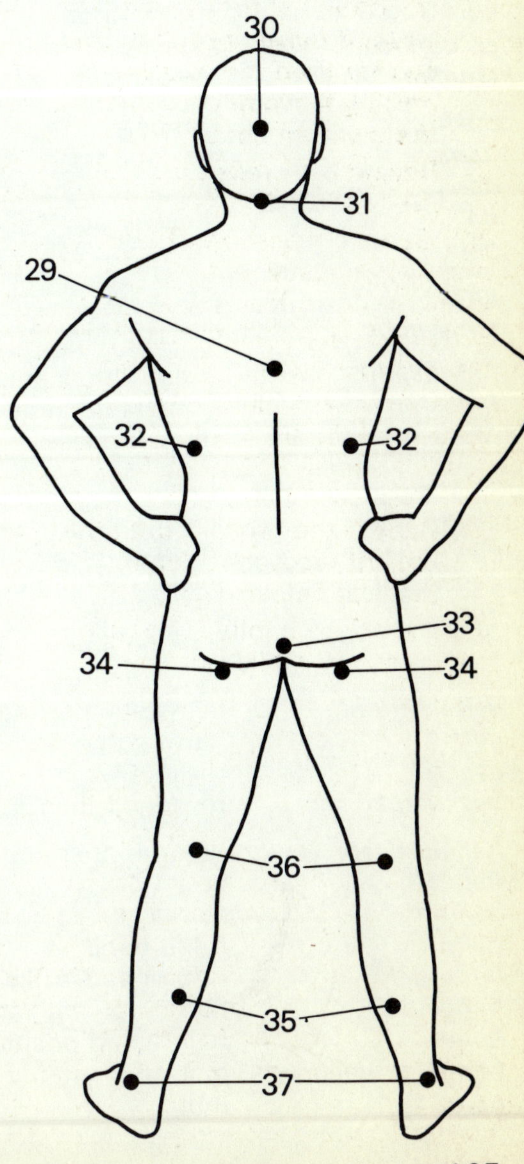

age-uke	rising block
age-zuki	rising punch
aikido	self defence art based on harmony of body and spirit
ai-uchi	simultaneous techniques by both contestants
aka	red
ashi-barai	leg sweep
ashi-waza	leg technique
atemi	the body, esp. the vital points
atemi-waza	techniques of attacking vital points
awase-waza	decision wins
bassai sho	a kata
bo	staff
bu	military affairs
budo	martial ways
budo-ka	martial arts practitioner
bu-jutsu	martial arts
Bushido	moral code, ethic of the warrior
bushi-no-te	warrior's hands
cha-no-yu	traditional tea ceremony
chikara	strength
chikara kurabe	a fighting art involving kicking and emphasizing strength
chinte	a kata
choku-zuki	straight punch
ch'uan fa	fist way: Chinese martial art
chudan	middle level
dachi	stance
dame	no good
dan	man, black-belt grade
do	the way of . . .
dojo	the way place, training area
empi	elbow
empi-uchi	elbow strike
fudo-dachi	immovable stance
fudoshin	immovable mind
fumikomi	stamping kick
gankaku	a kata
gedan	lower level
gedan barai	lower-level sweeping block
gedan-zuki	lower area punch
geri	kick
gi	training suit
geta	traditional footwear
gohon kumite	five-step sparring
goju	hard/soft
gyaku	reverse
gyaku-zuki	reverse-punch
hachiji-dachi	natural, open-leg stance
hai	yes
hajime	start
haito	ridge-hand
haito-uchi	ridge-hand strike
hangetsu	half-moon - a kata
hanmi	half-facing position
hangetsu-dachi	half-moon stance
hansoku	foul

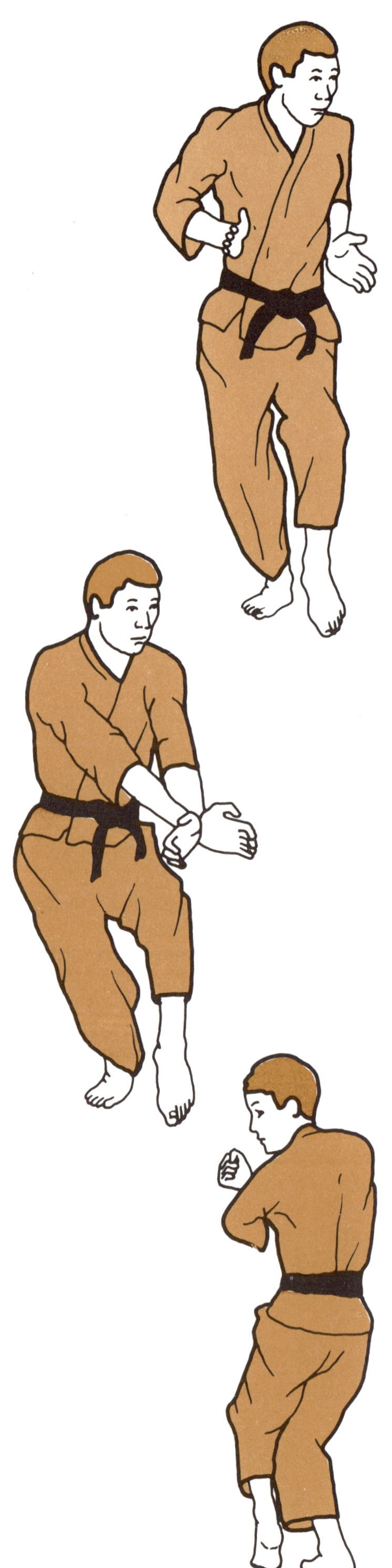

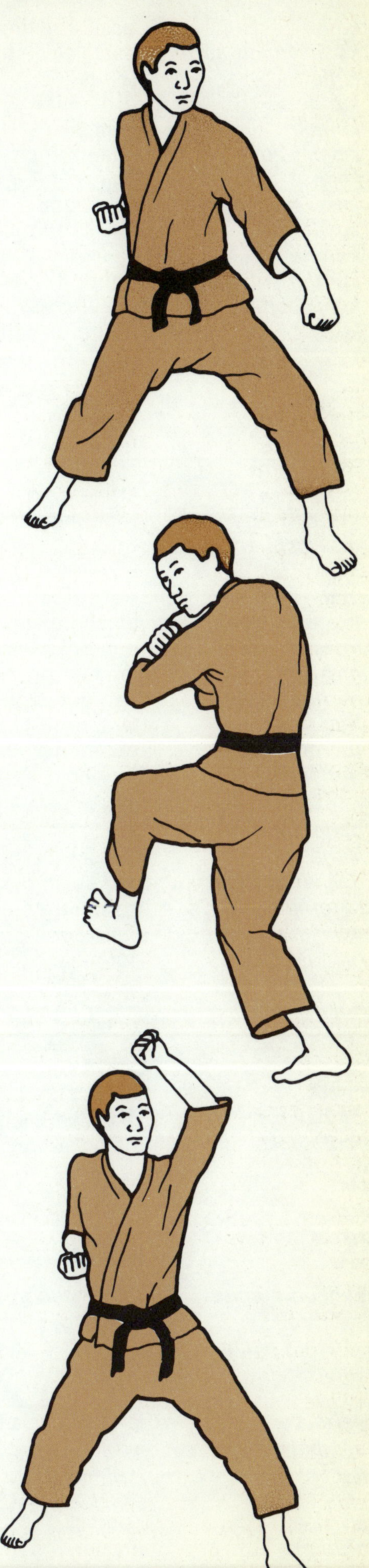

hantei	decision
hara	belly, lower abdomen, concept of spiritual centre
hara-kiri	lit: 'Belly cut'. Slang term for ritual suicide by disembowelling ***(seppuko)***
haragei	art of developing ***hara***
heisoku-dachi	informal attention stance
hidari	left side
hikiwake	drawn match
hiraken	foreknuckle fist
hiza (hitsu)	knee
hiza-geri	knee kick
hombu	main ***dojo***, headquarters
hyoshi	timing
ibuki	breathing method (esp. ***Kyokushinkai)***
iee iie	no
ippon	one point
ippon-ken	one-knuckle fist
ippon nukite	one-finger spear-hand
ippon-shobu	one point contest
jion	a kata
jitte	a kata; alternative spelling of jutte
jodan	upper level
jogai-chui	warning for leaving contest area
ju	soft, pliable, free (and the number ten)
ju-dachi	free stance
ju-ippon kumite	semi-free one-step sparring
ju-jutsu	art of flexibility, method of combat
juji-uke	x-block
ju-kumite	free sparring
jutsu	art
jutte	a kata; ten hands
ka	person or practitioner
kage uke	hooking block
kage zuki	hook punch
kaiten	round, wheel
kakato	heel
kamaitte	action
kami	Shinto spirit/deity
kamikaze	lit: 'Divine wind'. World War II suicide pilots
kancho	Master of the House
kanku	a kata
kanku dai	a kata
kanku sho	a kata
kansetsu	joint
kara	empty; Chinese
kata	pre-arranged sequences of techniques
kata garuma	shoulder wheel throw
katsu/kappo	resuscitation methods
keage	high kicks (snap kicks)
kekomi	thrust
kempo	fist way: Chinese martial art
kendo	the way of the sword
kenjutsu	the art of swordsmanship
kenpo	alternative spelling of ***kempo***
keri (geri)	kick
ki	spirit, inner power
kiai	shout used to help unite ***ki*** and physical power
kiba-dachi	straddle or horse stance

kihon basic (technique(s))
kihon-ippon kumite basic one-step sparring
kime focus
kin-geri groin kick
kinteki testicles
kisami-zuki snap punch
koan Zen riddle or problem
kokutsu-dachi back stance
koshi ball of foot
kumite sparring
kumite shiai-jo fighting contest area
kumi-uchi ancient grappling art
kun motto or oath
kyu boy: rank below black belt

ma-ai correct distance between opponents
mae front
mae-geri front kick
makimono scrolls
makiwara striking post
mawashi-geri roundhouse kick
mawashi-zuki roundhouse punch
mawatte turn
migi right side
mikazuki-geri crescent kick
mizu no kokoro mind like water
mokuso meditation, contemplation
mondo Zen question and answer
morote-uke two-hand block
morote-zuki two-hand punch
mushin no-mind, impassivity

nagashi-uke sweeping block
nage-waza throwing technique(s)
Naha-te Okinawan school of karate
nakadaka-ken middle-finger one-knuckle fist
nami-ashi inside leg block
nekoashi-dachi cat stance
nidan-geri double kick
nihon nukite two-finger spear hand
nukite spear hand

O big, great
obi belt, sash
oi-zuki lunge punch
Okinawa-te Okinawan school of karate
osoto gake major outer hooking throw

rei bow
ren-zuki combination punching
riken back fist
ryu traditional system (s), school (s)

sanbon kumite three-step sparring
samurai classical warrior of the feudal period
sanchin dachi hourglass stance
satori enlightenment, ultimate knowledge
seiken forefist
seiza kneeling position (meditation posture)
sempai senior
sensei teacher
seppuko ritual suicide
shiai contest
shihan master
shin mind

shinpan	referee
shinken shobu	fights to the death
Shinto	Japanese national religion
shiro	white
shizentai	natural stance
shobu	competition
shuto	knife hand
shuto-uchi	knife-hand strike
sochin-dachi	diagonal straddle-leg stance. Alternative name for *fudo-dachi*
sokuto	edge of the foot
soto ude-uke	forearm block from outside
soto-uke	block from outside
tai sabaki	body shifting
tameshiwari	testing by breaking
tate-zuki	vertical fist punch
te	hand
teisho	palm heel
tekki nidan	a kata
tekki shodan	a kata
tetsui	hammer/bottom fist
te-waza	hand technique
tobi	jumping
tobi-tetsui-uchi	jumping hammer-fist strike
tode	the hand arts
tokui	favourite
Tomari-te	Okinawan school of karate
uchi	(1) strike (2) inner
uchi ude-uke	forearm block from inside
ude	arm
uke	block
ura	opposite, reverse
ura-zuki	close punch
uraken	back fist
ushiro-geri	back kick
wa	harmony
wu shu	Chinese martial arts
waza	technique(s), skill(s)
waza-ari	near point
yakusoku kumite	pre-arranged sparring
yama-zuki	u-punch
yame	stop
yoi	ready
yoroi kumi-uchi	grappling in armour
yoko	side
yoko-empi	side elbow
yoko-geri	side kick
yori-ashi	sliding technique in which the body position is maintained
yudansha	holder of black belt
zanshin	state of calm concentration
za-zen	Zen meditation (usually seated)
Zen	form of Buddhism based on meditation
zenkutsu-dachi	front stance
zuki no kokoro	mind like the moon

PRONUNCIATION HINTS

The pronunciation of Japanese is relatively simple for the English speaker, since most of the sounds occur in English. Specialized books are available on the subject; but below are detailed one or two points of interest to the karate-ka.

The consonant ***n*** is pronounced as in English when it forms a syllable with a following vowel, and when it is followed by ***s,z,t,d*** or ***n.*** Where it occurs before ***b,p*** or ***m,*** its sound is like the English ***m***; thus, ***sanbon-zuki*** is pronounced ***sambon-zuki.***

The consonant ***g*** is pronounced as in English when it occurs at the beginning of a word; otherwise, it is pronounced as the ***ng*** in singer (not as in finger). Thus, ***age-uke*** is pronounced ***ange-uke:*** the sound should be a cross between ***n*** and ***g,*** voiced nasally.

The vowels ***i*** and ***u*** are unvoiced; that is, they are not fully sounded. This usually occurs between voiceless consonants ***(p, ch, ts, s, k, sh)*** or after a voiceless consonant at the end of a word. Thus, ***shuto-uchi*** is pronounced sh'to-uch' rather than shoe-toe oochee.

Where long vowels occur, it is important to give them their correct stress, since they are considered to be different letters from the short vowels. Not to do so would be to invite confusion:

tori = bird
tōri = road
toru = to take
tōru = to pass

Remember not to follow the English pattern of stressing certain syllables. Japanese does not possess a strong stress system, therefore each syllable should be pronounced distinctly and given only a moderate stress.

The English ***f*** and ***v*** do not occur in the native Japanese sound system, but sometimes occur in borrowed words. Likewise, there is no ***l*** sound in native Japanese. When it is necessary for a Japanese to use ***l*** he will usually substitute an ***r*** sound in its place: thus, table becomes teeburu; lemonade, remonēdo; London, Rondon, etc. Remembering these points will help the student better to understand a Japanese instructor's English.

Kanazawa ***sensei,*** with the help of instructors J Weenan and E Whitcher, demonstrates flying double kick, a technique requiring excellent co-ordination and flexibility.

THE NUMBER SYSTEM

Japan possesses two number systems, one of which is native in origin, the other Chinese.

The Japanese numbers are used in statements concerning age, and when discussing quantities of objects; the Chinese numbers are used for measures, money and distances. Beyond 10, only Chinese numerals are used.

	Japanese	Chinese
1	hitotsu, hito-	ichi
2	futatsu, futa-	ni
3	mittsu, mi-	san
4	yotsu, yon yo-	shi★
5	itsutu, itsu-	go
6	muttsu, mu-	roku
7	nanatsu, nana-	shichi
8	yattsu, ya-	hachi
9	kokonotsu, kokono	ku
10	to, to-	ju
11		ju-ichi
12		ju-ni (and so on)
100		hyaku

★Because in Japanese ***shi*** is the root of a word meaning death, the Chinese ***shi*** for 4 is rarely used; more commonly employed is the Japanese ***yon.*** The use of the two systems is complex, but the karate-ka will generally get by with a knowledge of the ten basic Chinese forms.

SELECTED WUKO RULES

MATCHES

Article 2

In principle, the contestant is not allowed to wear bandages or supporters. He should wear a clean, white and unfigured karate-***gi*** (suit), and keep his nails short. As a general rule no protective devices may be worn, unless specifically permitted to prevent hazard.

Referees shall wear an attire specified by the regulations of individual events.

Article 3 (criteria for establishing the winning team)

Under the number-of-winners method, the result should be decided on the basis of the number of individual winners. Should both teams have an equal number of wins, the winning team shall be the one with a greater number of ***ippon*** scores. Should this also be indecisive, judgement shall be based on the number of ***awase-waza*** (decision wins) by ***waza-ari***, and decision wins without ***waza-ari***, in descending order of priority. Victory through a foul or disqualification of the opponent shall be counted as ***ippon***. If, following these criteria, the result is still a draw, the decision will be made according to the result of a match between a representative of each team.

If the extra match exceeds two rounds, the representative of each team shall be replaced by another member.

Under the successive-winning method, the winner shall continue to fight new contestants of the opposing team until he is defeated, and the victory shall be awarded to the team whose member defeated the last opponent of the opposing team. A system of limited successive wins (under which a contestant who has successfully won three to five rounds is withdrawn from the match) may be adopted.

JUDGES AND ARBITRATOR

Article 4

The judgement of a match shall be made by one referee and four judges.

An arbitrator shall be appointed to ensure fairness of the conduct of matches and judgements rendered.

CONDUCT OF MATCHES

Article 5

Matches shall be conducted exclusively under the instructions of the referee.

VICTORY AND DEFEAT

Article 7

Victory or defeat shall be awarded on the basis of ***ippon***, victory by decision, defeat due to foul or disqualification. Attack targets shall be limited to the following parts of the body: the head, face, neck, chest, abdomen and back.

CRITERIA FOR DECIDING AN IPPON

Article 8

An ***ippon*** shall be decided on the basis of the following considerations:
When an accurate, effective and powerful ***zuki, uchi*** or ***keri*** is delivered to the recognized attack targets under the following conditions: When a contestant has scored two ***waza-ari*** in a match, these in combination shall be considered as an ***ippon***. Techniques will only be

PERIODS IN JAPANESE HISTORY

Period	Dates	
Tumulus period c.	AD 250 - 500	Early Period
Asuka period	500 - 710	
Nara period	710 - 794	
Heian period	794 - 1160	
Taira period	1160 - 1188	
Kamakura period	1185 - 1333	Medieval Period
Muromachi or Mashikaga period	1336 - 1573	
Monoyama or Azuchi-Monoyama period	1573 - 1603	
Tokugawa or Edo period	1603 - 1868	
Meiji period	1868 - 1912	Modern Period
Taisho period	1912 - 1926	
Showa period	1926 -	

considered effective if the following conditions apply: good form, good attitude, strong vigour, ***zanshin***, proper timing and adequate ***ma-ai*** (distancing).

If a technique is delivered simultaneously with the time-up signal, it shall be counted into the score. No technique delivered after the referee has called ***yame*** will be counted into the score.

Techniques delivered outside the match area shall be invalid. If, however, the attacker was within the match area at the time of delivering such a technique, it will be considered valid, provided that it was executed before the referee's signal of ***yame***.

A technique, even if incomplete, shall be reckoned as an ***ippon*** if delivered:

at the very instant the opponent was thrown off-balance by the attacker;

with combined use of *nage-waza* (throwing techniques) and any of the other attack techniques;

when the opponent had lost the will to fight.

A technique, even if fulfilling the above criteria, will not be deemed ***ippon*** if:

a contestant fails to deliver a decisive blow the moment he seizes his opponent;

a contestant fails to deliver a decisive blow the moment he throws his opponent or tumbles him down.

CRITERIA FOR DECISION
Article 9

In the absence of ***ippon***, or defeat due to a foul or disqualification, a decision shall be awarded according to:

(1) whether there has been a *waza-ari*.

(2) whether there has been warning of a foul.

(3) the number of escapes outside the match area.

An early photo of Asano ***sensei*** when he first arrived in England, performing ***hangetsu kata***.

(4) whether there has been a *jogai chui* (warning against stepping out of the match area).

(5) relative excellence in the fighting attitudes.

(6) ability and skill.

(7) the degree of vigour and fighting spirit.

(8) the number of valid attacking moves.

(9) relative excellence in strategy.

PROHIBITED TECHNIQUES AND ACTS
Article 10

(1) Attacks to the face with *nukite* (spear hand) or by open hand.

(2) Attacks to the testicles.

(3) Persistent attacks directly to the shin.

(4) Direct attacks to the hip-joint, knee-joint and instep.

(5) Unnecessary grabbing, clinching or bodily crashing against the opponent.

(6) Dangerous throws.

(7) Excessive moving out of the match area or moves wasting time.

(8) Any unsportsmanlike, discourteous behaviour such as calling names, provocation and unjustifiable utterances.

FOUL AND DISQUALIFICATION
Article 11

If a contestant, having once been warned, repeats prohibited acts, the referee may announce his defeat on account of a foul.

When a contestant commits any of the following acts, the referee shall announce his defeat:

(1) If he fails to obey the orders of the referee.

(2) If he becomes overexcited to such an extent that he is considered unfit for engagement in the match.

(3) If he wilfully violates the rules, or is considered malicious.

(4) If he has received two *jogai chui.*

(5) If he commits any acts which are deemed to violate the rules of the match.

PROTEST
Article 13

No contestant may personally protest to the referee and/or the judges against their decision. The officer responsible for the person or team involved may protest to the arbitrator against the decision.

(When an appeal is brought to the arbitrator, the referee, with the help of the judges, shall explain to the arbitrator in detail the circumstances that led to the appeal. In case the arbitrator demands a re-decision, correction or confirmation of the decision must be made upon consultation among the referee and judges. ***Rules of Judging, Article 8).***

The foregoing represents a selection of WUKO rules for the conduct of competition matches. It is advised that serious competitors make themselves thoroughly conversant with the full rules.

MEDICAL RECOMMENDATIONS

A selection from the medical recommendations of the Martial Arts Commission of Great Britain:

(i) Supervision at Competitions
A qualified medical practitioner, preferably one versed in karate and/or sports medicine, should be present at all championships or matches in which more than 20 karate-ka participate. In addition, local voluntary first-aid organizations should be in attendance.

(ii) Medical Officer's Duties

(a) Preliminary examination of competitors, if required by officials.

(b) Advice to officials regarding protective equipment and dressings.

(c) Advice to adjudicating official as to severity of any injury and fitness of a competitor to continue.

(d) Treatment of injuries

(iii) Fitness for Competition

(a) Following a knockout or concussion to a competitor, he should not be allowed further participation in the tournament, or participation in any other competition for a period of not less than one month following, subject to final examination by a medical practitioner.

(b) Following a bone fracture, a competitor should not be allowed to continue in the tournament, nor must he take part in any competition for a period of not less than six weeks from the date of the injury, subject to final examination by a medical practitioner.

(c) Following an eye injury, a competitor should not be allowed to participate further in the tournament, nor must he take part in any competition for a period commensurate with the severity of the injury, subject to final examination by a medical practitioner.

As soon as possible following an injury, a competitor should be examined by a medical practitioner to ascertain the nature and severity of the injury. It should be the responsibility of the team manager or other responsible official to inform the organizing body of a competition of any recently injured competitor, so that his or her fitness to participate may be verified.

It is a responsibility of the medical officer to report any of the above category of injuries to the organizing body of a competition so that these recommendations can be complied with.

(iv) Major National and International Competitions

It is recommended that major teams or groups competing should be accompanied by their own medical practitioner. At such events, each area should have a medical officer in attendance.

THE MARTIAL ARTS COMMISSION

The UK Martial Arts Commission was inaugurated on January 1 1977 following discussions between delegates of the martial arts and representatives of the Sports Council and government departments.

One of the functions of MAC is to identify all proficient instructors of the martial arts. These instructors possess and issue MAC registration slips bearing the distinctive MAC logo.

In addition to guaranteeing recognition, the slips also serve as insurance certificates and the holder is indemnified against basic accident risks. Holders are eligible to obtain enhanced coverage at special low rates.

In addition to providing a means of recognition and an insurance coverage, the full-time staff of the MAC also work to support and develop the martial arts themselves. Administration work is undertaken and MAC provides a pool of specialized medical knowledge plus an excellent MAC travel service.

MAC encompasses not only karate but also the Chinese and Korean martial arts, plus the full complement of ***budo*** activities. Coaching, refereeing and training courses are held by the nine governing bodies and their member associations.

The technical functions of each martial art are carried out by the governing bodies.